HALFWAY

To

PARIS

A Trilogy

Volume Two – The Elephant Conspiracy

Owen Quinn

"A leader is a dealer in hope"

Napoleon Bonaparte

For

Owen, Harry & Sebastian

Other works by Owen Quinn:

Separating Sheep from Ghosts

The High Places Beyond the Pyrenees

Pilgrim Who is Calling You?

PROLOGUE

Chapter 1	WHERE IS WORKINGTON?	Page 1
	Face to Face with Reality	
	Leyland National	
	The Neighbours from Heaven	
	Case Study & Resolution	
	In the Midst of Life	

Chapter 2	HQ CALLING	Page 52
	On the Move Again	
	Al's Chinese Cracker	
	Leyland Olympians	
	What's A Pourer?	

Chapter 3	THE BATHGATE ENIGMA	Page 83
	The MD Drops a Bomb	
	136 + 15 (OK Less)	
	The Elephant Conspiracy	
	The Ayatollah & A Perfect Storm	
	Rough, Tough Hombres	

Chapter 4	THE HOLY FATHER'S TRUCK	Page 129
	The Leyland Popemobile	
	You Can't Buy Us, You're Bust	
	Are You a Salesman?	
	Mike's Mind Games	

Chapter 5	WHEN IRISH EYES ARE SMILING	Page 165
	You Mean Oliver Cromwell?	
	You're A Fine Big Fella	
	Hermann & The Men from Harvard	
	Paris J'Arrive	

Chapter 6	A DEALER IN HOPE	Page 210
	What's The Plan?	
	Motivating A Sales Team	
	Nicole Taieb	
	The Professor Tackles Churchill	
Chapter 7	VAN GOGH & THE BONNIE LASS	Page 243
	The President of Presidents	
	Christmas in Paris	
	Auberge Ravoux	
	The Bonnie Lass O'Corsica	
Chapter 8	TERROR COMES TO PARIS	Page 275
	Ghaddafi & The Gardener	
	Talking Trucks at the Tower	
	Moonlight On the Seine	
	Jerome's Bar Mitzvah	
Chapter 9	AU REVOIR ET A BIENTOT	Page 308
	Paris Salon	
	The Crown Prince Talks Trucks	
	Christmas 1986	
	Did You Say DAF?	
	The Scottish Mafia	

PROLOGUE

Business is simple really, even when the numbers are big. Sell for a copper more than you buy and live happily ever after, of course as soon as you think you have grasped what business is all about something arrives from left-field to make you think again. This is especially true if you are trying to breathe life into an industrial giant limping towards oblivion.

In my pursuit of business success and happiness, I had a few left field issues hit me, for example where is the management handbook to guide you through closing 'un bordel' without outraging the staff and clientele to the risk of life and limb? Who knew being President would involve being pursued by a gang of international terrorists, intent on kidnap and mayhem? Then there was the fat guard and the one eyed dog!

There were many challenges to be confronted and overcome from Halfway to Paris, thankfully not all of them life threatening.

Halfway, is a mere thousand kilometres from Paris, but the chic capital of France, with its wide boulevards and stylish architecture could be on a different planet from my childhood home in a small dark hamlet dominated by mountains of coal slag. Fortunately, I felt very much at home in Paris and just as comfortable meeting and greeting Princes, Presidents and Prime Ministers.

The journey was exhilarating, inspiring and occasionally a wee bit intimidating.

Come, join me.

'Owen Quinn is a typical Scottish high-flier, who carved a career in British Leyland, ending up as President of Leyland Europe in Paris then joining the MBO of Leyland Bus Group. He became a company doctor, and spent five years in Australia turning round companies and recovering debt in the car industry'.

Glasgow Herald 27th August 2003

CHAPTER ONE

WHERE IS WORKINGTON?

"Where exactly is Workington?" was Isobel's first question when I told her I was thinking of applying for a job with British Leyland in that town. My Dad, my Mum and my brothers and sister were also a bit perplexed, perhaps because most people associated the motor industry with the great centres of Detroit, or Coventry but not with Workington. In the 1950's my Dad had worked for Standard Motors, which subsequently became part of the Leyland Motors Corporation, and when I told him of my plans, he just looked at me and like Isobel asked, "Where is it"? I knew exactly where it was because I had visited the place on one of my adventures in the van with Junior and wee Shuggy. I sent off my application for the job as Management Accountant with the Leyland National Bus Company, based at Lillyhall on the outskirts of Workington. In the library I found that Workington was 32 miles southwest of Carlisle, to the north of the Lake District and access was via difficult winding roads, across the A596 from the M6 Motorway. What more do you need to know? Ronnie Barker was later to slander the town by writing to his wife from Her Majesty's Prison

Slade and telling her that he was incarcerated 100 miles from civilisation and 5 minutes from Workington. I suppose the town's greatest claim to fame was that the Romans cared enough for the town for the Emperor Hadrian to include it in his new province by building his famous wall just north of the town. I drove to Workington on a fine sunny day, had a really good interview with the Financial Controller and a walk round the factory, which was very modern but not terribly efficient looking. After the tour I drove back home, confident I would be offered the job.

On the way home I picked up a couple from Peru and their tiny baby, who were hitching around the UK, with no money and no real plan, brave indeed. Both parents were charming, erudite and spoke beautiful English but they looked to be careworn and a bit down at the heel, possibly they were giving one last hurrah for the hippie lifestyle, now they were parents. Isobel had packed me a very substantial picnic, which I was never going to eat, being anxious to get home as quickly as possible and let Isobel know all the news from Workington. I asked the hitchhikers if they had had lunch and when they said they had not I told them to help themselves. The way they attacked the picnic I don't think they had eaten in days. As we drove northwards, we chatted about Scotland and its various cities and over the course of the drive they decided they would visit Edinburgh, for no reason other than the discussion we had in the car. I dropped them off on the outskirts of Glasgow at the main road to Edinburgh, and wished them the best of luck. When I arrived home, Isobel listened to my news and thought it sounded promising enough to think about planning our departure from Scotland. and then we waited for the result of my interview. A few days later I received a job offer and a nice package, we were off and our life of globetrotting was about to begin. I had to give ITT one month's notice and it gave me great pleasure to leave that company despite knowing I had learned a lot and improved greatly in the almost three years I had been with the company.

The new post was Management Accountant at Leyland National Limited, which employed 600 people making single deck buses, in a brand new cutting edge factory, just outside Workington in Cumbria. This move was to prove the making of me and the start of a great relationship that lasted almost twenty years. My association with British Leyland shaped and formed me as a businessman, and as a person, and my new job turned out to be more like a company doctor's project than a normal post, in fact my entire career with British Leyland followed that same line. I was excited at joining the motor industry and looked forward to building on my experience so far, and perhaps I was a little in awe some ways, here was I from the hills of Scotland in the employ of the mighty British Leyland one of the highest profile companies in the UK, I was thrilled.

Being born into a working class family in a tiny village in central Scotland might not seem the most obvious place to start climbing the ladder of success in business. In the bleak post war period rationing was still in place and life wasn't easy although not many thought of themselves as poor because there is equality in deprivation that makes all men equal in the eyes of God and his fellow man. Of course, in those gentle far off days the consumer society with its inexhaustible demand for things, had not yet been imported from the United States so we did not know that we needed 50 inch TVs, laptops, iPhones or two cars. That tiny village with its cramped housing was a long way from the bright lights of Paris, New York or Beijing and dining with Princes and Presidents and the odd Prime Minister. It was a whole world away, but that was where I was heading. I ended up working on five continents and living in five countries. I found much in common with people on every continent, once we had made ourselves understood to each other. How much more could our species achieve if not for the dreadful barrier of language? The wrathful God of Genesis gave us a terrible punishment for trying to build that tower at Babel.

Childhood and adolescence had been carefree with freedom to explore intellectually and geographically, although on occasion I pushed the envelope to breaking point. The teenage years brought great adventures watching one of my buddies eject himself from a blazing sleeping bag and another pal chasing sheep with a bull whip, as I looked for the long dead Ghosts of massacred Highlanders. A venture into the vehicle building business as a ten-year old prefigured my business destination with British Leyland. And that was where I was now heading the huge British Leyland

Corporation, I decided that since I was joining such an important high profile company I should do a bit of research to find out what I was getting myself into. British Leyland's turnover was one billion pounds per annum equally split between domestic and export, it sold one million vehicles per annum, employed 280,000 in 67 factories in the UK and 26 factories overseas.

This was some company was I ready for this?

Well I was pretty confident in my business ability, in my time at Singer I had received a terrific grounding by working in many departments. This gave me a good solid grounding in business and particularly in the manufacturing business. I had some great mentors who guided me and advised me as I made my share of mistakes and they offered me wise words when I was in danger of getting too serious about myself. Singer also knocked me into shape as far as the daily discipline of work was concerned and as a callow youth it gave me an insight into the goings-on in the hallowed environs of the boardroom. Singer provided me with the opportunity to assume real responsibility while still in my teens and I left that company with great experience and well prepared to take on new challenges. My time at ITT, taught me a rigid discipline, the job had to be done at all costs and it had to be done right and most importantly of all it had to be done on time. ITT gave me my first taste of people management and the space to make mistakes and to learn from them, as well as in depth knowledge of accounting practices across the whole finance function. While there I became expert in reading Profit and Loss Accounts and Balance Sheets, and equally adept at forecasting and compiling budgets that made sense. I was also quite good at persuading colleagues from other departments to return information to me when I needed it rather than when they had a spare minute to deal with it. I learned the techniques of forensic analysis and in depth reporting. It was not enough to simply identify variances from plan, these had to be explained in detail and plans put in place to repeat good habits and to eliminate negative ones. My monthly reporting was in turn subject to scrutiny in our national head office in London, our regional HQ in Brussels and our Corporate HQ in New York. I learned about hierarchical reporting and its importance in a group with diverse business interests and a global span. This was not a particularly enjoyable phase in my career but I undoubtedly learned a lot and grew up in business terms. In both Singer and ITT, I was fortunate to work for managers who had enough confidence in their own ability to allow me the scope I needed to grow without fear for their own position within the group.

FACE TO FACE WITH REALITY

While both Singer and ITT gave me a brilliant platform for the business world, I had two other periods of employment that equipped me for life in the real world. The first of these was my summer job working in a debt collection agency in Glasgow. In this job I learned some lessons about how harsh life can be and how the folk at the bottom of the social ladder are exploited and manipulated by the system. In addition to face to face meetings with people who were behind in their repayments by working on the counter on Friday afternoons I could read first-hand the evidence of this exploitation in the files I was busily re-arranging for my employer. Those files also contained details of the other agencies we dealt with, the Sherriff Officers, known as Bailiffs in England. These were heartless men empowered by the law to wreak havoc on debtors. In Scotland in the 1960's, most people who owed money failed to answer a summons to court for various reasons but mainly because they were embarrassed. By not responding they became open to many charges and the full force of a cruel and punitive system. If, after judgement was granted they still did not pay what they owed, my company would instruct Sherriff Officers to carry out a warrant sale. This involved valuing their possessions and then having a forced sale on their premises, often the goods were massively undervalued in order to make a quick sale and recover what was owed. By the time of the warrant sale the amount owed could be many times the original sum. A cruel, cruel system which took little heed of circumstances. We also dealt with Private Detectives who would be required to track down some difficult to find defaulters. There was one of these gentlemen who often called into our offices, always bringing sweets for the girls. When he happened to arrive at lunchtime he would join me for a cup of tea and a sandwich and regale me with tales of his trade. He was an unprepossessing wee man, short and slightly built, he always wore a coat with the collar up and a trilby hat, neither of which I ever saw him take off. He looked unkempt and he was a wee bit smelly with a furtive sneaky way about him. The only Private Eye I had ever seen was Sam Spade, played by Humphrey Bogart, our wee man was no Sam Spade. More like Wee Willie Weasel than Sam Spade.

He told me stories about following women as they left their homes to go to work, he would follow them on buses and he described how he sought cover to ensure they did not realise they were being followed. Once he had determined where they were employed, he would supply us with details and through our lawyer we would instruct their employer to 'arrest' their wages, which meant making a deduction and remitting it to us. Willie Weasel was very proud of his investigative techniques. I think he was a bit of fantasist and actually thought he was a Hollywood Private Detective cracking big, complex cases instead of following hard working women around and dodging behind post boxes. Nasty though this business was, I learned about real life and that is always valuable. There were some good things I took away as well from my short spell in that company, like being much more comfortable in the company of girls and ladies. There were 46 girls and me working in this company, and they alternately fussed over me or teased me mercilessly and I learned to cope with both. I joined this company, never having worked a day in my life or earned an honest coin, I came with a naïve and somewhat sheltered view of life and a wide eyed mid-1960's flower child /

hippie optimism, and I got a large dose of reality. This was a short spell and despite the nature of the work or maybe because of it, I grew up quickly and I was definitely a more aware person when I departed than when I had arrived.

While I was working at Singer I took a part time job in a bar in Cambuslang, it was a rough and ready establishment with a bunch of regulars who charmed and appalled in equal measure. Life as a part time barman brought a further degree of reality to an otherwise sheltered existence. Watching drunk men cajole, threaten and wheedle another drink from their mates while bar owners skimmed and cheated was a real eye opener. The pub gave me a chance to meet characters whose idiosyncrasies made 'larger than life' such an inadequate description of them and their behaviour. There was one man in that working class bar in Cambuslang who was a published author and playwright whose work was broadcast by BBC Radio. This man also held the Military Medal for his deeds of derring do during the war, when he was captured behind enemy lines, while on a commando raid. After three failed attempts to escape from a prisoner of war camp he eventually succeeded in escaping and made it back to his own regiment to continue his personal odyssey against the fascist hordes. Like my own father this man struggled with Post Traumatic Stress Syndrome and when it came upon him he retreated into a world of nostalgia, bitterness and sadness. In my eighteen months working as part time barman I established a good relationship with this man whose name was 'Big Andy', and we often chatted about music, art, literature and politics in fact anything and everything except football. After I had known him for about six months I plucked up the courage to ask him what he did with the 12 bottles of fortified wine he bought about once a month, and he told me. He did not have an ordinary job but he received regular royalty cheques from the BBC and when they came in he went on the razzle dazzle and bought copious quantities of his favourite tipple, in this case it was 'Lanliq' a popular brand of fortified wine. After getting drunk at home he and his large Alsatian dog would decamp to the local cenotaph and Big Andy would spend the night with his dog, his bottle and his memories of his mates. Andy was erudite, witty and hard as nails, and I loved talking to him.

At the other end of the spectrum was a round, fat guy called Gilbert whose favourite trick was to buy a pint and go for a sleep on one of the wooden benches around the edge of this very large bar. He would wake every now and then and have a drink from his pint and then go back to sleep, after a while he would wake up and finish his beer and then he would move up to the bar and start chatting to anyone who was there. Whenever someone went to the toilet Gilbert would slide over and drink from the man's beer, if nobody was watching. It was always a struggle to keep on top of his antics if the bar was busy and he would often get a slap from some offended drinker who caught him at his beer. This man Gilbert was another complex character, he had been in some sort of accident which caused the sleeping problem and apparently he was unaware that he was drinking other people's beer. The regulars were normally able to keep him straight but for visitors it was a real problem.

Saturday night after closing time we had another couple of regulars who would drop in for a fag and a wee dram. In the days when policemen still walked the beat we had two constables who kept an eye open for us, especially when we were closed. When they came in they always got twenty fags and a large dram of real whisky (as opposed to the stuff the regulars were served), they would stay for twenty-minutes, have a chat about the weather and how bad the other pubs were and then leave for the rest of their evening patrol. The bar I worked in was at the end of the Main Street and there were three other bars before us, so on cold nights our constables would be well fortified against the weather. One Saturday as the bar staff were sitting having a chat and a drink, waiting on the police, there was a knock at the door and I went to open the door expecting to find the police but instead I was greeted by a drunk, dishevelled and distinctly pale faced young man. He mumbled something to me but I couldn't make out what he was trying to say, due to a combination of the fact that he was drunk and that he was missing his top teeth. After several attempts at speaking in a toothless, halting, mumbling drawl, he managed to convey to me that he had lost his upper plate and thought it had happened in the toilets when he was being sick. I told him I would go and look for him and locked the door again and left him with his thoughts, bad breath and no teeth. The bar staff had responsibility for tidying the bar, the glasses and the gantry but the actual cleaning of the bar, the lounge and the toilets was left to two nice ladies who came in early every morning, and scrubbed and rubbed until the place was shining. You need to have that piece of information to grasp the magnitude of what followed. As I walked into the gents I was met with a horrific sight, no I was met with an utterly revolting sight. Somebody had been violently sick all over the floor and there right in the middle of all this vomit was a wee pink shiny piece of plastic with some white sparkling false teeth attached. The bugger had been sick all over the place and now his false teeth were sitting there grinning maliciously at me. My stomach was churning at the prospect of picking up these offensive items and I was tempted to walk back out and tell him I could not find them. My good nature got the better of me, so holding my nose with one hand I bent down and picked up the wee guy's falsies with my other hand. I marched quickly to the door opened it and handed him back his teeth. He popped them straight into his mouth and clearly said, "Thanks, pal, I appreciate it." Yuk.

I was very conscientious in my bar work and when the manager realised that I was studying accountancy I was also hired to do the books. This was not a very arduous job since there was a set of prepared schedules that needed completion showing a simple trading account and various operating percentages there was another schedule used for doing a weekly stocktake. After completing these schedules, I prepared the cash deposit for banking the takings, for the manager to take the night deposit safe.

I was also responsible for ordering and part of my role was to work out the optimum number of quarter bottles of whisky to buy for decanting and selling over the bar. You see a skilled barman can get a better yield out of four quarter bottles than the pub will achieve through off sales. Although we did weekly stock audits in the bar, the brewery sent in their own auditors each quarter to do an independent stocktake. This quarterly audit was a hoot with bars swapping barrels of beer with each other, and one particular trick I thought was very inventive was filling aluminium lager barrels with water. Somebody had invented a tool for opening these barrels and replacing the seal to fool the auditor. It was all very dodgy but I watched and understood that these things were happening elsewhere and not just in a small bar in Cambuslang. I learned things in that bar that they don't teach you on ICWA courses, I can tell you.

LEYLAND NATIONAL

Was I ready for British Leyland, I think that Singer, ITT, debt collecting and bar work had equipped me to cope with most things the world could throw at me and I was up for this new venture. My boss was the Financial controller Arthur Hall and on day one I went into his office as he was puffing on his scabby old pipe and flipping through heaps of really old paperwork and mumbling to himself. He was only in his late thirties, but he had a shock of white hair that made him look older, so somehow the pipe seemed in keeping with his general persona. Maybe the pipe helped him to keep his composure, because he was a really calm bloke. Arthur was a top notch accountant who told me he was engaged full time on structuring an Investment Grant claim for the enormous Capital Expenditure it had taken to build and equip this state of the art facility. I was surprised to hear that and asked him why he needed to work full time on that, to which he replied "How long have you got?" He went on to say, "I haven't been in post for very long and before me there was only part time cover, two days a week. Nothing had been done about the claim, none of the paperwork was at hand and since we are owed about four million quid, we need to get on with it."

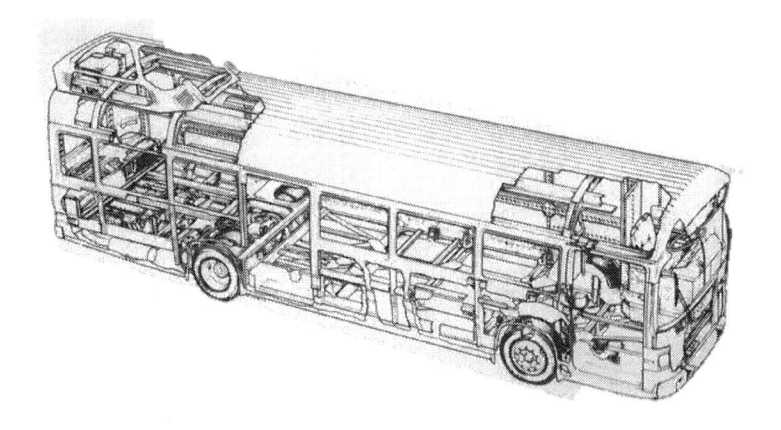

The revolutionary Leyland National Bus

Arthur continued, "The project was conceived and run by engineers whose focus was to get the factory built and running. The factory opened two years ago but the project goes back a further three years before that, now I have to somehow find the necessary documents and then put them into some sort of order to justify the claims for the sums we have actually spent. In a shed outside the factory we have an archive with boxes of documentation, I have been told that nothing has been thrown out but until you check you don't really know. I've had a look at it and it looks more like an abandoned graveyard but I am going to make a start with the help of one of the girls".

Within the Truck and Bus Division of the Leyland Group being offered a job in wee Leyland National away up in the wilds of Cumbria was not seen as a plum posting and there had been trouble recruiting from the senior ranks. Having become geographically mobile in pursuing my career objectives I found it strange that many people in the North of England were extremely reluctant to move from their home area to take up a new post. As a result of this reluctance, the Finance function was only just getting started at Leyland National. Amazingly when Arthur arrived, only basic procedures were in place and then only in terms of bookkeeping and wages, no reporting of any sort. Arthur had recruited an old colleague Andrew Barnard to run the Financial Accounting Department and reporting to Andrew were two external recruits, Tommy Relton and Eric Newton, both qualified accountants, the rest of the employees were local recruits.

Eric and Tommy were the same age as me and we became friends, as did Roy Nicholson a local man who was a supervisor in the financial accounting department. Andrew had a very strong team. Arthur told me he had recruited me to create a Management Accounting Department from scratch and to try and to install a cost accounting system also from scratch, and that I would have a lot of scope to do my own thing while he sorted out the Grant. He would leave me to get the management accounting routines in place. I had a strong CV in all aspects of finance and I knew my way round a set of accounts. I was technically strong and had lots of experience in costing, budgeting, forecasting techniques and P&L reporting. I was also able to analyse problems, offer solutions, to make decisions and accept responsibility. I was comfortable in my own skin and I wore responsibility and authority very easily. I had experience of running small departments and managing people. I was 25, very confident in my ability. And now I would have freedom to do my thing. Lucky boy.

Arthur told me it had been noted that I arrived for my interview in a Hillman Avenger car and now I was driving a Ford Cortina, someone wanted to know if I did not like Leyland cars. In those days of extended lead times it had taken more than three months for my new Ford to arrive, I waited for six months and sold it at a significant loss to keep faith with my new employer. On leaving Arthur's office I sat in my own little cubby hole and had a good long think about how to proceed, I took a leaf out of the book of one of my lecturers and created a case study paper as a formal report for my new boss, so he and I would have a road map to measure progress on this job.

THE NEIGHBOURS FROM HEAVEN

To join Leyland National, Isobel and I had to leave our nice modern flat in East Kilbride and move into a rented semi-detached house in Whitehaven. It was a lot more primitive than our flat, and needed a bit of work to knock it into shape, but we were young and in love and nothing was an obstacle. By this time Isobel and I had expanded our family, we now had a blue roan cocker spaniel, called Misty. We arranged the removers and headed off to Whitehaven, arriving three days before I was due to start at Leyland. The house might have been disappointing but our neighbours were fantastic people, we never really had much to do with our neighbours in East Kilbride, we were too busy working during the week and socialising with our friends at weekends. Misty knew the neighbours better than we did, because the local children came to ask if they could play with him. The kids taught our dog some bad habits we were to discover when the man who ran the local ice cream van charged us five bob for cones he had given the dog during the course of the week.

Our new address was number 2 The Oval, and our next-door neighbours were Jim and Tina Denver and their son Alan. Jim worked a shift pattern at the local colliery and Tina worked as a waitress in the Directors Dining Room at the local Chemical works of Albright and Wilson. As soon as we moved in Jim and Tina decided that we were lost souls and they took us under their wing. We could not have had better neighbours on our first time away from home. They came round to see us and to introduce themselves and by the time they left you would have thought they had known us forever. They took away one of the keys to our front door "in case the postman needs to leave something and you are not home from work".

Isobel and I both started work on the same day, me at Leyland National in Lillyhall and Isobel in the offices of Albright and Wilson in Whitehaven. When we arrived home from work it was to find the dog had been walked, the fire was lit and the kettle was boiled ready for a cup of tea. Tina asked us if we liked salmon steaks, (this was a time before farmed salmon made this fish so plentiful, it was still relatively scarce, expensive and slightly exotic.) When we said we did like salmon Tina presented us with two large steaks straight from the Directors Dining Room. And so it went on for the next 14 months, they babied us and looked after us as though we were their own children. It turned out that Tina finished early in the afternoon and because Jim worked shifts he had large parts of the day where he would do things for us, around the house or in the garden. We never asked but we didn't need to, they just looked at what needed doing and went about doing it. They were among the most remarkable people I have ever met. As well as being warm, kind and generous they were also very interesting and clued us in on all things English and Cumbrian. Jim was a cricketer and he loved that game with a passion. I wonder if it was just a coincidence that he lived in a street called the Oval? When I asked him his position he said he was a stumper. I asked if that was the same as a wicketkeeper and Jim said "some people think so but I don't, I'm a stumper. I'm there to get batsmen out not to watch the bowling." Jim was then 60 years old and still played regularly in the North Lancashire League, (the NLL) which is a very high standard. Many of the clubs in the North Lancs. League, including Whitehaven had overseas professionals on their books. Jim had also played minor counties cricket for his county side, Cumberland and Westmorland from its inception until just after his 56th birthday. And for all their accomplishments Jim and Tina were both self-effacing, gentle people and we came to love them dearly just like our own parents.

That first summer Jim decided my education was sadly lacking and took me down to Whitehaven Cricket Club for an NLL match. While Jim stumped right and left, I sat on a deckchair with a glass of shandy and watched proceedings. Jim converted me that day and I have loved cricket ever since. Although it was an unsettling time for us moving away from our home, our family and our friends in Scotland and trying to establish ourselves in Cumbria without knowing a single soul, Jim and Tina smoothed the way for us and helped us in so many ways. Their kindness went a long way to helping me settle quickly in to my new job and in helping Isobel and I settle into life in a foreign land!

CASE STUDY

THE GROUP – Having done some research on my new company I was to learn that the reality was a bit different from the claims I had read. British Leyland Ltd – BL was a mish-mash of companies not a corporation in the general way of things, it had been forced together in an act of Political will, a visionary move but one that needed support through the dramas that would lie ahead. Would the Government that had the vison to establish this initiative have the stomach to accept the changes that would be needed and to provide the funding needed to re-tool and re-equip these factories? The answer to that question would determine how successful this nascent corporation would be in the white hot heat of the motor industry. I was to discover that some managers running substantial businesses were not up to the task, many lacked any formal education in the principles of management. The various companies which formed BL, had enjoyed massive success until the outbreak of the Second World War, when many of their overseas operations were suspended and the UK manufacturing base was given over to the production of armaments.

The post war years were hard for the auto industry, with significant investment required to reconvert factories to peacetime activities and to design and develop new products. Against this background, in 1968 the Labour Government created a company to compete on the world stage. It would be known as British Leyland Limited, and was a merger of two independent conglomerates British Motor Holdings (BMH) predominantly a car company and Leyland Motors Ltd, which manufactured commercial vehicles. It was decided Leyland Motors would be the dominant partner, the Leyland management team would take the senior positions in the new Corporation, and the Leyland name would be prominent in the branding. The new British Leyland Ltd was a Global Corporation with factories throughout the five continents and 280,000 employees. In 1974 the Corporation ran into major funding problems and was bailed out by the government, and from that moment on it became a political football and a metaphor for all the bad things that existed in British industry, indeed in British society. The company struggled to compete, as plans for rationalisation and cost cutting were rejected as being politically unsellable and vote losers. With hands tied behind their backs senior managers inevitably failed to deliver in line with plans. Then they were fired, and replaced by men from the second tier, clever and competent people but inexperienced. These new sacrificial lambs were given little time to acclimatise before being fired for the same reasons as their predecessors, only to be replaced by more of the same in a pointless exercise of expedient hire and fire. This depressing policy was more aimed at pacifying critics than planning the renaissance of an industrial giant.

THE COMPANY - Leyland National was a joint venture company 50% owned by BL Ltd and the National Bus Company, (a Government owned company), to manufacture a unique bus, a single deck advanced vehicle which allowed one-man operation. The vehicle was produced in exactly the same manner as a car, where all the components arrived at the start of a production line and as the line moved the components were added until the vehicle was complete. The raison d'etre for the Leyland National factory had been the reluctance of British unions to allow one-man operation of double deck buses. One-man operation of public transport was seen as fundamental to the future profitability of the industry and in the face of determined union opposition it was decided to introduce the single decker, where one-man operation was acceptable to the Unions. A major investment decision that looks odd in the light of hindsight. As construction commenced on the Leyland National factory, the unions dropped their objections and allowed the introduction of one-man operation on double deck buses to go ahead. This change of heart had a profound effect on Leyland National, because the guaranteed volumes of 2,000 standard buses per annum from National Bus Company was slashed to 250 units per annum. Now that NBC could have their preferred option of double deck buses with one-man operation they no longer had the need for a high volume of single deckers.

Significant political capital had been expended on this flagship project, including the building of new roads, and other infrastructure improvements, so construction of the factory had to go ahead. The decision to proceed with the project with this reduction in guaranteed volumes from NBC, meant the Leyland Sales Team would have to find replacement volumes from other customers and that meant the export market. Incremental volumes were necessary to make the numbers work and for the factory to operate profitably. The difficulty with this was that the equipment could only cope with the strict requirements of the standard NBC bus for which it had been specifically designed. This left Leyland National between a rock and a hard place, the products and the factory should have been re-engineered but in a classic political fudge a halfway house accommodation was deemed acceptable. The factory would run as designed and the standard vehicles would go through as planned but at the derisory volumes of 5 units per week. Any other sales would be engineered on a one off basis and 'knife and forked' through the factory, thus condemning the business to be inefficient forever or at least until all the factory equipment could be replaced. This was an easy decision for a politician to make but a hard one to live with at the coal face.

THE ROLE – Management Accountant – responsible for profit planning and reporting

THE TASK – To review the business and decide on the systems and processes that were needed to allow the construction of annual Budgets against which the actual performance of the business could be measured.

In my meeting with my boss I got the message, this was going to be a major development role but not for me it was for this leading edge company I had just joined. He told me the company lacked any sort of management accounting systems or procedures, which was honest of him but what else did it lack? The Financial accounting manager showed me what he had and it was effective but basic, costs were allocated properly in line with Finance

Manual procedures but we operated with a single costs centre for the entire factory of 600 people. There was no allocation between any departments because we did not have any. We did have a set of financial accounts and they were accurate but with no budget to compare them with nobody had much idea of what we should be expecting, in the way of profitability. The other department heads were as forthcoming as my colleagues in finance had been, and they did not have very much in the way of controls either. There were no standard times in place, no grouping of labour by work centre, no bills of material to determine the components which needed to be purchased, we had a remote sales team who did not report to our MD and who set prices in isolation of any factory input. So we could determine current results but we did not know if that was in line with plan because there was no plan. We could not forecast where we would be in future because we didn't know how, but we had lovely shiny equipment and a bus with no sales volumes. This should keep me out of trouble for a wee while! At least I knew what I had to do, easy really, so get on with it.

This little company was part of a huge organisation and as such I knew there would be manuals available for most aspects of the business. I borrowed a copy of the Finance Manual, all three volumes, and was pleased to see it had a familiar ring. The BL manual was very similar to the one I had used while at ITT which had been plagiarised from the granddaddy of all Finance Manuals, the one created by the Ford Motor Company. Why re-invent the wheel when Ford had done such a good job? Pretty sensible if you ask me to use the industry standard. So that was all good, I was right at home and knew my way around this book. I looked to see what it had in terms of structure and organisation and started my task by making a list of the departmental names and codes for the production and stores departments, as defined in the BL Finance Manual

I needed to meet the senior personnel, starting with the Production Director, John Clark, who took me on a tour of the factory, and I was very impressed with what I saw, both the manufacturing concept and the equipment being used were very advanced. This was the industrial equivalent of walking on to the USS Enterprise, with a lot of bling to catch the eye. The factory was totally unique, the only one in the world trying to build complete buses in the same way as cars are built, John Clark and I spent a lot of time going through the details of the products and the production process. I like factories and felt very comfortable wandering around and poking my nose in to see what was going on. John told me they only had assembly instructions for the standard buses and that was a major challenge as most vehicles sold had to be engineered by varying from the standard vehicle. This often involved an engineer walking the vehicle through the factory and working with the production team as they encountered difficulties. Coping with multi specs was not just inefficient, it was a nightmare for production management. When I asked him how his supervisors managed their charges without any recognised departments he laughed and said the foremen have sorted out their own informal work groups, based on the individual operations. Well done them, but why has nobody picked up on this? John Clark was in his first Director's post and to some extent was still finding his feet, he was very proud of the factory and trying very hard to overcome the hurdles and obstacles placed in his way. He became a close ally as I started to introduce changes. I spent an entire morning with the production director, who assured me that he would provide me with any assistance I needed.

Neville Brownlow ran the engineering departments, and he was a competent experienced engineering manager. I was particularly interested in getting my hands on the build manuals, the projected timings and to see whether or not we were getting close or not to those forecasts and most importantly I wanted a list of the operations as planned. Neville gave me one piece of information that stuck with me my entire career. He told me the planned build time for both variants of the original Leyland National Bus was 120 hours, start to finish, for the completed vehicle through the factory, through the test centre and ready for collection by the customer. He added that of course with the change of direction from a standard product to a more bespoke production plan it would be unlikely to achieve 120 hours build time. Neville had re-set the build target for non-standard products to 150 hours to reflect the added complexity. At that meeting with Neville these numbers had no real impact on me, they were numbers in isolation but later when I had a chance to compare these numbers to other types of manufacturing I realised just how revolutionary this concept was. It was not unusual for a completed bus, chassis and body to absorb up to 2,000 hours for assembly, while coaches could be more than double that. These, I was to learn were stunning numbers and a bench mark for other bus builders in years to come. I asked him why the production team did not have any build schedules and he said they didn't really need them because they could work from the standard schedules and the resident engineer could fill in the gaps. I was aghast!

Ken Sewell a fellow, Scotsman with a weird mid –Atlantic drawl and a big ego was the Materials Manager. I quizzed him about the purchase of materials and his systems, his controls and checks and his approvals procedures. I was very interested in establishing the link between our original projected costs and the actual purchase prices and I did not get a good feeling when talking to Ken. He told me bluntly that his department was by necessity run by the seat of the pants and every day was a crisis trying to get parts into the factory in impossible lead times. In a calm moment during our chat Ken told me that his wife was Cambodian and that he had bought her, for a case of Johnny Walker Red Label Whisky. I thought this was a very interesting thing to tell someone on your first meeting. I knew I was going to have my work cut out getting an insight into the materials department and getting Kenny boy to think about anything other than shouting at suppliers, for faster deliveries.

The HR Manager, Mike Howell was a bright, expansive, gregarious man who was extremely helpful and was able to give me a lot of data on our employees. In particular I wanted to know how they went about determining how many employees they needed, as well details of rates of pay for employees and their various grades. Mike was very straightforward and said that the manning levels were based on the original production levels of 40 standard buses per week at 120 hours each. But once battle was joined at the reduced build rates they simply allowed the foremen to deploy the workforce as they thought appropriate. Really? How awfully democratic. In answer to my asking if we had any overmanning Mike simply replied, "probably, but we get the buses out." Well that's ok then. I was also interested in his views on our shop floor employees. Mike told me that the majority of our employees were either ex miners or fishermen and that many were still coming to terms with being inside a factory all day every day. The vast majority of tasks within the production department had been de-skilled to a semi-skilled basis, and with on the job training over six weeks most people adapted well. He added that most but not all, were now house broken.

We did not have a sales department at Leyland National, our sales resource was part of a centralised team who were responsible for selling the production capacity of all the bus and coach manufacturing plants within the Group. In reality there was one man who looked after the NBC account (5 units a week, guaranteed as part of the deal in the aftermath of the unions agreeing to allow one-man operation of double deckers) and another man who dealt with export opportunities. Not having any authority over this function would have been a great frustration for me had I been the Managing Director of the business, with forecast sales programmes always late, and deficient in numbers and clarity of specification requirements. This lack of control of sales was a real pain because for the most part the bus sales personnel were quite unique, regarding themselves as something of the "Gentlemen Sellers" and above other mortals. With no justification because in truth they were order takers working in a captive environment rather than aggressive pointy nosed sellers of capital equipment. They were a slippery lot.

THE RESOLUTION

After my meetings with the senior personnel I launched the first part of my strategy, to organise the production team into recognisable departments in order to assemble some cost schedules. I formed a little team of the maintenance manager, an industrial engineer, the factory superintendent, myself and a large pot of paint and a brush. With brush in hand I got all three to agree to what constituted sensible work groups in line with the Finance Manual requirements, and with agreement reached I painted the department number on the floor and copied it into my notebook, to create the company's first list of departments. The Maintenance Manager, Dennis Hayton, proved to be an interesting character, he was a former Merchant Navy Officer and a first class engineer, but he had a reputation in the factory for being the grumpiest man in the world. Dennis and I got on famously and I found him to be a true professional and like so many ex Merchant Navy engineers, he was well organised, resourceful and great in a crisis. My appearance on the factory floor caused a lot of comment and no small amount of interest as everyone speculated the purpose of my little exercise. I had thought I would be a country hick compared to the hard-headed guys from the motor industry, in fact the reverse was the case, and I quickly established a reputation as a no-nonsense operator.

Armed with my new structure I started to change our way of grouping costs, starting with the payroll, my colleague the Financial Accountant and his team were not wildly enthusiastic because they had grown used to the freedom they had from the way they did things. I arranged a seminar for all the members of the finance department, and briefed them on what I was doing, why I was doing it and what the benefits would be to the business. That turned out to be a good move because once they understood what I was up to, I got all sorts of helpful insights that made the task a lot easier. Communicating with the folk at the coal face was not an established principle in that part of rural Cumbria, but it became a wee bit more frequent after my arrival. After my meet and greet tour of my colleagues I formed the opinion that in the hurry to build this factory and to commission all this ultra-modern equipment, the joint venture partners left some administrative details until later. And later was now.

Once I had the payroll anlaysed I had one part of the equation to start creating a budget cost of sales.

With a brand new list of departments and the beginnings of a labour budget the next stage was to talk to my countryman Kenny Sewell to see what he used for Bills of Material, (BOM) and that was a lot of fun. Poor old Ken had been left with the original spec for the standard products that had formed the design phase of project Leyland National, so that every time there was a non-standard product ordered he had to get an engineer to work with him to list what the differences were, then he had to work out who if anyone manufactured, or even could manufacture such a component, then he had to get an engineer to raise some piece of paper to get this component an allocated part number. Only then could he place an order. Placing the order was often the beginning of another drama because the majority of vehicles were specials this meant large sections of the original bills of material were obsolete and new components were engineered very late and sometimes were actually engineered by our suppliers, with grave consequences in terms of costs. He told me he would often get a design for a component from the design engineer and be expected to have it in the factory within a week, including tool design, manufacture and delivery all the way up to Workington from a supplier's factory in the Midlands. This timescale was unachievable and the result was delayed production, inevitable cost overruns and large numbers of obsolete parts being ordered unnecessarily to lie in the stores - forever. With the side benefit of high blood pressure and ulcers for the buyers working in that department, there was a lot of swearing and threatening of suppliers going on. This was a terrible environment to work in, a job with zero possibility of success, how can you order components for a bus that hasn't even been designed? Everyone was in a state of conflict with their suppliers and running around like the proverbial blue arsed fly and must have been knackered when they left for home in the evening. Kenny might have been a smart arse but he was actually smart, he had a tough job and the poor guy was on a hiding to nothing. But I knew how to help him. So I took copies of Kenny Sewell's BOM's and I got a list of all the buses in the order book, passed them to the engineering department and asked them to supply me with a list of the additional components.

About ten minutes after I asked the guy to do it I had Neville Brownlow in my office demanding to know what I was up to. Neville was a terribly nice man and awfully polite, but with an exaggerated sense of his own importance and full of bluster. Neville took himself very seriously and I have always though that is a dangerous thing. Although I take what I do very seriously, especially my work, I try to remember I was born in the Halfway, so I try never take myself seriously. I think Neville was also a bit niggled that a Johnny come lately to the auto industry should be ordering his engineers to do things that he had not even thought of, in an attempt to make the production process more simple, as well as simplifying the ordering of materials for the products.

Neville like many British managers of his generation was acutely aware and protective of his status and was determined to defend "his turf", a small minded attitude all too prevalent I was to find in some quarters of the company. To be fair to Neville he was upset at me going directly to his people and in effect re-priortitising their work schedule. Neville and I chatted for a while and I explained that when I spoke to his colleague he told me they had all the information available from the design team, I briefed him on where I was going with this exercise and its value to the business. I apologised and said I should have spoken to the head of the department before sending his guy off on a fair amount of work.

A lesson learned and a mistake not to be repeated.

Simultaneous with trying to understand the data I could collect in-house I was wrestling with a budget request from HQ and preparing some basic schedules from the scant information available to me. Then I received an invitation to a Budget meeting at head office, Lancaster House in the town of Leyland. So off I went, taking with me various reports I had been working on. I was looking forward to this meeting and thought that I would be super impressed by the head office staff and that my poor opinion of the company thus far was just because I was out in the sticks and at a plant where it was difficult to persuade the best people to move. When I arrived I was presented with a pack of schedules, together with completion instructions to be used in compiling the following year's budget, in a pretty binder with the company logo on the front. A cursory examination of these schedules showed the basis of next year's plan would be last year's actuals. The HQ staff would be using a system of historical comparisons pioneered by Noah in planning the feedstuff for the animals on the Ark. This system was far from being realistic yet nobody seemed bothered and talked as if we were discussing state of the art proposals. The man in the chair said that they had run out of time last year and the budgets had been compiled without any input from the factories, what? This was just ludicrous how can HQ people possibly know the needs of a factory, the budgets could never be right, this was amateur hour at the Lancashire Working Men's Club.

They were nice people but without much of an idea on how to run a meeting, let alone a major Finance operation and their lack of discipline and lack of focus on deadlines was worrying. The people preparing these budgets knew they were wildly inaccurate so they had developed a neat technique which they called consolidation adjustments (this was simply loading the costs and depressing sales price increases until they had a bottom line they could live with). This meant that the individual factories were managed against an unforgiving set of budget targets but the consolidation adjustments ensured that the whole looked ok. The plants then got a ton of flak for underperforming but the HQ team were praised because the company results were ok. Talk about having your cake and eating it. It was either frighteningly cunning or frighteningly naïve, but it was hardly the basis for driving a company forward, was this really the much vaunted motor industry, at work? Quelle horreur!

All in all, this was a pretty disappointing meeting, it was a bit like a parody of how to do things professionally and yet these men were not fools and not without the scars of experience. I just could not get my head around this it was Mickey Mouse stuff compared to the depth and forensic thoroughness of planning and reporting at ITT. People would have been fired for this lackadaisical approach to planning in my old company. I asked for and got a copy of what had been previously submitted on behalf of Leyland National, which, as expected bore no resemblance to what the company was doing, or was even capable of doing. From now on Leyland National, at least, would be submitting professional budgets based on fact and realistic targets and objectives that the company had a chance of achieving. Meeting over, off I went back to the wild rural idyll that is Workington, extremely disappointed with what I had encountered at head office, determined to get to grips with my case study and drag Leyland National into the 20th century as quickly as possible.

Changes were coming thick and fast at Leyland National and everyone seemed to be keen to buy into the idea of more control, first we started producing weekly reports showing production performance, simple things like output volume, numbers employed, absence, overtime and factory efficiency. The production Director was in his glory, he actually had something to talk to his team about, it had only taken two years! We then added material costs and order book details to the weekly report and made sure it was available on a Monday and still relevant. From there we produced simple in house quarterly forecasts of profit and loss accounts and after 6 months we had a fully functioning budget covering 12 months and supported by monthly rolling forecasts of full year performance. By the end of year one we were a fully functioning finance department and our reporting routines to HQ were timely, accurate and well received. By the end of my second year the place was utterly changed we had installed a proper standard costing system, thanks to Tom Relton's hard work, we had proper budget routines in place, with enormous input from Kenny Sewell we had accurate Bills of Material for all of our buses before they were released to the production team. We even had a pretty full order book and the manufacturing team were consistently building in excess of 30m units per week, lower than the planned 40 but including much more complex products. Arthur Hall had managed to reconstruct the Grant paperwork and that money was safely in the bank. We had produced a five-year plan that showed a pretty solid future for our little business. In terms of my original Case Study paper I had prepared I was pleased that we had managed to achieve so much in such relatively short time.

The factory was a happy place and then we got a bit of a shock, when it was announced that we needed to be bailed out by the Government, which was the result of the Ryder enquiry earlier that year. From now on British Leyland would become a bye word for the ills of British industry and British society, we became political football, to be kicked by any and every politician trying to score a point over the opposition, and reviled by newspapers with no idea of what the company was about. After the visit from the Ryder Committee one of the managers at Lancaster House, telephoned asking me if I could provide him with a full year forecast, with an analysis of variations against budget. When I asked what was going on he said there was a flap on and he needed the forecast super quick by the end of play that day, a full three hours. I said it was going to be pretty rough and ready and was assured that would be good enough. Despite the assurance that quick and dirty was good enough, I then spent the next three weeks answering questions from various people at head office on a series of documents that took a couple of hours to construct. The people who were asking these various questions had been with the company for a long time and had got used to the old way of working. It was clear they were now marching to a different drumbeat and the pressure they were under was evident in the phone calls. Somebody was pulling the strings and wanted a more serious approach to forecasting, and that person was the new Finance Director, Jerry Glancy, an Irishman with a soft accent and an iron will. Things would change still more in the near future. Back in Workington I was happy with my lot although beginning to get a bit restless, I was on top of my own job and because I had spare capacity, I was able to spend time helping

37

colleagues with issues that concerned them I worked in the stores with the materials manager and on improving build schedules with the production director, for example.

In the 1970's the United Kingdom was lurching from one crisis to the next, in 1974 a hung parliament meant two General Elections in one year, we experienced strikes, power cuts, three day weeks, streets full of rubbish, recession, depression and soaring interest rates. Interest rates were phenomenally high and costs were rising steeply on a daily basis. As was the case during the Second World War we were subjected to rationing when the Government issued coupons for buying petrol. The impact was evident in the shops as prices rose sharply and the weekly shopping bill became ever more steep. British Leyland was not spared the pain as the costs of materials went through the roof. We were revaluing our inventories every month because of the cost escalation, some months our cost of sales would increase by 15%, it is almost unbelievable but that was what happened. Naturally with the cost of living going through the roof there was great pressure on wages with unionised employees and non-union staff demanding salary increases just to stand still. Economically the United Kingdom resembled the hyper-inflation beset German Republic of the 1930's, it was a dreadful time.

We had become a Banana Republic.

In response to this national emergency the Government took leave of its senses and passed an act of Parliament imposing a wage and prices freeze which prevented companies from awarding general pay increases to employees but they could promote a person and award an increase in salary as a result of the new job, or alternatively award a tax-free perk. The prices freeze was widely welcomed by the public but caused great damage to companies who could not absorb the cost escalation and needed price hikes to keep their heads above water. The wage freeze, however caused general outrage, a massive increase in job mobility and the birth of a new tier of employees who had "manager" added to their job title, without the responsibility of managing anything. Many people continued to do exactly the same job but with the new title they were able to receive a pay rise. Another unintended consequence of this stupid legislation was that in a bid to retain key employees, companies began offering them company cars. This naturally had an overflow effect as other employees demanded parity with their colleagues with cars, and soon the UK had the highest number of company owned cars in the free world. This was all done in an attempt to retain the services of valued employees, and prevent them leaving in order to get a salary increase, and the impact was felt for decades to come. Hard as it was for individuals those days of hyperinflation took a heavy toll on companies and the economy, there was so much uncertainty. Running a business is always tough and it seems that governments (at least UK Governments) never seem to learn that stability is the greatest gift they can give their companies. Of course stability is not a word in the politician's lexicon, after all they exist to pass new laws just to show they are important.

In the meantime, Isobel and I were coming to terms with life in Whitehaven, making friends and getting out and about. We socialised with other young people from Isobel's work at Albright and Wilson and with some of my colleagues from Leyland National. I started supporting Workington Reds who were in the English fourth division at the time, it was not quite up to the standard of Celtic who were winning everything in Scotland and doing well in Europe. But there was no pressure and it was enjoyable and I had another group of friends I met through the football. I also joined the Round Table, and Isobel joined the Ladies Circle and that added yet another dimension to our socialising. When asked to join round table I was bit hesitant, from the little I knew it didn't sound like my sort of thing. It had a reputation for exclusivity in Whitehaven but I had a drink with a couple of members and found them charming, clever and funny. They told me the Round Table is a truly international organisation with over 35,000 members in 60 different countries and aims to promote fellowship amongst young professional and business men, while raising funds for various charities. Members who are aged under forty, meet on a monthly basis, in a formal minuted meeting and regular attendance is expected. Joining Round Table really opened up our social life, while some may view it as a distinctly white middles class club of social climbers, it gave us a ready-made group of friends and helped us to settle in a new town.

Round Table did some great things in terms of charity work and at the same time the members had a lot of fun. In 1974 we revived a long forgotten Spring Carnival, which was an immense success. The Carnival consisted of a parade of floats funded by different organisations, a Carnival Princess and a weekend of jollity and festivities. The Table float was naturally a replica of a castle with a bunch of be-armoured knights and their ladies flouncing to great effect in a mocked up castle. The focus on fund raising was still there and people were throwing money onto the float if they could not reach the land based knights with the collecting buckets. It was all great fun and so successful was the fund raising that we decided to go round the pubs and try and raise some more money from the local drinkers. I was assigned the local bikers pub, full of hairy, leather jacketed and tattoo festooned tough guys and their gals. Nothing ventured. As I rattled my bucket the response was absolutely brilliant and it fairly filled up with the generosity of the bikers. There was, of course one guy who tried to take the mickey, and he eyed me up and down in my pretend chain mail, tabard, helmet, sword and shield. After a moment he said, "Are you not embarrassed going outside dressed like that?" To which I retorted, "In an hour I will remove these clothes and once again I will look normal, what will you do?" at that the place erupted with laughter and his mates gave him a right good ragging, and to be fair he also laughed and put a pound in my bucket. Later that year we decided to organise a fireworks display on the cliff tops overlooking the sea and a poignant memorial to lost miners. This was part of our Guy Fawkes bonfire night and we organised a few stalls selling burgers, crisps, sweeties and drinks. We also managed to persuade a man with a steam organ to come along hoping to get a couple of hundred people to turn out. Almost ten thousand people turned up to make it an unforgettable experience and to further improve the bucket collection.

The following Spring one of my fellow table members asked me if I would accompany him on a pony trek with his two sons, aged fourteen and twelve. We arrived at the stables in Ennerdale and I was reminded of the only other time I had been on horseback, also in Cumbria, about three miles away on the beach at St Bees. My two pals, Junior and Shuggy and I were touring the north of England in our heroic van, VS886 and we had camped for the night at St Bees. I had gone for an early morning stroll along the beach when I met a girl exercising her horse, and as we chatted she offered me a chance to have a trot along the beach on her very calm steed. When I returned to the van to recount my adventure to my sleeping buddies, they refused to believe me, claiming I was a fantasist. Jealousy is not attractive in young men!!

Back at the stables my colleague was very careful about choosing suitable horses for his sons and asked me if I was experienced with horses. I said I wasn't and asked for a peaceful cuddy. The stable maid was an efficient young woman, if a touch serious and she organised an old horse for me and something similar for the two boys. My pal asked her for something with a bit of life for himself as he would like a decent gallop, the girl looked at him and reminded him this was a trek not a race but she would give him a horse with some spirit. The boys and I were already mounted when she returned with this very large brown and white horse that looked like a refugee from a rodeo, jumping and stamping. This creature looked utterly mad with wild bulging eyes, he was snorting and harumphing as he pawed the ground with impatience to get at his victims. His mane was unkempt and the hair was sticking straight up in the air, this creature looked positively scary. We set off very gently and the kennel maid rode alongside me for a bit and said my mount was a lazy old sod and if I wanted him to go faster I needed to show him the crop, with which she handed me this instrument of torture with a silver coloured handle. Whenever my poor old horse saw this crop he tried to hobble a wee bit faster, so I stuck it in my belt and let him meander along the trail, at his own pace since I was in no hurry. A few hundred yards from the stable was a large field stretching about a mile, relatively flat but covered with boulders strewn higgledy, piggledy as far as the eye could see. My brave chum decided this was his chance to find out what the crazy horse could do, so he dug his heels in and whacked it with the crop. The thing took off like a bat out of hell, with my mate clinging on for dear life. He and the horse went scudding along the valley and, miraculously the horse picked its way through all the boulders, they then disappeared over the brow of a hill at a rate of knots. Fortunately, he managed to hold on but if he had fallen off he would have been battered to smithereens on those boulders. It was one of the funniest things I have seen, this wee fat man hanging onto this mad horse, even his two sons were laughing fit to burst.

One of my colleagues in Round Table was an estate agent called Robbie Burns, and I got talking to him about buying a house. Isobel and I had been talking about buying a house and the implications, like moving away from our wonderful neighbours and getting a mortgage. Now that I was sure of my career at Leyland we decided it was time to stop renting, and with Robbie's help we found a new house on Thornton Drive, in Hensingham, only a couple of miles from where we were living in the Oval. With Robbie's help we negotiated a mortgage from a very traditional (i.e. old fashioned) manager at the local Building Society. He sat us down and explained the implications of taking on a debt for twenty-five years, the commitment we were making and then he said that even although Isobel and I were both working only my salary would be considered.

In the days before everything had to be politically correct he told us we were young and would probably be having a baby soon and possibly several others, so it was important for us and for his Society that we did not overstretch ourselves otherwise our home might have to be repossessed. He was a jolly chap, the optimistic sort. He told us the rules were that we could borrow up to two and a half times my salary, but in his opinion that was reckless. He suggested we should pay a deposit of 25% of the purchase price and only borrow the balance of 75%, which equated to two times my salary. We had a strict policy when we got married, no debt and we had been very clear about that and now here we were taking on a mortgage of 200% of my salary to be paid over the next 25 years.

We moved into our new home with the help of my family, Mum, Dad, Billy, John, Patricia and her husband Stephen, all of whom came down over a weekend and got us established. We rented a van and the whole team pulled together to get our belongings from the Oval and drive the short distance to our new home. While we were moving in the furniture my Dad and Stephen got on with all the handyman jobs that needed doing and the move was easy, as the saying goes many hands make light work. It only took one day to get everything moved and for us to be settled in. I was the first member of the family to own their own home, progress. After a hectic weekend my family returned home leaving Isobel and I proud as punch in our new home.

Life carried on, I was happy at work, Isobel had good friends in the place where she worked and we were both very happy in Thornton Avenue, even if it was something of a building site for the first twelve months we lived there. Once again we lucked out with our neighbours, Pat and Brian Martin who were very supportive and helpful, I think we intrigued them, with our different ways and the different cars on our driveway every other week, we might have seemed a little exotic. Some of our other neighbours proved to be quite interesting but not always interesting in a good way. One of our neighbours was a policeman who was caught stealing materials from the building site and forced to give them back, another one had a tendency to cause a fuss on a Friday night and often ended up in a domestic with his wife. Both of these neighbours left soon after arriving and things settled down to mere suburban intrigue. Like every other house on the site our garden was a mess and filled with rubble and it was hard work bringing the garden under cultivation, because it sloped two ways both up and across. But I resolved to terrace my garden and to create asymmetric vegetable beds and a lawn. Living on a building site has certain advantages; it means you have a ready place to dump garden rubbish for example. The weekend I started to excavate the garden I first removed all the rubble and rubbish left in the garden by the builders, bits of broken pipes, slabs of broken concrete, bits of wood and glass. I had to clear all that up just to let me assess the site. When I started digging I quickly hit clay and lots of it, although I was not much of a gardener I knew nothing would grow in clay and worse water would shed off the clay and cause problems for my new house.

So I started digging out the clay, barrow load by barrow load and dumping it along with the building rubble at the back of the newest part of the construction site. I had been working at this for hours and, fit as I was at the time I was pretty tired. As I was wearily planting my spade into yet more clay, I felt a tap on my shoulder and turned round to see my neighbour Brian Martin, who said, "Move over and have a rest lad, and I'll give you a spell." What a relief that was but I was to learn that was typical of Brian who was a great neighbour and a really good person. By the end of the weekend I had moved 146 barrow loads of rubble and clay and laid some land drains in preparation for the next stage of my terracing project, which would have to wait until the following weekend. During that week Isobel saw an advert in the Whitehaven News, for dressed red sandstone, so we ordered ten tons to build our terrace walls.

Two nights later I arrived home at 6:45pm to find my driveway blocked with a mountain of red sandstone. I had been in plenty of time for my squash match at half past seven but before I could play squash I would have to move this sandstone to the back of the house. So I parked the car, changed into my jeans and started barrowing the sandstone up the drive to the back of the house. I finished at 7:20pm and, sweating heavily, I grabbed my squash bag and went off to play my match, which I won. Those were the days! Isobel and I built the sandstone walls and then ordered some topsoil for the vegetable beds and turf for the lawn, and a month after starting the back garden was finished and looked great. It was the first time we were able to provide for ourselves with vegetables grown in our own garden, and they tasted fresher and better than any from the shops. Forty years after they were built, those walls were still standing I am pleased to say.

IN THE MIDST OF LIFE

On 8 November 1975, a Saturday morning I was up and about, thinking about work as always, I was at the dining room table with papers spread out in front of me, trying to finalise a pricing system that would give me an accurate basis from which to guide our sales team through the process of quoting to our customers, at prices where we could all make money. The responsibility for sales was with the central team who did not report to my Managing Director and as a result were something of a law unto themselves. Leyland National sold to the Sales Division on a cost plus basis but I was amazed at how those figures had been arrived at since there were no accurate costs for any of the products. Sales pricing was a black art in those days, which goes some way to explaining some of the Corporation's difficulties. If you don't know how inefficient you are how can you eradicate inefficiency? The Sales Division had a pricing policy and did not know if that resulted in a profit for the business or not. While I understand that pricing and the cost base are not necessarily inextricably linked, neither are they mutually exclusive, after all it is useful to know if you are selling profitably or not. If you are not selling profitably what is the point?

As these big thoughts were rattling around my head on a dull November morning, the phone rang. I was a bit irritated at the interruption but brightened when I heard my little sister on the other end of the phone. Then she said to me, "Owen you need to come home Dad is dead." I was stunned into silence. Isobel and I had visited Scotland the previous weekend and stayed at my Mum and Dad's house, and we had a great time. It had been a lovely weekend, even if ten-year-old John borrowed ten bob, with a promise to pay me back when he got a job. John illuminated my parent's lives, especially coming so many years after their first born, John was 18 years younger than me. Billy, Patricia and I were all married and out of the house and John had become the total focus of my Dad's life, he adored Johnny boy (as we all did). That last weekend Dad and I chatted about many things but mainly he wanted to hear about what I was doing and where I was going with my career. Dad had been my first and best mentor and was very proud to see me carving my way through the business world, and now he was dead. My Dad was dead. Bloody hell, I can't believe it, he was gone and was never coming back. I was confused, and felt as though I was about to collapse, a million thoughts ran through my mind. "Dad, dead? no, no, no, that can't be right, dear God, please don't let that be right. How can my Dad be dead he is only 52 years old? How can this possibly be true?" I was stunned, my Dad is a giant, he is indestructible, he's my Dad, how could he possibly be dead? No this can't be right it's too horrible to think about. As Patricia spoke, I was trying to control myself, I understood the words well enough, but it was not sinking in I just couldn't believe what I was hearing. But I did understand that I had to be with my family as soon as possible so without thinking too much we threw a few things together, jumped in the car and headed for Scotland. Isobel didn't drive at that time, so I took the wheel, but I have absolutely no recollection of how we got there, none whatsoever, however we arrived at my Mum's somehow. Thank God for Isobel who was a tower of strength. Isobel had been through this when her own Mum died at the age of 37, when Isobel was only 13 years old. When we arrived, Isobel made tea for everyone and then we sat around trying to comfort Mum and each other. Then we started the process of closing ranks in a way that only a really close family can, and we were a very close family, we shared our sorrow and our grief brought us close together. The only others allowed into this circle were Isobel, Janis and Stephen, our spouses, and we closed ranks to protect ourselves. One of the best compliments I have ever had was that "you Quinns are so close you could not squeeze a bus ticket between the whole lot of you."

My Dad was a much loved, accomplished, complex man, devoted to his family and much respected by all who had the privilege of making his acquaintance, he had survived the second world war as a sailor on a flimsy Motor Torpedo Boat in the shooting and bombing war that was the Mediterranean Campaign. A man who inspired his three sons and daughter to be the best they could be and not to settle for less, was now taken from us at the ridiculously young age of 52, destined not to meet five of his six grandchildren and none of his nine great grandchildren. The funeral was a trying time but our closeness and the circle we formed round Mum got her and us through. Such a terrible loss.

I had arranged for two weeks leave of absence, and when all the arrangements were over, Isobel and I went back to our own home on the outskirts of Whitehaven and I went back to work, I retreated into myself for a while and threw myself headlong into work with a renewed intensity. I debated whether or not I should be going back to live in Scotland now that my Mum was on her own and trying to raise my younger brother, John, all by herself. I talked to my Mum about this and she thought I should carry on with my career pointing out that Billy and Patricia both lived very close by. But I started to go back to Scotland most weekends for the next twelve months or so. Back in Whitehaven, everybody was very kind but I really did not want sympathy I just wanted to be alone to work things out for myself. The first Saturday after we returned home our friends from Round Table had a party for us, and that was when I started drinking alcohol, consuming almost a bottle of vodka and dancing the night away until our host insisted I should change my shirt for one of his.

That was a frenetic night that passed in a blur of music and vodka.

CHAPTER TWO

HQ CALLING

The Group Finance function was being shaken up, the new Director appointed a new Group Financial Controller, another Scotsman, Ken McIver from the Isle of Lewis. Ken McIver was a single minded and driven individual, who had spent his entire career at the Ford Motor Company. One day I got a call from his secretary who invited me to a meeting with Mr McIver at his office to discuss Leyland National's planning routines. In the meeting he told me I had something of a reputation as a person who got things done and Leyland National had a reputation as the best run Finance Department in the Group. I thanked him and said we had all worked hard up there and it was a strong team of people. We then talked about the future and he offered me a post at Head Office, I apologised and declined the offer saying that it was not possible for me to move from Leyland National at that stage because of my family circumstances, and I told him about the recent death of my Father and my Mum's need to raise my younger brother. He offered me his condolences and said he understood my need for space and time, and I went back to Leyland National and thought no more about it. About three months after my meeting with Ken McIver I received another, uninvited offer of a job and once again this was to be based at head office, and once again I respectfully declined, on the grounds of my need to be close to my family. To be honest by this time I knew I needed to move on from Leyland National because I had outgrown that job and I needed a new challenge. I had worked hard with my colleagues to ensure we had a fully functioning standard department, an efficient and timely set of reporting procedures, local management and head office management were bang up to date with operational results for the factory. On a personal level I had become something of a guru on all aspects of short term planning and reporting within the Group and I usually ended up chairing the Head Office Budget meetings. Leyland National was running like a Swiss watch and I was getting bored and spent my time sniffing out waste or developing ways of dealing with the spiraling costs of production as a result of high interest rates. On the other hand, my head was still reeling from losing my Dad and I could not bring myself to move further away from my Mum, not to mention the small matter that Isobel was now pregnant and that complicated life still further as far as a move was concerned.

Isobel had quite a difficult pregnancy with Nicholas, she was ill for most of the first six months and had to finish work earlier than planned to take care of herself and our baby, it was a worrying time. Isobel is a single-minded girl and had decided that as soon as she was pregnant she would give up work to be a full time Mum, and I was in total agreement with that (not that I had any say in it – Isobel had decided and that was it). And now we were having our first baby and both families were absolutely delighted that we were expecting a baby, it would be a first grandchild for Isobel's Dad, Jimmy and her step Mum, Frances and a second for my Mum, Billy's son Bevan was already four years old. When talking to my Mum on the phone she asked me if Isobel had any cravings since she became pregnant and I had to admit that I did not know. My Mum then told me that when she was pregnant with me she had a craving for coal, and would always have a piece of washed coal in her handbag whenever she went out, and she would nibble on the coal when she got a craving. I laughed but my Mum said it was normal to have daft cravings like that. Isobel and I started talking about this and she said "I do have cravings, I often take a fancy to toast with tinned peaches and I have that quite often as a snack. The only other thing is that I keep thinking I smell fish in the kitchen cupboard under the sink, but there has never been any fish in there and there is no fish in the kitchen but I can still smell it and it makes me nauseous."

I suggested this might be an excuse to avoid going into the kitchen and escaped from the room before she belted me. The following weekend I was out at a football match and Workington as ever were well beaten but I had a good time with the group of blokes I met up with at the games. When I returned home it was about 5:30pm and I was met at the door by Isobel who said to me, "I have a craving for a cream cake you'll need to go and get me one from the town." I said, "But you don't even like cream cakes and besides look at the time the shops will be closed". Isobel insisted, "I need a cream cake, and I need one now, so please go and get me one." Isobel can be very persuasive when she needs to be, especially with me, so off I went in search of cream cakes. I jumped into my car and sped off to town and parked the car illegally to run through the town's bakeries looking for a cream cake. Most of the bakers' shops were already closed and those that weren't had no cakes left never mind cream cakes. Now what to do? Ever resourceful I headed to the freezer shop and asked the man who owned it if he had any cream cakes and "Aye, mara we've got tons of the buggers how many do you want?" I checked out his stock and picked two large gateaux, paid the guy a small fortune and then headed to my lovely, pregnant wife with my trophy to satisfy her cravings. I felt like the guy in the milk tray advert, "Because the Lady Likes Milk Tray."

I jubilantly showed Isobel these magnificent cakes and she said, "Oh its ok the craving has passed!!"

ON THE MOVE AGAIN

In April 1976, Ken McIver called me to a meeting and I guessed I was about to be convinced I should move. Isobel and I went gone through the various scenarios and discussed what I should do if another job offer was made. Isobel was by now in her 5th month of her pregnancy with Nicholas and that together with my wish to be near Scotland meant that we had a lot to talk about, but we were both ambitious. My dear wife even as a young woman always had a great way of getting straight to the heart of the matter. Isobel said to me, "if you do get an offer it will be the third one in less than six months, it's clear that they really want you to move to Head Office. But if you don't take this one you might have to accept you will never move. Is that what you want?" I said, "No, that's not what I want, because I really want to work at Head Office and I think it would be good for me, and I agree with you that if I don't accept the next job I might never get another one. And I guess if you think about it, if we were to find a house near Preston we would be a lot closer to the Motorway than we are now. It would probably not take us much longer to get back to Glasgow from Preston than from Whitehaven." So it was decided if I was offered a job and thought it was right I would accept it.

The meeting went very well and Ken got straight to the point and offered me a dream job to reconstruct the short term planning department at Truck and Bus Head Office. The plan was to re-organise the entire department and for me to come on board and implement the sort of procedures we had installed at Leyland National. I was delighted with the offer and accepted the job offer on the spot. The following day I spoke to my boss Arthur and to the Managing Director, the civilised and ever courteous John Battersby, both of whom were delighted for me. John Battersby invited me for a cup of coffee and a chat in his office, which would have to have been the finest office in the whole of the Leyland

Group with magnificent, sweeping panoramic views across the bay to the lowlands of Scotland's border country. John first asked me how old I was and when I told him I was 27, he asked me what I thought I would be doing when I was forty. An interesting question but I replied that I would be concentrating on doing a good job over the next couple of years. John was a cautious man and maybe he suffered from vertigo. He added that he would be really sorry to see me go because he felt I had made positive changes to the company and I was a key part of his team.

As we chatted John, who was a confirmed Cumbrian, having been born and raised in Ambleside, became a little mischievous and said to me that he couldn't understand why anyone would want to leave Cumbria. He then added that the plains of Lancashire were very plain and very boring, "They don't have any hills down there, if you stand on a soapbox you can see the sea from twenty miles." I laughed at that but he wasn't far wrong because West Lancashire is indeed a very flat county, East Lancs. is another matter and the towns nestling in the foothills of the Pennines have their share of hills although not quite to the standard of the Cumbrian mountains. Our conversation concluded with John wishing me well and then another chapter of my career closed and a new and exciting chapter was beckoning at the Group Headquarters of Leyland Truck and Bus in Lancaster House in the town of Leyland.

But far more exciting than any fantastic job was the fact that we were expecting our first born in a few months. After the depth of sadness which I felt at the death of my dear Father, here I was with the great blessing of a new baby coming into my life, and irony of ironies our baby was due to be born on what would have been my Dad's 53rd birthday, nine months after his death. Isn't life so very strange?

Leyland Truck & Bus HQ – Lancaster House

By the time I took up the post in head office on 3rd May 1976, I was much more confident in my own ability and it was just as well. Before I got my team established I went to a Budget Planning Meeting, where the Financial Controllers from all the Truck and Bus Divisions were in attendance. This was a big meeting and I was just one more attendee in this august body, that is until one hour before the meeting started when my line manager, decided he did not want to attend and asked me if I would chair the meeting. A nice gentle baptism then. Fortunately, for me the purpose of this meeting was to launch a completely new set of Budget procedures and schedules, all designed by me. Chairing that meeting turned out to be a real stroke of luck for me because it set the "Pecking Order" between me and the factories and that was to be helpful in the future.

My boss did me a favour there, the law of unintended consequences very much working on my behalf. On taking up my new post I realised that I had arrived at Truck and Bus at an important crossroads in the company's history. Ken McIver was part of a new breed of manager, and was in the vanguard of a concerted attempt at improving the quality of management, in both substance and style. Ken was an import from the Ford Motor Company and was a genuine new brush, and I learned that the reason he was impressed with me was because my background was 100% American with the Singer Corporation and ITT Inc. Ken McIver ran the whole of the Financial Services area, Budgets, Short Term and Long Term Planning, Pricing, and Capex and he reported to the Finance Director, Jerry Glancy. Our Financial Accounting arm was run by Tony Rose, another Scotsman, who had been with the Corporation for a number of years. As the new man Ken was determined to lift the standards of the entire Truck and Bus operation, starting with Financial Services. There would be no more of those sloppy, old fashioned British management behaviours, such as I had witnessed on my earlier trips to H Q.

These were going to be exciting times.

While Ken was very focused on driving his departments forward to embrace modern methods and systems the Financial accounting team were more traditional, mostly long term company employees. They were a group of talented people but a wee bit suspicious of change and wary of the brashness of the newcomers. There was a slight culture divide to some extent between those who thought of themselves as Accountants and those who regarded themselves as Finance People. This created a wee bit of an "us and them", between Financial Services and Financial Accounting.

When I arrived to take up my post I realised there had been an impressive recruiting campaign going on, there had been a clean out of the former headquarters personnel and just about everyone was replaced. I found myself as one of the longest serving employees in the whole of the Group Financial services area. Ken was determined that his ideas would be quickly implemented and that the changes would be made to stick. I had my new team in place very quickly and what a brilliant group they were. First on board was Peter Nuttall, a smart man, a good accountant, a really nice bloke and a big fan of Burnley Football Club. Stevie Piper from Paisley was next, he was quiet, strong and very logical, and another terrific man and a great colleague, even if he did give me a nickname that stuck. Stevie had decided to call me "Mighty Quinn", which he then shortened to a simple, "Mighty" after the Bob Dylan song that was popular at the time.

Next was John Millet, articulate, opinionated, excitable, headstrong, a very smart man, another good guy and a supporter of Coventry City Football Club. Then there was John Mockett, a bluff Yorkshireman whose favourite saying was "Laugh? I nearly bought me own beer!" This saying struck me as a particularly strange thing to say and I thought it was an example of the English love of irony. After I had known John for a while I realised it was not irony that was really how John did feel about things. Mockett really was careful with his finances and the old cliché "a Yorkshireman is a Scotsman with deeper pockets and shorter arms," described John perfectly. John was a hard working lad, a good member of the team and idiosyncratic to the point of eccentricity. Uniquely within the team, John was always addressed by his surname. Then there was Alan Findlay who was yet another Scotsman, Alan was a Glaswegian and he was bright, sharply witty, a bit bohemian and belligerently left wing with a wickedly dark sense of humour.

There was a lot to be done but our first task was to start the process of putting in place a consolidated budget for financial year 1976/77 for the vast number of companies across the group. By the time we got started we were already weeks behind the regular schedule, just one more little hoop to jump through among so many others. We would have to be very focused and so would the individual companies in order to hit the necessary dates and to have everything in place for the start of the new financial year.

AL'S CHINESE CRACKER

Although we were a newly formed department there was no time to spare for training or getting to know each other, that would have to come as we got on with our tasks. Because we were already well into the budget timetable by the time we came together as a department, we had a backlog of work. The scale of the task in hand was enormous and effectively meant compressing a twelve weeks work schedule into half that time. This resulted in a lot of hard work and extended hours but I had a team of very hard working and committed professionals so we got on with what we needed to do.

The sheer scale of work resulted in our group working late every night, (often not finishing until after 9:00pm) and because of this the Company bought us dinner, or rather we bought dinner and claimed the cost back via expenses. Dinner was always a take away, something we could rush down as we continued to work. We had a steady diet of fish and chips and Chinese take away meals from two local establishments. The team had developed a very democratic rota for collecting the food, a different person went each night, and this worked very well, most of the time. But there was one particular time when it was Alan Findlay's turn to get the grub, when things didn't go quite so well.

On this particular night there was one other department working late and when they discovered we were getting a Chinese take away they asked if we could get some food for them as well. Alan did not really want to go for the meal that night because he wanted to finish the job he was working on, and more importantly he did not particularly like the bloke who was the manager of the other department, who offended Alan's bohemian sensibilities and his devout socialist principles. This guy came across as very false, he was everything Alan was not, with a terribly posh southern accent, while claiming to be a native of Liverpool. Most of my colleagues shared Alan's disdain of this man. But we were all hungry, so we got out the Chinese takeaway menu and gave Alan our meal number which he carefully wrote down next to our names, he was very thorough, and off he went to get the Chinese takeaway, armed with all the appropriate meal numbers.

About forty-five minutes later he was back and started doling out the meals, matching the meals to the names and numbers on his list. There was a howl of disgust from Mockett, who asked, "What the F*** is going on? You've given me the wrong meal, Finders." (he was Al to everyone but to Mockett he was Finders). Alan was all of sudden polite and said "are you sure John?" everybody knew at that point something was afoot because he never, ever addressed Mockett by his Christian name. Mockett was now in a strop and said "Listen you bloody Jock, I know what I ordered, check that bloody list." Alan said "here it is Mr Mockett (oh dear, it's getting worse) number 26, against your name that's right isn't it? What is the number on your carton?" "It is number 26 on the carton, but I ordered fried chicken and beansprouts, with boiled rice, I don't know what this shit is," replied Mockett. Then all hell broke out, everybody had the wrong dish, or to be more precise everybody had a meal that was different from the one they thought they had ordered. Some people even had fish and chips and other English meals and at this point we were on the brink of a lynching. Alan remained completely serene and composed and simply said "I can't understand how that happened, I made sure the Chinese man took all the right numbers and I asked him to write the numbers on the cartons. (Al never did this.)"

And then John Millet who was smarter than the rest of us said "did you go to the normal Chinese Restaurant, Al? Innocently Alan said, "Nah I couldn't go there because it was closed, it's always closed on Tuesdays, it says so on the take away menu. I went to the other one in the town centre." John Millet said "but Alan you took the numbers off the menu from the other take away restaurant, the one we always go to?" Alan retained his composure and with a straight face and in an absolutely deadpan voice he said "but all Chinese take away restaurants sell exactly the same meals, do they not all have the same numbers on their menus?" Apart from Mockett we were all laughing but the other department never asked us to get their meals again, which I suppose was the object of the exercise. Mockett ate his mysterious meal without further complaint. Working with this group of men was among the best times in my career, we worked very hard and we became friends and still are to this day. We achieved much in a very tight timescale, and not without incident.

While I was rampaging through the planning systems of Leyland Truck and Bus, I stayed in a hotel in Preston from Monday to Friday and returned home for the weekend, leaving Isobel with all the pressure of organising our move to Lancashire. Poor Isobel, who was now in an advanced state of pregnancy was left with the pressure of organising the sale of our home in Hensingham, Whitehaven in Cumbria. Fortunately, the home sold very quickly and we were able to go house hunting in Lancashire and found a lovely dormer bungalow in the village of Longton about five miles from Preston and about the same distance from my office in the town of Leyland, across some delightful country lanes. Isobel arranged the removal and we moved into our new home on Wednesday 4th August 1976 and there was still a lot to do. We needed a lot of new bits and pieces to make our new house a home, meaning that weekends were spent shopping. Isobel, even in her advanced stage of pregnancy was determined we would get it all completed before the baby was born, the date Isobel had been given was the 6th September, just one month after the move.

On the Saturday after we moved in to our home in Longton, we went shopping in Preston, I dropped Isobel at the top of the hill beside the main railway station, while I parked our car at the foot of the hill. When I arrived up the hill Isobel was blushing to her roots and giggling uncontrollably. When I asked

65

her why she could hardly talk for laughing. Isobel said, "when you dropped me off to park the car, I was thinking about what we needed and was absent mindedly looking in the window of that shop over there." She said pointing across the road. "I wasn't looking in the shop just standing there thinking about what we needed, when I turned around I suddenly realised that people were looking at me and laughing and I got embarrassed. When I looked around to see what they were all laughing at I realised that I was standing outside a sex shop." We both started laughing as we quickly moved away from the offending premises with Isobel protesting "I wasn't looking in the shop, honest."

Our son Nicholas was born almost two weeks early on Sunday 22 August that year, exactly 18 days after we moved into our new home in Longton. On the Saturday night we stayed home, Isobel went to bed early and I stayed up to watch Match of the Day, getting to bed about 11:30pm. The next thing I knew was that Isobel was shaking me saying "my waters have broken, it's time to go to the hospital." Isobel meant for me to get myself dressed, get her suitcase which had been packed for over a week, get the car out of the garage and take her to Sharoe Green Maternity Hospital in Preston. I knew exactly what she meant but instead of doing what any responsible father-to-be would do, I went back to bed and fell fast asleep. I hadn't actually woken up, I suppose. After a few minutes Isobel returned and gave me another shake and this time I did wake up and the seriousness of the situation got me moving quickly.

We left just after 1:00am, the traffic was light and we got to the hospital very quickly we went straight into the delivery ward where my assistance was not required, when I offered to help a very business-like sister said, "you've done enough damage, just go and take a seat in the waiting room and we'll keep you informed of progress." So off I trooped to the empty waiting room and I waited. After an hour the nurse came back and said I could go and talk to Isobel which I did but she was very tired and the pains were there but not yet at the critical point, and after half an hour I was sent back to the waiting room to find another man had arrived. We struck up a conversation and he asked me if this was our first child and when I said it was he told me it looked like it. I guess I looked very concerned. He went on to tell me he had a daughter of eight but it was so long ago that he also felt like a first time father. We chatted and the hours went past. A third man joined us about six o clock in the morning, but he was a bit taciturn and not at all interested in chatting. He left the waiting room and was pacing the corridors of the hospital, we decided that he must be a first time father also because he looked so nervous and worried. The following day we realised he was no first time father when he arrived to visit his wife and brought his seven other children to see their new baby brother. He had the most beautiful children, very well behaved and a credit to him and his wife. How wrong can you be?

At two o'clock in the afternoon Isobel had been in labour for over 12 hours and the doctor told me I would have to leave because this would need to be a forceps' delivery so I was kicked out of the labour ward and told to amuse myself. Two hours later I was allowed back in to find out I was the father of a bouncing baby boy, and both he and his Mum were healthy, although Isobel was exhausted. I suppose I was no different from any other new parent but I could not stop staring at our baby and I could not believe that we were parents of this beautiful, little human being, he was perfect, absolutely perfect. I remember feeling so full of pride and emotion that I thought I was going to burst. I also suspect I had a gormless smile pasted to my face for weeks afterwards.

We spent the rest of the afternoon and evening together and we had already agreed that we would call our new baby Nicholas, which we had decided upon as soon as we knew Isobel was pregnant. When I had composed myself (??) I slipped out to phone my Mum and Isobel's Dad and I have no idea what I said or if I was making any sense. But they seemed to understand what I was saying and they agreed to ring around both families with the news. My Mum was very, very emotional at the news of her first born's first born. One thing I remember very clearly is that I was happy, ecstatically happy and walking on air, and that continued for a week – at least. Isobel and I were blissfully happy with our beautiful baby boy. And as a bonus Nicholas was very well behaved, sleeping and feeding on cue. Around 8:00pm the nurses persuaded me that they would look after my wife and my son (I was a dad, wow) and it would be ok for me to go home and let them both get some rest, and reluctantly I left that hospital ward.

Our neighbours of 18 days Bob and Bett Denton, came round when they saw me arrive home from the hospital. They had prepared a meal for me to eat in my own home and then they educated me on a lovely little local custom. In our village when a new baby was born tradition dictated that a soft toy should be placed in the window of the home, to let the neighbours know, pink for a girl and blue for a boy. Not knowing whether we had had a boy or a girl, Bett had brought a pink bear and a blue bear for me and congratulated me on the birth of our son, and left me with the blue bear. They were doubly delighted with our choice of name as they had a grandson also named Nicholas. And then happy that I was ok they left me to enjoy my dinner. What a lovely gesture by two delightful people, once again we had lucked out with our neighbours.

That night, 22 August 1976, I was all over the place emotionally and all sorts of things were rattling through my mind. It was nine months since my dear Dad had died, and now we were welcoming our first child into the world. Nicholas was born two weeks prematurely and had he arrived, as scheduled on September 6, he would have shared my Dad's birthday (incredibly his own son, Harry was born on September 6.) To her dying day my Mum regarded Nick as a really special boy and although we never discussed it, I knew exactly what her thoughts were when she held Nick and watched him grow. I decided I would call in to the office in the morning and then take a few days off to be with Isobel and Nicholas.

When I was chucked out of the hospital at lunchtime I had gone for a walk around Preston city centre. I dropped into a record shop where I saw a Harry Chapin record on sale. I had been looking for one of his records but had been unable to find any until that moment. Harry Chapin was not all that popular but I had heard his track W.O.L.D., which was only a minor hit in the UK but I loved it and kept checking out record stores to see if I could buy his album. The choice wasn't great in Whitehaven but I found it at my first attempt in Preston. Big city.

When Bett and Bob left I had my dinner and I put on my new record which has many great tracks and it remains one of my favourite records to this day. Harry Chapin is a great storyteller and a wonderful wordsmith and the lyrics of his songs are powerful. There was a song on that album that stopped me in my tracks and which had a profound effect on my work pattern from that day on. The track was "Cats in the Cradle" and tells the story of a man who was so busy working he missed his son growing up, always promising to do something with his son except he always seemed to be too busy working. It came as something of a shock when his son grew up and turned out like his Dad. I found the third verse an absolute stunner:

> *I've long since retired, and my son's moved away*
> *I called him up just the other day*
> *I said, "I'd like to see you if you don't mind."*
> *He said, "I'd love to, dad, if I could find the time*

You see, my new job's a hassle, And the kid's got the flu
But it's sure nice talking to you, dad
It's been sure nice talking to you."
And as I hung up the phone, it occurred to me
He'd grown up just like me, My boy was just like me

© Harry Chapin

I played that track over and over because Harry Chapin was talking about me. To that point I had been a workaholic, I was driven by the need to get the job finished; for me work was all absorbing. To be honest I enjoy hard work, and I got a real buzz from my work. It took me many years to understand that I have distinctly obsessive tendencies in many things but I am particularly obsessive about my work. On that night, the day of my son's birth I vowed to change my ways and to ensure I made time for my wife and family in the future. I thought about my vow over the next few days and decided that I really would change and so from then on I would not work at weekends, my career could have Monday to Friday but weekends would be for my family. I also made sure I would be home every night for baths, prayers and bedtime stories and I held true to this principle for my entire working career, with very few exceptions. Thank you Harry Chapin and Nicholas James Thomas Quinn.

I was away from the office from Monday to Friday of the week Nicholas was born, and when I returned to work it was to a meeting with Ken McIver, who wanted to update me on events. A major re-structure of the company was about to be enacted. From being a very centralised organisation we would become five separate business Groups, Heavy vehicles, Medium vehicles, Buses, Parts and Special Products plus a rump of a Central Function.

So by the middle of September, with a new born son and having only been in my new home for 4½ weeks I was told that the Company wanted me to take up a new job in Edinburgh. I was to be part of the new Head Office team for the proposed Medium Light Vehicle Division, to be established in spring 1977. It was an obvious appointment and it brought promotion and more money and it also meant I would be taking my new son back home to be with his ain folk. But it was hassle. This re-organisation was a big thing, and involved a colossal upheaval across all the functions of the Group and a major movement of personnel around the country in order to staff the new organisation.

One division would be The Heavy Vehicle Division (HVD) concentrating on the design manufacture and sale of trucks of 16 tonnes gross vehicle weight and above. This included Leyland Truck Manufacture in the town of Leyland, plus Scammell in Watford, Guy Motors in Wolverhampton, AEC in north London. This division also included a number of other sites involved in re-manufacture of engines, and Service Centres around the UK. The HVD team would be located in Lancaster House in Leyland.

Then there would be the Medium Light Vehicle Division (MLVD) which would be the high volume producing division, concentrating on vans, trucks up to 16, tons gross vehicle weight plus agricultural tractors. This new division would include all the Group's Scottish based operations on the Albion site in Glasgow and the former BMC site in Bathgate. This division would be headquartered in Edinburgh.

There would be a new organisation to be known as Leyland Bus and that would include all the passenger vehicle operations of buses and coaches, including chassis builders and body builders. This division included chassis and axle build in Leyland, Bristol Body, Park Royal in London, Eastern Coachworks in Lowestoft and of course Leyland National. The Bus Division HQ would be located in the Farington factory offices in Leyland. Then there was Parts Division, based in a brand new headquarters in Chorley Lancashire and finally Special Products Group which included such things as road rollers, graders, heavy dump trucks and other specialist products.

We always referred to British Leyland as the Corporation and so did the media but the truth was very different. The BL Group was actually an amalgam of many companies which had different systems, different cultures, styles and ways of doing things, and many of them jealously guarded their "own" way of doing things and actually some resented being known as "Leyland". Many even saw other parts of the "Corporation" as rivals, with products fighting for the same market share and the same share of a meagre research and development budget. British Leyland was a political concept, created by forcing many independent companies with a long history of their own (and fierce rivalry with their new bedfellows) to come together with the alternative being going out of business altogether. And as they say Hobson's choice is no choice. They had to be part of BL but they did not have to like it. Attempts at product rationalistion met with stiff opposition from plants guarding their little empires and met even stiffer opposition from MP's worried about losing votes if they lost jobs in their constituency. I suspect this re-organisation was at least in part aimed at addressing some of these lingering structural problems.

But for the moment my team and I had to continue in our current roles and accept the additional task of managing the devolution of budgets. Peter Nuttal, Stevie Piper, John Millet, Alan Findlay and John Mockett bonded brilliantly into a highly effective team, we were tight and totally supportive of each other, a hard working team that achieved great things in difficult circumstances. This period turned out to be very short and in the end we were together for only twelve months before the major re-organisation into the new divisional structure took place in April 1977. This part of my career left me with some life-long friends both in my own team and among other members of the head office team. It was a highlight in my career and taught me a very important lesson, that with a motivated team focused on a common purpose, great things can be achieved. But with this re-organisation the pride (and relief) my team and I felt in completing the consolidated group budget was quickly replaced by a sinking feeling at the thought of the work involved in de-constructing that plan and re-assembling all the data to match the new business divisions. Ho hum, very fulfilling!

But we cracked on with the creation of operating plans for the new divisions.

I have always been a people watcher and I am endlessly fascinated by the way people conduct themselves and the games they play with each other as well as the way some people set about manipulating others. At Lancaster House I was particularly fascinated by the office politics that took place and I formed the opinion that I was not going to be a player for a few reasons. Firstly, there were some very clever blokes in that organisation, guys with a devious turn of mind who seemed to have an awful lot of time in which to make their moves. Secondly I had no time for that bullshit, I had a job to do and I did not want to be diverted from that, I loved my job in spite of the crazy hours that I needed to put in to get through the workload. It always seemed to me that what most people considered to be "politicking" was no more than gossip and tittle tattle or much worse it was sneakiness or butt kissing, what is clever or desirable about that nonsense? It was a bit ironic that because I refused to participate in cliques or conspiracies some people assumed I was pretty smart. A case of keeping your mouth shut and letting people think you are dumb rather than opening it and proving them right. Can you imagine that?

That Christmas the Quinn family from Lancashire went back to its Lanarkshire roots, in Scotland for New Year and while there we told the family we would be returning on a more permanent basis. A glass or three was raised by both families who were delighted that they would be seeing a lot more of the new baby. Isobel and I started the process of house hunting during that spell in Scotland and found the house we eventually bought the following spring.

Back at the farm, the New Year found the departmental workload greater than ever with the fall-out from the de-centralisation of Head Office functions but as ever we got through it and still managed to have a bit of fun together. The months of January and February saw the Personnel department stretched to the limit trying to populate the new organisations and I was delighted that Peter Nuttal and Steve Piper had agreed to join me in Scotland as had Tom Relton my colleague from Leyland National. I knew with these blokes on board we would be successful in our efforts to set up a decent finance function for this new venture. I was less sure about the wisdom of this whole enterprise of divisionalisation, it seemed a bit of an irrelevance if I'm honest.

LEYLAND OLYMPIANS

In March 1977 some of the more socially minded people at Head Office decided that this was such an auspicious time in the Company's history that we should mark it in some way. After many pints of ale in the company's wonderful social club it was decided we would stage a sort of mini Olympic Games. The Games would be restricted to the Finance Department and would be contested between the Financial Accounting Function (the Recording Angels of the Business) and The Financial Services Function (the Clever Boys and Girls). After much negotiation it was decided that we would contest these games solely for the honour of our Department and for the prize of a die cast scale model of the wonderful Olympian bus. There would be ten events:

1. A Five a Side Football Tournament with each function fielding four teams
2. A Swimming Gala, with three events, Crawl, Breaststroke and Backstroke
3. A Golf Tournament with eight players from each function
4. A Lawn Bowls Tournament open to all
5. A Tennis Tournament with eight players from each function

6. A Darts Tournament with eight players from each function
7. A Dominoes Tournament open to all
8. A Hockey match with mixed male/female teams from each function
9. An Eleven a side Football Match
10. The Final Event was a Boatrace, where an Eight-person team from each function would compete to drink pints of beer faster than their opponents

A lad called John Cairns was organising the eleven a side football team and he asked me if I would play, I said I would be delighted but that I had recently given my boots away to a friend and I did not feel like buying a new pair for one game. Quick as a flash John said, "that's not a problem if you go to Tommy Ball's in Preston you will find he has football boots on sale at 27 pence a pair." I burst out laughing but John insisted it was right, so at lunchtime I visited this famous bootery and found he was absolutely right. Mr Ball had established his Preston store as a clearing house for all sorts of standard and exotic footwear and everything was dirt cheap. There were two problems about taking advantage of Tommy's bargain prices, firstly you had to sort through hundreds and hundreds of pairs of footwear to get your size and then somehow disguise the tiny hole in the heels made to keep them together, with fine twine. But right at the front of the store was a rack full of modern football boots all bearing George

Best's autograph and available at the ludicrous price of twenty-seven pence.

The real Leyland Olympian

I purchased a pair and returned to my office where I was besieged by anxious football hopefuls anxious to examine Tommy's bargain boots. On the day of the match most of the twenty-two participants, the six substitutes the referee and his two linesmen all took to the pitch in Tommy's footwear. Our team consisted of some good players and included Peter Nuttal, Stevie Piper, John Millet and myself and we were all reasonably fit through playing five a side every week in the gym at the company's training college. The game was remarkable for its unremarkableness and although I remember that we won, I forget the final score. At the end of the game in the changing rooms one of my team mates, Fred Noonan (another bloke with a wonderful sense of humour) broke the lace of his boots when taking them off and Fred picked up the boots and chucked them out of the pavilion window saying, "I'll buy a new pair of boots, it'll be cheaper than buying a pair of laces. Needless to say we were all hooting as we headed off to the pub for a pint and to celebrate our famous victory.

WHAT'S A POURER?

In the Eagle and Child pub, we were crowing at our defeated colleagues when talk got around to the impending Boatrace. Our Recording Angel friends reckoned they had something of a secret weapon in one of their chaps who was a "pourer". (A pourer is a person who swallows his drink straight down, by the simple expediency of pouring it down his throat.) This was a surprise to me as I had never heard the term before and anyway I was not much of a drinker. In fact, during my audition for the Boatrace team, in the Social club, it was decided to do without my services when after half an hour I still had a half full pint glass. I never made the team.

Back in the Eagle and Child (or the Bird and Bastard, as it was more commonly known) John Millet bristled at the thought of us being beaten by the wimps of the Accounting Division, John was never one to let a challenge go without a response and he told the assembled audience that we would win the Boatrace by a mile because we had Fred Noonan (of new boots not new laces fame) and he was a proper pourer, not one of your gulpers. I looked at Fred but he just smiled, no he smirked back, liked the cat that had supped the cream. As chance would have it the Recording Angels' Champion, Jim Creighton who was a pal of Alan Findlay's, arrived in the pub, just as Fred was downing his fourth pint of the night. Inevitably a contest before the contest was arranged, after all John Millet was in the house, so he got the pints in for Fred and Jim. Remember this was Jim's first pint of the night and Fred had already drunk four pints. What happened next will live in my memory forever because I have never seen anything like it before or since. Imagine the scene, a crowded pub, twenty odd young guys in their twenties, yelling, one lot despondent in defeat the other lot resplendent in victory and two gladiators championing their respective teams' hopes, with the spotlight on them and a full pint in front of them. The air was thick with war cries and testosterone. John Millet had appointed himself referee and official timekeeper and now stood over the contestants, watch in hand. With wary eyes the two protagonists stared each other down as John called them to their starting positions "Please lift your pints, gentlemen, and I will count you in, when I say go you should begin to drink." Jim and Fred raised their pints as John began his backwards count, "Five, four, three, two, one, go!" says John. And it was all over before it even began, as Jim raised his pint to his lips the mighty Fred placed his empty glass back on the table. It was as quick as that, for a moment there was a stunned silence and then wild cheering burst out and Fred was an instant folk hero –

actually he was already a folk hero, now he moved up the pantheon a few notches. The actual Boatrace was a complete anti-climax after that episode but we went through with it because it preceded the final presentation of the Leyland Finance Trophy and it was another chance for the "Clever Boys and Girls" to do a bit of posing and bragging.

This post at Leyland Headquarters hadn't been destined to be the longest job of my career and lasted exactly one year, but we had crammed three years of work and experience into that time. Within the narrow framework of what was required of us we had been successful, quite what that meant in the overall affairs of our company I am not sure but it was over and once again change was the order of the day. Now we were off to Edinburgh and the Medium Light Vehicle Division Headquarters in the suburb of Westerhailes.

CHAPTER THREE

THE BATHGATE ENIGMA

The move to Edinburgh through the creation of the Medium Light Vehicle Division was quite an emotional time for me, the death of my father was still raw and now I could be very close to my family once again. It was also significant in that here was I coming back to Scotland from England with Isobel and Nick, the same as my own Dad had done all those years before when he brought us back home from Coventry. Another coincidence was that while in Coventry my Dad had also been working in the Motor Industry, with a Leyland subsidiary. The new organisation kicked off in April 1977, by which time Isobel and I had a new home in beautiful Dalgety Bay on the shores of the majestic Firth of Forth. Our early house hunting worked very well and our house move coincided perfectly with the move of personnel from Head Office in Leyland Lancashire to Edinburgh, Westerhailes to be precise. We took over a two storey office block in this working class suburb south east of Edinburgh, and began the task of creating a regional head office to manage the financial affairs of the major volume producer in the Leyland Truck business. This location proved to be a real culture shock for many of my English colleagues who struggled with the local accent and some strange words that they heard me and others use. My line manager was Ric Turner whom I had first met in Lancaster House, and he told me I had three accents, one in the boardroom, another when talking to the natives at Bathgate, and a third one when I returned from a weekend with my family. He had a sharp ear did Ric, and he was a very clever chap as well, not to mention a good bloke who would play a major role in my life, further down the line.

From the vantage point of our third floor eyrie we had a bird's eye view of everyday life in Westerhailes as we overlooked the bus terminus, the taxi rank and the main pub in Westerhailes, which at the time was called the Parrot Cage, and it's fair to say that all human life passed beneath our windows. One day one of my colleagues pointed out the window to a line of people standing outside the pub at 10 o'clock in the morning, and asked what they were waiting for. I explained that opening time was eleven o'clock and they were simply killing time until they could get into the pub. The goings on outside that pub in Westerhailes were different from anything I had seen before and provided a daily drama for our team. We could not really hear what was going on but we became experts at reading the body language of the locals.

One day there was a huge rumpus when a very drunk couple fell out, apparently over more alcohol, the woman wanted to leave and the man wouldn't let her, and was threatening to hit her with his crutch, as he hopped around, long John Silver like waving his crutch and threatening who knows what. Eventually the woman slipped his grasp and jumped into a taxi, undaunted our erstwhile Pirate leapt in front of the taxi, barring its way. After an impasse of a few minutes when nothing was moving and everyone was getting involved the brave taxi driver got out his cab – and chucked the woman out. Gallantry took second place to self-preservation for the taxi drivers of Westerhailes. Fortunately, she got out by the far away door and scuttled off to safety from the crutch wielder but the argument continued between the taxi driver and crutchieman. The disappointed drunk was very angry that the taxi driver had allowed the woman to escape and take with her his drinking fund, to fritter away on groceries. Westerhailes was a rough and ready place, and we were viewed as foreigners especially me, a "weegie soap dodger", who was considered more foreign than my English colleagues. We were certainly very different from the locals but to be honest we never had any agro or hostility just looks of wonderment. For hostility and agro we had to look closer to home, to our new colleagues at Bathgate and Albion plants who were very resentful of our presence and let us know clearly that we were not welcome, none of us. Bathgate had entered the Leyland fold from the car giant that evolved into British Motor Corporation and for my entire time in Scotland it was referred to as the BMC never as "Leyland" by local management. I was singularly unimpressed by the local management team who were running an operation of four factories employing over 5,000 people. Nepotism was rife, perks were jealously guarded, small mindedness was the order of the day and many managers were unworthy of the title, but that would all change.

THE M.D. DROPS A BOMB

The first Board meeting of the new Division was held at 3:00pm on the Monday morning after we arrived and I was tasked with presenting the budget targets and talking the board through the devolved numbers. I arrived in the Boardroom at 2:30pm to set up my presentation and my ultimate boss, the Director of Finance, Geoff Richardson arrived at 2:55 pm followed by the Managing Director, Harold Musgrove. Three o'clock came and went and there was only the three of us there, none of the other executive team were on time. They straggled in over the next twenty minutes, each with an excuse as to why he had not been able to make the meeting at the appointed time. As these men came into the room the Managing Director did not acknowledge them or their whingeing apologies, he sat quietly looking at his papers but I could see there was a crimson tide rising up from his neck to the top of his bald head and the tension in the room could be cut with a knife. Eventually the last of the recalcitrants arrived and as he started to apologise he caught the feeling in the room, shut up and sat down.

After a moment the Managing Director stood up and glared around the room then he took his wristwatch off and threw it into the metal wastebasket by his chair, the resultant noise sounded like a bomb going off in a phone box. Harold then said in a quiet but menacing air "that fucking watch is wrong, that fucking watch says 3:20pm and that must be wrong because I asked you to be here at 3 o'clock and no bastard is ever late for my meetings." Now if you please Mr Quinn, let us hear what you have to say. When I had finished my presentation 20 minutes later the place was hushed and Harold Musgrove said to me, "that sounded very clever but I'm afraid I did not follow a lot of it, I think I need a refresher course in finance, will you come to my office after the meeting please?"

I went to his office after the meeting and every day for the following two weeks to walk our Managing Director through all the numbers, their relevance to his business objectives and how we could use these to guide the business, a mutually advantageous time. *(This was one more important lesson; it's not about appearing clever it's all about ensuring the message is pitched correctly for its intended audience. If my Managing Director, a smart man, had trouble understanding my presentation, what chance did some of the other, less gifted attendees have?)*

It soon became clear that the divisionalisation was causing more problems than it was solving, there was little respect on either side and it was becoming impossible to make any progress. Bathgate Plant appointed a new Plant Director, the bright, energetic and classy Derek Harris who was everything that the managers of Bathgate were not and they hated him for it. Derek was intellectual and keen to change outmoded working practices and attitudes. When he accepted the Bathgate job, Derek had inherited a management team that was dedicated to conflict with the unions, with each other, with Divisional staff and most especially with the New Plant Director. Derek had asked me to a meeting in his office to go through his targets and I arrived 5 minutes early and met one of his managers leaving the office. I knew this man by name so I introduced myself to which he replied, "And who the fuck might you be?"

I was astonished at such crass aggression and angrily I replied, "I'll tell you who the fuck I am, I am the fucker that will clip the wings of fuckers like you and bring some discipline to this fucked up operation, that's who the fuck I am." To which he replied, "what's the matter with you?" I think he was genuinely surprised that I had taken offence at the way he had spoken to me, these blokes were so used to being aggressive with each other they did not realise what they were doing. They would learn. Derek had overheard the conversation and we discussed it when I went into his office and after we went through the numbers, he said to me, "do you fancy being Financial Controller for this plant, I really need somebody on the same wavelength as myself to bring in the level of changes that I need." I thanked Derek for his confidence in me and I said that he would first need to talk to my boss, the Director of Finance, but yes I was interested. And the following week I became Financial Controller and I can tell you the local

Management were well and truly pissed off, they knew change was going to happen and quick.

136 + 15 (OK LESS)

Together Derek and I worked at making changes, whipping people into line putting pressure on them to achieve what they had committed to, completely different from the way the previous pussycats in Finance had operated. My first production meeting was brilliant as a lesson in how to get an understanding of the cavalier way Production Managers regarded the reporting of their output figures. Derek was in the chair and the General Managers of each of the four factories were in the meeting which lasted for hours and which was the most important meeting on the site. In this meeting everything was laid open to view, not just production output but material supply, expediting, engineering support and finance, because everything ultimately affected production output, which was the whole point of our existence. We had no control over sales which was still the responsibility of a head office based team who distributed our domestic products through a UK dealer network and our export products were sold through our own wholly owned overseas subsidiaries.

This production meeting was particularly important because auto plants and their managers live and die by production output. This was a testosterone fueled meeting where coarse language was the lingua franca and where fists thumped tables in time with aggressive assertions of right while daring anyone to disagree. What a sham. I listened with interest until I heard one General Manager claim that he had produced 136 trucks plus 15 ok less which meant he had beaten his target for the week, by one unit. He glared round the room and I quietly asked if he could tell me what "ok less" meant. He patronisingly explained this was a common concept in most truck plants where production could claim products which were complete apart from some minor component. There was a lot of sniggering around the table, so I took the signal and decided I would investigate this "ok less" category of production output and pull an audit on the Truck claims. Outside of the meeting this man sought me out to reassure me that there was nothing to worry about, how interesting, he was worried at his bravado in the meeting and he was right to be worried, he was about to be rumbled.

Of course the audit revealed that "ok less" was a con and there were products in that claim which were missing engines, axles, and gearboxes as well as minor components. One truck had been claimed even though it did not have a cab. At the next management meeting we unclaimed more than 300 units more than two weeks' production output and we dispensed totally with that ridiculous category and I had made a mortal enemy in the process. Over-reporting was endemic, for years the cheating culture had been submitting phony numbers and then working holidays and overtime to make up the shortfall but it was like the emperor's new clothes as long as nobody queried this nonsense the farce continued. Everyone could now see the king was in the buff. I applied the same forensic procedure to the other categories of labour and the Group Managing Director started to take notice and at first he was not pleased with Derek and me, because production shortfall ultimately lands on his shoulders and he was decidedly unhappy about that. Derek and I took him through the changes we had made and what he could expect in the months to come and he was pacified at least for the moment, and told us to make sure we got output up. At least he now had the truth in front of him.

This was a time of massive change in British Leyland, the company was something of a political football and after nationalistion we were always in the public eye and it seemed we no sooner had a new Chief Executive than he was deemed to have failed and sacked to be replaced by another then another. In 1979 our Chief Executive was Michael Edwardes, who had formed quite a low opinion of some of the men running the various parts of this great unwieldy, monolith of an organisation and decided enough was enough and that some fundamental changes were needed to the senior management corps. He and a psychologist friend introduced a pretty revolutionary concept, he would send his senior people for psychological assessment and use that technique to create a management profile, against which ever senior person would be assessed. Exciting times.

The initiative of the shrink sessions was being planned just as I had decided that I had had enough of running finance operations. I had now been working for British Leyland for nearly six years and had broad experience of finance. I had worked at the coalface as it were, in the Leyland National factory and also at Bathgate with its four Factories, and in each of these posts I was up close and personal with the products, the people who made them and in those roles there is no hiding from the realities of business. I had also had two-year spell as an apparatchik deep in the centre of the organisation, at Central Head Office and then in Divisional Head Office. In these roles products and customers were distant things, which only occasionally intruded into the reality of desk top planning. In these roles my real products were long term business plans, annual budgets and monthly and quarterly forecasts, in which we showed how clever we were at manipulating numbers to create those wonderful analyses of actual results compared to the forecasts we had made. These comparisons were proudly displayed in J curve graphs which demonstrated clearly how rotten we were at forecasting, either that or they showed how rotten our factories were at doing what they were told. Our customers were the Directors, the Media and most worryingly of all the Mandarins and Ministers from the Department of Trade and Industry. In those roles I could have been in any business or none. Working at Bathgate had shown me where I wanted to be, and it was definitely not in a Finance role. I wanted charge of the complete business, that is where I found a real buzz, and that was where I saw my future career.

Exciting times or not the intrigue continued at Bathgate and after one Production meeting one of my colleagues, the General Manager of one of factories invited me to his office for a chat and a cup of tea, which I gladly accepted. He was a long time Bathgate man who had joined the company from University where he had graduated in engineering. He told me of his career and how he had risen through the ranks and was very proud of what he had achieved (quite rightly). He asked me how I was enjoying life in the Bathgate Plant and I was happy to tell him I was enjoying life and my job very much but what I saw as my destiny was running a business not just a part of it. He confessed he had no real ambitions in that area as he found the whole finance thing a bit confusing and best left to experts. Was this a message, was he looking to form a coalition and playing a long game? He probably was but I was not interested so I did not pick up on that line, and left the conversation dangling for a bit and sipped my tea.

He tried a different tack, and said to me, "You are very different from the other managers, you always seem calm and happy, nothing seems to get you upset, how do you do it?" Oh that's an interesting observation from one of the most enthusiastic proponents of shouting, swearing and table thumping. I continued sipping my tea and then I said, "Well I guess I am pretty relaxed by nature (aye right, driven and obsessed more like) and that influences how I approach the workplace. The other thing is when you work in a close environment and see the same people every day, they pick up on your body language and your moods. When I come in every morning, smiling and whistling, everybody around me gets the idea of the kind of person I am. If, however one day I come into the office and I am not smiling or whistling, then everybody gets the message that something is wrong. They will take notice and watch me, it's called learned behaviour (now who was playing a long game?). If another day I come in scowling they will pick up on that as well and might be prepared for fireworks, because people are really smart and know the score. So you see there are many stages I can go through before I get angry and that is why you never see me angry. And just because I am not visibly angry it does not mean I am not cross and my people will always know when I am not pleased about something without the need to yell at them". I did not elaborate any further and we chatted for a little while longer about the items on the meeting agenda and then I left my colleague, more in the dark about me than he was when I entered his office.

At this time, I had started to think differently about my career progression, which to that point had depended on gravity and had been directed by others. Sure I had taken the decision to leave Singer and then to leave ITT but those decisions apart, others had guided me into new posts and endeavours and I had not been in charge of my own destiny. To be fair, those who had been influencing my career had done a pretty good job, I was successful, highly paid, I had loads of perks (including three cars) but there was something missing. I was now thirty-one years old and it was time for me to find out how much of a businessman I could be by stretching myself. I had outgrown finance, it no longer satisfied my needs and I found myself increasingly getting bored with numbers and recording, important as it was to understanding the business it was not actually the business. I had watched some distinctly average performers mucking up business decisions and I knew I could do a whole lot better. And now I decided this was the time when I should try to get just such an opportunity. My then boss, Derek Harris and I had a long chat about this and as always he was incredibly supportive and advised me to try for a plant director's role but not at Bathgate because that was his job!! I spoke to the Personnel Director and set the wheels in motion.

As a result of my conversation with Derek Harris and the HR Director I was invited to consider a new post in one of our Bus factories in Bristol. This wasn't a huge factory and only employed about 350 people manufacturing bus bodies but the job was a good one, as Finance Director and Assistant Managing Director. The current Managing Director was nearing retirement age and the plan was that I would run Finance and shadow him for one year when he would retire and then I would become the MD when he retired. Perfect absolutely perfect, I could not have written a better job description, I love Leyland, and Leyland seems to love me as well! Isobel, Nicholas and I were enjoying life in Fife, we were blessed in all that we did, and now we were going to add to our family Isobel was pregnant, again. It was becoming a habit this, me getting job offers that involved moving home, when Isobel was pregnant. On Wednesday 28th February 1979 I went to Bristol to be meet the MD and talk about the new job and because Isobel was now past her due date and could give birth at any moment, I did not want to be away from home overnight, so I tried to work out a way to get to Bristol and back in one day. There were no direct flights from Edinburgh to Bristol so it was going to be complicated to organise myself. But as always where there is a will there is a way and after all, I worked for a major corporation with factories, people and cars all over the UK so here is what happened. I flew to Heathrow where I was met by two colleagues from one of our London factories, who brought me a car, a white MGB and I drove along the M4 to Bristol, had my meeting and then returned the same way, to be home with my pregnant wife and our son before nightfall. The interview went very well, I had a look round the factory and we agreed terms and I accepted the offer, easy as that. And I went home to await the birth of our new baby and to organise our big move. The irony was not lost on me, here I was again about to make a career move that would see us move to the other end of the country, with a baby on the way.

On Friday 9th March 1979, Isobel was already two weeks past her due date and it was arranged that she should go into the local cottage hospital in Dunfermline, and be induced. So off we went to this lovely little maternity ward with professional, caring and friendly staff. After half an hour it was decided that Isobel needed to have a drip fitted so that the process of inducement could begin. Isobel detests needles with a passion, and the insertion of the needle started her labour pains. At first the nurses refused to believe that Isobel had really started but a quick inspection confirmed that the baby was on the way. Twenty minutes later our beautiful baby was born, and what a welcome improvement from the more than 12 hours labour it took before Nicholas was born. The baby appeared into this world with a little red face, eyes closed tight and blowing bubbles. The midwife gathered up this precious little person and handed me this wriggling, beautiful bundle who was all ours, our second gorgeous baby. And the baby's mother, my darling Isobel, who had done all the work, looked up at me and said "do we have a girl or a boy?" In my state of heightened emotion and absolutely bursting with pride, I looked down at our baby with the umbilical cord still attached and straggling across the baby's abdomen and said "we have another boy, darling. At this the midwife and her attendants burst out laughing and said, "if this is a boy, he's some boy. It's a girl, you are a complete eejit, that's the umbilical cord you are looking at." And that was when my dear Princess, Carrie Simone, entered the world and made our family complete. Nicholas and I were left to look after the house and each other, and we coped admirably with a little help from neighbours and family. My Mum came through to help look after Nicholas and on Monday 12th March I went back to work for a few hours. While at work I arranged that Isobel and I and our two children (I really loved being a dad) would be going to the south west of England to go house hunting. The factory I would be working at was in Keynsham, to the east of Bristol, so we decided to stay in a hotel in Frome, Somerset which would allow us to easily cover the area. We decided we would drive down as that would give us the flexibility of stopping whenever we needed to look after the baby.

As luck would have it I was due to change my company car which was a beautiful triumph 2000 in British Racing Green, registration ORM 55P, to which I was greatly attached. I had discovered to my pleasure (more like vanity) that this was the very car used by UK Government Cabinet Ministers and I had become used to being saluted by Policemen and car park attendants. But it was time to change and I was persuaded to have one of the new Austin Princess Cars which I took delivery of exactly one week after the birth of my own little princess. This car was the most spacious car I have ever owned; the designers had created something of a miracle in maximising the space inside the car, which was ideal for us with a new baby and the need to have a carry cot secured in the rear seat. The boot was also very capacious and allowed us to easily carry everything we needed for us and the children. The drive down was uneventful save to say that the weather was miserable the whole time we were in the South West, it rained non-stop. This did not help the house hunting, a damp mood on a damp day is not conducive to making big decisions.

Although we did not know the area we had some advice from colleagues, so we decided to avoid the city of Bristol and to look at the rural areas around Bath but not further south than Shepton Mallet or further north than Chippenham. We looked at a lot of properties but remained unimpressed with any of them. We were most impressed with our hotel where the staff went to great lengths to make all four of us feel comfortable. Each night we would head for the dining room with Carrie asleep in her Moses basket and Nicholas in his pyjamas. Nicholas caused a stir in the hotel, he was already a carnivore at the age of two and each night the manager would make a great show by asking "what will you have tonight, Nicholas." The answer was always the same "steak, please." The manger was really taken with him, but he gave us a fright when he disappeared from the dining room one night and I found him perched on a stool at the bar with a bottle of juice and holding forth on his favourite subject which was auto products especially, tractors, trucks and jaguar cars, about which he knew a lot.

Each night over dinner the hotel manager was interested to know how we had got on with the house hunting. Actually we were becoming quite despondent about finding a house to buy when the manager of the hotel suggested that looking in Bristol might not be a bad idea and he gave us a couple of districts to go and have a look at. So the following day, Saturday we went into Bristol in the afternoon for a look around, without having any specific houses to view, and of course it was bucketing down, as usual. It was a very dull day and the city was not at its best and we kept getting lost, eventually at five o'clock we decided to head back to our hotel, through the rush hour traffic. For some reason that particularly Saturday both Bristol Football Clubs, City and Rovers were playing home matches and the rush hour traffic was a nightmare. At that time Bristol had a proliferation of traffic lights and we made stop go progress through the city traffic. As we approached a set of traffic lights in my one-week old car, I changed gear and found myself with the gearstick, swinging freely in my hand, with the car stuck in second gear. Now what? I couldn't afford to panic with my precious cargo, my wife our son who was only 2 years old and our daughter who was only eight days old. And anyway there was no time to think let alone panic, the traffic was everywhere, no place to pull over.

I nursed the car through the city in second gear, feathering the clutch, slowing as much as possible as we approached traffic lights trying to anticipate the change pattern. I would accelerate as hard as possible (in second gear) when the lights changed to green. There were many angry drivers that wet Saturday night and I did my best to ignore their angry honking at me. I understood, people were anxious to get home after the footie or a hard day's shopping, and were getting hot under the collar with some joker playing games in a car. I managed to get the car through the city and through the country roads back to the hotel in second gear without stalling, a distance of about 25 miles. I arrived back at the hotel like a washed out rag, I never want to experience anything like that again. It took four days to fix the car and for the rest of the house hunting expeditions the four of us and all the baby gear were squeezed into a mini which was the only vehicle available from the local Leyland garage. Perhaps not surprisingly we went back home without having seen anything we wanted to buy and just a bit chastened, we would have to return and go through the whole process again, sometime soon. Or so we thought at the time.

Back in the Bathgate factory things were moving very quickly, Michael Edwardes' revolution was moving apace and a number of senior personnel across the Group seemed to vanish from sight after they had visited the psychologist for assessment. We had a new Managing director for the Medium Light Vehicle Division, a young Scotsman called Ian McKinnon, one of the most impressive businessmen I have ever met and who was to become a close colleague of mine. Together with Ric Turner, Ian McKinnon would play a key role in my career and my life. My boss Derek Harris left the company, for reasons that were nothing to do with psychologists, Derek got fed up banging his head off a brick wall and decided he would move on. I had a new immediate boss in a man called Tony Jordan, who spoke with a very broad London accent, and called everybody John when the whole world knew that all Scotsmen should be called Jimmy. In the meantime, I was still busy trying to organise myself for the move to Bristol and to make time to go house hunting again.

The week I got back from Bristol I had an appointment with the shrink in London and I went down for two days of assessment. I quite enjoyed the experience even if the Psychologist thought I was Irish not Scottish. The two days of sessions with the Shrink were concluded with a chat lasting an hour or so where we discussed the experience and where the Psychologist took the opportunity to go over some aspects of the assessment and provide a de-brief. One thing he wanted to explore with me was the questionnaire I had completed in advance of the assessment. One of the questions in that form was *"if there was part of your character you would change what part would that be?"* Before replying to this question I thought about it carefully as to what the question was trying to get from me. I had colleagues who had become obsessed about this question and there was a story that one guy in a fit of pique had written that he would like to be six foot five with blonde hair and blue eyes instead of being five foot six and bald with glasses.

But questions like this can be over thought and in the end I decided that honesty was always the best policy so I simply wrote "I would not change any part of my character." In the closing interview the Psychologist picked up on this and said "would you care to elaborate on this answer?" To which I replied, "well I think I know my strengths and my weaknesses and I'm able to cope with them. To change any part of me would have a knock on effect and who knows what the result would be." A bit literal but that is what I truly believed. This man was smoking a pipe, which he puffed for a bit without saying anything. Eventually he said to me, "in twenty-five years of doing this job, that is either the most honest or the most arrogant answer I have ever heard."

Well there you go!

I got local feedback, a short time afterwards and it seems I did ok, I guess the answer was considered honest rather than arrogant. It was now only three weeks before I was due to leave to take up the new job in Bristol, and although we were receiving details of houses from estate agents in the South West of England, we still had no idea of where we would live. But our own home was now on the market and we decided I would start the job and go house hunting in the evenings and proceed from there. I was still getting stuck into my job at Bathgate and after a Bathgate Plant Review meeting the Managing Director of the Division, Ian McKinnon asked me to stay behind for a chat. Ian is a straight shooter and got right to the point and said "why are you leaving Bathgate?" I told him of my career ambitions and that I wanted to run companies not just finance departments. "So why Bristol? He asked, and I told him about the job and then he dropped a bombshell when he said, "I don't want you to go and I have a much bigger job here at Bathgate, and it's yours, if you stay." I said "but I am due to start the job next week they are expecting me." "Don't worry about that I can fix it with Centre, do you want the job or not?" Ian said, as ever getting right to the point and dispensing with the unnecessary in his own unique way.

Now I had a dilemma should I stick or twist, the Bristol job was a good job and gave me the comfort of the Financial Director post while I acclimatised to running the factory. On the other hand, this could be a much bigger post and I was very impressed with Ian McKinnon and believed there could be exciting times ahead. I looked at Ian and said, "I don't even know what the job is or what the terms might be."

"That's better" said Ian, "let's talk about it." The job Ian was offering me was Manufacturing Engineering Manager, a completely new job which merged all the diverse engineering functions on the Bathgate site, to focus on supporting production while being able to review, monitor and report from a completely independent perspective, which had been lacking to that point. Strangely the various engineering departments for which I was now responsible had previously been spread across different departments, including Production, Design Engineering and most bizarrely the Materials & Procurement department. The new department brought together Industrial Engineering, Production Engineering, Jig and Tool Design, Utilities, and Maintenance of machinery, roads railways, and miscellaneous assets. (This was all engineering functions directly associated with running and controlling the factories, it did not include product design or research and development.)

The point of this new organisation was to make engineering independent of the rest of the company and to provide a clearer view of how manufacturing was performing and more importantly how it could be improved. These departments provided not just a support service but also a control function which could be wrongly subjugated, if they were not independent of those they sought to control. Ian McKinnon was an extremely sharp operator and he quickly spotted the way things were set up at Bathgate, there was a conspiracy of silence by a confederacy of dolts. The whole thing was incestuous where departments charged with exercising independent control were being managed to protect the status quo. This structure kept the stories consistent and the truth buried, Ian wanted more than that and knew how to get it.

The total headcount of the new department was in excess of 800 and this gave me a fantastic opportunity to gain experience running a cross section of employees, hourly paid, clerical and management. I accepted on the spot and started the following Monday. The terms and conditions were excellent. The only slightly sad part of this new post was that I took over the office of my colleague and friend Derek Harris who had left the company. His successor, Tony Jordan de-camped from the heart of the factory to the front office block where he could be closer to the MD, Ian McKinnon and the Finance function. I also inherited Derek's PA, the gentle, fragrant Mary. Backing out of the Bristol job did create some bad blood, for a little while, but it did not harm my long term career prospects I am happy to say.

Before taking up my duties as Manufacturing Engineering Manager, I had a meeting with the personnel manager a Welshman called Berwyn James, who was a great help to me. The appointment of a finance man to run the Engineering departments came as a shock to everyone but none more so than the senior engineers who already ran the individual departments, which some of them had done for a number of years. There was at least one bloke who was offended by my appointment and it got back to me. When Berwyn ad I were going through the files of the senior guys in the organisation, I took particular care in reading the file of a certain "Mr Disgruntled of Bathgate".

It seems this man had been unhappy about a number of things for some years and thought he was under appreciated, and looking at his contract I agreed with that view. I asked Berwyn if he was properly graded and Berwyn said he probably wasn't but he had been such a pain in the neck that nobody felt inclined to do anything about it. Bloody typical of all that we were trying to change in this plant, if your face fitted, or you were a butt kisser you were looked after, if not too bad for you. So Berwyn and I hatched up a little plan that we would enact at an appropriate time. I arranged a series of interviews with the senior guys and ran through my ideas for merging the departments and set some priorities with these men. This was my first posting away from

Finance and I realised I was going to have to work at establishing my credentials, something I had no need to do before, because there was not much I did not know about the departments I had run before I had become an Engineer.

This was going to be quite different and I would need to develop some techniques for managing outside my knowledge base, and comfort zone. And I would need to learn quickly, because these blokes were polite but pretty cold and distant for the most part, and certainly they were not yet "on board" with me on the good ship Manufacturing Engineering. One of the first things I put a stop to was people trying to blind me with technical terms and bullshit. There were a couple of guys who were pretty smart but who were also intellectually lazy and on one occasion one bloke was waxing lyrical about some piece of equipment he said we needed and which he wanted me to spend an awful lot of money on. I could not see any benefit from this project and it sounded to me like this was a guy who wanted a new toy. So I asked a simple question "how will this benefit the company will it make us more efficient, will it reduce down time on the production line, where is the payback?" He started blustering with bullshit like "well it's kind of technical, Owen, you see its complicated to explain." I kept up the questioning, "I have time, please explain it to me in non-technical terms." After a couple more attempts at blustering his way through he finally admitted he did not know the answer to my question. The truth is he should have done his homework but laziness and precedent meant that he got away with that level of sloppiness and goodness knows what rubbish he had bought in the past. This was one more lesson in life, for me. It is easy to accept what experts tell you and sometimes we demur from asking questions because it can be embarrassing to admit you don't know something, especially if you are responsible for it. I learned that daft questions can often get dafter answers and that you should always follow a conversation where it leads you, it can be surprising where you may find yourself. It was also a lesson for those in the room and word got around quite quickly, nobody else tried bullshitting me after that incident. Although it took about six months of hard work I got them into my way of thinking and in the process I created a good department.

Eight weeks into my new appointment I had a meeting with "Mr Disgruntled of Bathgate" who I had come to regard as a consummate professional and, even if he did resent me in this job he knew his stuff and was on top of the job. He was also a shrewd operator and never got himself into the kind of pickle his blustering colleague did, and he also understood the need to ensure your boss got his strokes. At our meeting we went through the departmental business and then I told him the annual review was due and could he let me have his thoughts on the performance of his own team over the previous twelve months. This was the signal for him to make known his dissatisfaction with his own terms and conditions, as I had hoped. Even shrewd operators want to look after themselves, and this gave him an opportunity to open up to me. I apologised and said it wasn't something I had been aware of, (liar!) but I would pick up on it and get back to him. I added that I couldn't promise anything. I called Berwyn James, the personnel Manager and talked through my chat with my colleague and I asked Berwyn to implement our plan, so we arranged for Mr Disgruntled and I to meet with Berwyn. At that meeting I asked Berwyn if he could initiate a review of the grade and salary and passed a review paper to Berwyn making a case on behalf of my new colleague. As previously agreed the re-grading went through quickly and resulted in a significant salary increase, both were well received. Later that year he and I went to the USA to inspect water based lubricating systems. In a week-long visit to the cities of Detroit, Philadelphia and New York we cemented our relationship. The US tour, together with the salary increase, secured me my staunchest ally and supporter, and that was beneficial for the department and the company, as well as me.

THE ELEPHANT CONSPIRACY

My main access into the production departments was through the industrial engineering department, which had a wide brief from me, that could be summed up as "anything to improve the efficiency of the factory operations." Some people still referred to Industrial Engineering Department as the "ratefixers" and admittedly one part of the department's function was to establish the times required to complete standard operations but that was a small part of the brief. One day the manager of that department Stewart Hayes, came to see me and to tell me that he thought we had a major theft going on in the factory. Stewart was bright and innovative, an energetic young manager who had initiated an audit of the trucks at the company railhead, as part of our crackdown on factory waste.

What his team had found was that some vehicles had a lot more diesel fuel in than they were supposed to have and this was naturally creating a substantial cost variance within the truck factory. Each truck was supposed to have five gallons of fuel but some had seventy, and it applied to virtually every truck which led to the obvious conclusion that there was some sort of organised fraud going on. It appeared as though someone within the production department was in collusion with others to smuggle the fuel out of the factory. The theory was, after the trucks left the factory, another member of the gang was then syphoning the truck fuel tanks at some point between production and delivery to the dealer, but most likely at our own rail head where the trucks were loaded on flat bed rail wagons for onward shipping. Stewart started an investigation and he had fuel checks carried out, in the factory at the rail head, at the dealers' premises and he even had a couple of trucks followed as they were driven to their final destination.

His purpose was to establish what happened throughout the delivery process to check out the validity of the theory. He hoped to discover how and where the conspirators syphoned the fuel, and hopefully to catch them in the act. We were very security conscious in that factory because we had valuable components that had a ready resale market, and of our 5,200 employees, some had been caught thieving. There had been one recent incident which was funny, and was only discovered by accident. The site had three main gates where employees could exit and every now and then, on a random basis the security guards would close one or more gates and make employees pass through a close inspection routine.

It happened that there was a man in the engine factory who had developed a technique for smuggling truck batteries out of the factory. This man fastened two batteries together by means of a length of cord (also being stolen) which he then draped around his neck. Once he put on his overcoat the batteries were hidden from the scrutiny of the security men. Normally this man left the factory by means of a gate about 50 yards from the truck factory and then he had a further 100 yards to walk to his car before he could unburden himself of his ill-gotten gains. Back in those days, truck batteries were beasts and very, very heavy, and with the nearest gate now closed our weightlifter thief was compelled to walk a further 350 yards with his loot. This was not an easy task for the fittest of thieves, and when he arrived at the only remaining exit, he was jiggered and collapsed at the feet of the security guard on duty. To be honest I don't think it was a very great surprise when the guard undone his coat to let him get some air, and found the stolen batteries. The battery bandit was fired, so Stewart's team were right to be suspicious of a potential fuel felon.

Stewart came back to see me to report on progress and had to admit that their suspicions were ill founded and indeed nobody was stealing, just being inefficient. It seems that at the end of the truck production line, the fueling section had not really caught up with technology and the method used for determining the number of gallons a truck required was an informal one that had been in place for a long time. The rule was that to fill with exactly five gallons the operator had to insert the pump into the fuel pipe and then count as follows:

    One elephant   PAUSE
    Two elephants   PAUSE
    Three elephants PAUSE
    Four elephants   PAUSE
    Five elephants   PAUSE

And, hey presto that was five gallons. Simple really, simple to the point of complete idiocy. Amazingly it seems this dopey system actually worked quite well, just as long as the foreman was around. But the foreman wasn't always there and when they were by themselves the guys would chat to each other and the actual counting was more along these lines: "One elephant, did you see the game on the telly last night, Wullie, I thought it was crap, what did you think?"

"Two elephants, you don't mean to tell me you liked it, it was rubbish were you even watching the same game as me?" And so the conversation carried on until eventually the fuel filler eventually reached five 'elephant's paws' or the end of last night's TV programme, whichever came first. In the time taken to reach the fifth elephant and a full tank of fuel, the guy could have counted a complete herd of elephants dancing on a beach ball at the annual Christmas Circus in Kelvin Hall. Now we knew why some trucks had seventy gallons of fuel in their tanks when we dipped them. The problem was solved by the purchase of a simple ten quid metre, but the company must have squandered tens of thousands of pounds over the preceding years, although we had never had any feedback from the dealers who must have known this was happening. But here was another lesson, the company had spent millions of pounds equipping the truck factory and yet nobody had thought of installing a metre in the fueling section.

Life at Bathgate moved along, I enjoyed the process of being at the centre of things and although I had no responsibility for production I had responsibility for ensuring production was able to do that which it needed to do.

As I got to grips with the breadth of this role I discovered all sorts of little quirks that I was now responsible for. I was responsible for the five miles of roads, seven miles of railway lines, and a shunter ("Paul") to move rail wagons. I was responsible for the boiler house, which generated the electricity for the site. All of these things had to be maintained serviced and kept functioning and all of it fell within my remit. The new organisation was keen to keep in touch with everyone inside the organisation, locally and at HQ, as well as keeping the external world appraised on all things Medium Light Vehicle Division, so as the one with the brass neck, I was asked to set up a Communications Department.

That was different.

I also discovered part of the empire I was responsible for was the installation and commissioning of new machine tools and equipment, and likewise for de-commissioning and disposal of surplus or obsolete tools & equipment. Hidden away in this part of my organisation was a section responsible for moving major pieces of plant and equipment, and another section responsible for office allocation, furniture and moves. In addition, this section also was responsible for the allocation of internal parking spaces. If you ever want to see senior and middle managers at their grubbiest and most childish you should spend some time managing office accommodation and parking spaces. Sensible people park their brains and regress into monkey mode and they can go to amazing lengths to get one over on someone else or to ensure they get what they are "entitled" to.

I had one bloke complain to me that he only had a metal hat and umbrella stand while the guy in the office next door had a fancy wooden one. I gave him a piece of my mind and told him to grow up and get on with his job. And don't get me started on parking spaces, "I think I should have my name on the wall by my parking space, so nobody else will park in it." Aye right!

Having responsibility for over 800 personnel, meant I had a great deal of contact with the Unions and I found this part of my job utterly fascinating and I think for the most part I handled my relationships pretty well. Not long after I took up my new role I had a visit from the head of the Joint Shop Stewards Committee (JSSC), a man called Jimmy Swan a devout socialist. Because of the complexity caused by the number of unions on the Bathgate site, Jimmy was a full time official, paid by the company. He asked if I would treat him to a cup of coffee and I readily agreed to his request. As we chatted Jimmy told me that the JSSC was the longest serving management organ on the Bathgate site, having had the same members for many years while managers came and went. He added that it was in the interest of his members if I was as clued in as possible on the issues of concern to the workforce, and he offered to have a regular meeting with me to discuss the various issues affecting my departments as well as the company as a whole.

One theme that Jimmy returned to frequently during our meetings was the importance of trust between men in a negotiating environment. He said to me on one occasion, "I don't need to know all your secrets or even know your negotiation limits, although I would like to, but I do need to be able to trust that if you tell me something is fact that I can believe it." He added,

"Trust is something that has been in short supply in this factory and as a result conflict has ensued. If I don't trust you and I think you are telling lies what options are left to me except industrial action? He then told me a story about an annual review negotiation that had taken place in the factory before my time. The shop stewards gathered in the Personnel Director's office, who had three senior personnel men in attendance. Management asked the stewards what they were looking for and the union men submitted a claim for a weekly raise of £20, hoping they might be able negotiate a settlement of £7 per week.

So far, so normal and this submission was discussed for a while and then rubbished by the management team who trotted out all the old excuses, that the company was making losses, needed money for new products to protect employment levels and new equipment to keep employees safe. The unions responded with arguments about parity with English factories, the cost of living, the difficult working conditions. To that point it was the normal well-trodden path of industrial relations discussions, the old industrial relations two step, 'you lead, and I will follow'. The unions expected this response and also expected the meetings would last for many days and possibly weeks but in the end they would reach a compromise deal, they always did. But this year there would be a difference. The personnel Director said, "Look I am very busy and I can't hang around here all day talking to you guys I've got some real work to do". The message to the unions was this is not real work and these discussions on people's livelihoods are not as important as the lunch appointment I have in 45 minutes. You can imagine they were not terribly pleased to hear this and reacted angrily. Jimmy had to call his troops to order. The Personnel Director then reached into the bottom drawer of his desk and produced a bundle of printed and bound documents which contained an offer of an increase in basic rates for all unionised employees. The shop stewards asked for time to consider this document so the meeting was adjourned until the following morning and the unions left to examine and debate the offer and the personnel Director left for his real work in the dining room. The proposal was for two pence an hour increase for the largest group of employees covered by the agreement and for proportionately higher increases for the more senior grades of workers. This was totally unacceptable to the unions, an offer of less than a pound when they had submitted a backed up claim asking for £20.

When the meeting reconvened there were heated exchanges with the unions demanding this offer should be withdrawn and negotiations should begin to reach conclusion. The management team responded by saying this was a final offer, and they must take or leave it but there would be no alternative. One week later the Personnel Director had not changed tack and had taken four more pre-printed and bound "final offer" documents from his desk drawer. They were no further forward but the unions now realised this bottom drawer might have another twenty pre-printed final offers and if they kept going they eventually discover just how much they could drive up the "final offer". At that point the unions registered a failure to agree and asked for and got a national conference which lasted four hours and settled on £7 per week.

Jimmy concluded this story by saying from then on he never trusted anything that man said, because he had shown himself to be a liar when he thought he was negotiating. These meetings with Jimmy were one more valuable learning process for me and I gained unique insights into the way unions operated and how they dealt with issues before confronting management, from the most senior union official in the factory. Jimmy did offer one important piece of advice, "I am doing this because it will benefit my members, but I am not your friend and if you take your troosers doon then I will skelp your bare arse." That was me told and I never did let my pants slip down.

I learned that the best shop stewards have a proper long game plan, that communist members are always well organised and disciplined and that the union organisation has many very clever people. I also learned that it is not easy to be an elected official and it takes a great deal of shrewdness and mental toughness to be a successful union leader. I had a lot of respect for Jimmy Swan and I learned from him an enormous amount about the workings of industrial relations within factories and about the workings of unions, but I understood where we both stood. I have a lot to thank Jimmy Swan for.

THE AYATOLLAH & A PERFECT STORM

Jimmy Swan talked seriously when we had a major redundancy at Bathgate and at the other manufacturing plant in Scotstoun, Glasgow. We were reducing the headcount from 5,200 to 3,500, and as you can imagine every department was affected and the unions wanted to know what was going on. We made a presentation to the JSSC, and took them through the reasons why a redundancy was necessary and the details of how we would proceed. Basically Bathgate had found itself trapped in a perfect storm with three major markets collapsing at the same time. The markets were Iran, the USA and Nigeria and in these markets we were hit by currency problems, a revolution and a scandal involving corruption and cement. These three markets were unique in their own way and irreplaceable, and in losing them the factory lost a massive volume of products.

The Ayatollah Khomeini's revolution in Iran, resulted in one of our major truck markets disappearing. Leyland had a factory in the city of Tabriz in the north of Iran close to the borders of Armenia and Azerbaijan. Over the whole period of its existence the Bathgate factory had shipped large volumes of trucks to this factory to be sold throughout the region. We shipped vehicles in CKD kits (Completely Knocked Down), for assembly in the Tabriz factory. These trucks were rugged, dependable and simple to fix and were and were well suited to the Iranian market. They were able to cope well with the rugged terrain, the steep mountain climbs and the basic facilities in which they were maintained and serviced. Suitably tough as they were for that market they were not acceptable in the more advanced markets of the West, and the sales team were not able to source substitute markets, though they tried. We also shipped substantial volumes of engines, axles and other spare parts to the Tabriz factory, making it a very significant market for Bathgate products. We started to see shipments being disrupted towards the end of 1977 but by the end of 1978 all shipments had been halted and we withdrew our personnel in mid-1978. The political demonstrations were very bad in 1978, and these brought the economy crashing making it impossible to guarantee payment for anything even if there had been a demand for the products. Any possibility of resuming shipments to Iran ended with the arrival of Ayatollah Khomeini on 1st February 1979.

In the same year we began to have problems with the Ayatollah's mortal enemy, the USA as the value of the US dollar dropped against the pound sterling, resulting in our agricultural tractors becoming very expensive in the US and as a consequence our volumes crashed. Bathgate enjoyed a market share of 3% of the agricultural market in the USA, this was lucrative business for the company and although on the face of it 3% might not seem a huge share, the market was enormous and our volume was significant, indeed it was critical to sustain the factory production programme. In July 1977 the sterling dollar exchange rate was $1.71 to the pound and this made us highly competitive and the business was very profitable. With the May 1979 election victory of the Tories under Margaret Thatcher, the pound strengthened and reached $2.31 that year. This was not good news for exporters but it was disastrous for the Bathgate plant because we found that our products became instantly uncompetitive, sales stopped, importers sold the stock they still held at the old price but would not, could not order new stock. As a result, we were forced to withdraw from the US market, with the consequent loss of production volume to the factory.

The third element of this perfect storm was the loss of our market in Nigeria. We had a presence in Nigeria for decades but during the Second World War, we had mothballed operations only to resurrect our factory when the war ended. The factory employed many local people plus a large contingent of expatriates in the managerial and supervisory positions. The Bathgate plant supplied trucks up to a maximum weight of 20 tonnes while other Leyland products were shipped from our heavy truck factories, all of these products were also shipped in CKD kits, for local assembly. This was another substantial market for the Bathgate factory. With the discovery of oil in Nigeria in the 1970's the country looked set for an economic boom, and we expected to see export sales rise given the forecasts from the local management and from our international sales colleagues. But the economic miracle did not produce the volume windfall we expected, actually the reverse was the case. The sudden availability of lines of credit resulted in every country in the world selling everything and anything to Nigeria but the country did not have the infrastructure to cope with such a boom in imports.

This was particularly true of the Ports which lacked the capacity to accommodate the number of ships trying to unload cargo, nor did they have the manpower to move products or to clear paperwork. Shipments of our products arrived in port only to join the ever expanding queue of ships trying to get unloaded, and when they were eventually unloaded they were stuck at the dockside awaiting clearance by overworked customs officers. These problems resulted in the reduction of Bathgate production volumes for Nigeria with all those CKD packs being stored in different UK sites while waiting and hoping for an opportunity to ship, at some point. We were assured that demand for our products was still strong but it was just getting the products into the country that was the problem, and we continued to build kits albeit at the reduced volume, and store these kits in our factory.

At the start of 1979 a corruption scandal was uncovered, involving senior government officials and foreign companies, Nigeria was buying more cement than it could ever use at the rate of 1.6 million tons of cement being shipped into the country each month. Unfortunately, the volume of cement coming into the country was more than twice the handling capacity of the Nigerian ports, which were already at a standstill. The worst part of this scandal was the shameless complicity of western countries who were being paid $115 dollars a ton while charging the rest of the world only $25. The government had ordered 20 million tons of cement of which 16 million tons were for the Ministry of Defense. Subsequent investigations claimed that there was enough cement ordered to cover the entire country with a six-inch concrete blanket. Not surprisingly the scandal had repercussions, it caused a revolt which saw the overthrow of the regime of Gen. Yakuba as well as contributing to the redundancy at Bathgate. The perfect storm caused Bathgate volumes to crash and there was no prospect of these markets returning to normal any time soon. The specification of the vehicles being shipped to Nigeria and Iran were unique to the requirements of those countries. These models would have been unacceptable in the advanced markets of Europe and our International Marketing gurus could offer no alternative world markets so production had to be severely cut back, which in turn meant jobs had to go. This was my first involvement in a redundancy. Fortunately, in George Newburn, we had an impressive new HR Director, another Ian McKinnon appointment. George led the team that managed the redundancy programme and I was part of the team. Much of the planning fell on my shoulders through the Industrial Engineering Department to define the appropriate manning levels, and as a consequence the surplus manpower. We worked hard to ensure that we carried this redundancy through in a professional and dignified way, in compliance with the recent changes in the law. We were required to give employees 90 days' notice of redundancy, the idea being this would give the company time to find volunteers and to see if some of those people whose jobs were redundant could be found other posts elsewhere in the organisation.

This was a major operation and I worked very closely with George on this. From scratch we created a blueprint for a smooth redundancy, or so we thought. We believed we had covered everything, we had anticipated the questions we would be asked by the unions, by employees, by the media and by politicians, and from this we developed press briefings as well as counselling documents. Since Bathgate had a huge public profile in Scotland at that time, anything which affected that site was big news and the Scottish media would be all over the case. We carefully worked out individual entitlements, we negotiated a fair package with the unions, (this was, as expected, a pretty tough process), we reviewed every single post and identified the key core skills we wished to retain. We even created a productivity scheme to be implemented at the end of the redundancy cooling off period, to motivate those left behind. We organised special counselling areas for those whose jobs were redundant, we created detailed briefing documents for those who would be doing the counselling, we tried to cover every possible eventuality. And still we had a couple of glitches.

ROUGH, TOUGH HOMBRES

Anyway the 90 days rushed past and it came to the day where we had to inform those who had not been successfully redeployed that their posts were now redundant and to report to the central area where they would receive their redundancy package and the opportunity for counselling. Anyone in a bargaining group represented by a Union was informed of their rights through the Union officials. Managers and other senior personnel were individually counselled. That morning I had a surprise awaiting me, it turned out that two of my colleagues, who projected themselves as "tough" guys, actually turned out to have less backbone than they would have the rest of us believe. I had only completed my own first interview when my secretary told me that my neighbour, one of the rough tough hombres had not reported for work that morning, and he had a person waiting for a meeting. I called the HR Director who told me that the other rough tough hombre hadn't shown up either, which meant there would be a group of people due to be counselled that they were leaving the company and the men who had been designated to speak to them had thrown a sickie. Given that the plan called for everyone who was leaving to be counselled that day we had to make some swift decisions and the HR Director and I made space in our own schedules to take over the counselling our colleagues should have been doing. George also had someone phone the no show boys to find out what was going on.

On that fateful morning, there was a profound air of sadness all across the site because everybody knew this was a portentous day. Many of those who had been counselled that their post had fallen out of the organisation still held out hope that somehow they would survive the impending cull. I had struggled with my conscience about this redundancy, the first in my career. In my head I well understood the economic necessity but how do you come to terms with making 1700 people unemployed for no reason other than being in the wrong company at the wrong time. I could feel for people who were leaving although to be honest the first guy I spoke to was quite happy and told me he had already got a new job at more money and the redundancy was a bit of a windfall for him and his family. Many others among my team who were leaving the company echoed this sentiment, because they had 90 days to come to terms with their changed circumstances, proving the value of this so called "cooling off period".

My second person for counselling that morning was not in my department but his manager was one of the two tough guys who had not showed up for work. When I told this man he would be leaving the company he was genuinely thunderstruck and then he got really angry. As I was speaking he interrupted me and asked "What the hell are you talking about I'm not redundant and who the f*** are you to be telling me this?" it seems there were lots of rough tough hombres in production. I quietly and patiently explained that often we don't like to hear bad news but that my colleague had counselled him 90 days earlier and had told him that his position was redundant and if we could not find an alternative post within the 90 days then he would be leaving the company. This understandably extremely irate man came back at me saying "that's fucking rubbish, he spoke to me and said the company was having problems and that it would all be resolved in 90 days. He never fucking mentioned redundancy." That was a very difficult meeting for that man, because he had no preparation for this shock and such a massive change to his life, and sense of self-worth. When that poor man left my office (in bits) I called the Personnel Director and he had the same experience, with the other fellow's personnel who had lost their jobs.

It would appear that these two Production Directors, who were in charge of the two largest of our four factories on site, had decided to be "kind" to their subordinates who were losing their jobs. Instead of telling them the truth of what was happening and giving them a chance to come to terms with it, they chickened out by telling them the company was having serious difficulties and it would take 90 days to sort out. This meant that those employees left that first counselling session not realising their jobs were redundant nor did they understand that if we could not find alternative posts for them then they would be leaving the company at the end of the cooling off period. Those personnel were thus deprived of the opportunity to look for alternative employment during the three-month period. Then having bottled out of their responsibility in the first place they had the audacity to avoid it once more when the day of final counselling arrived and these two not-so-tough guy jokers failed to show up for work, citing man flu. It's impossible to imagine the shock and pain those poor men suffered that morning when they realised that their jobs were now redundant, and they would be leaving. Word spread quickly and by the time I counselled the second person from my colleague's department he had already learned of his fate. He was bitter, frustrated and very angry with his boss but in his absence the only person he could talk to was me, and he sat silently and listened to what I had to say and at the end he said, "Thank you, for taking the trouble to tell me this." It was an awful experience for these men, who had worked for the company for a long time and who deserved so much more than to find out that their jobs had gone in such a manner. They were floored by the news which was one of the most craven things I have ever experienced in business. And it was made worse because of the tough guy image cultivated by the two perpetrators.

On their return my delinquent colleagues had a brutal meeting with our MD, Ian McKinnon and HR Director, George Newburn, both of whom were genuine tough guys, unrelenting and unforgiving of such behaviour. To use a local expression that was current at the time, the craven ones were bored, screwed and countersunk and made to understand the magnitude of the company's disappointment with them. Courage is not about swearing and banging your fist on the table, courage is about doing the right thing even when it is uncomfortable. Another important lesson on the human condition and in organising a redundancy.

CHAPTER FOUR

THE HOLY FATHER'S TRUCK

Although I was employed by and paid by MLVD Bathgate plant I was nevertheless a Corporate resource and after two years running the Engineering functions at Bathgate I was summoned to Lancaster House for a career chat. My development as a manager with Leyland Truck Group would continue and it was time for me to take up a new challenge. I was appointed General Manager of the Leyland Truck Service Group. This was a business within a business, a fully owned subsidiary of Leyland Truck and Bus but for the first time in my career I would have full P&L responsibility of a business.

The Service Group consisted of seven factories located around the UK, there was one in Aldenham, north of London on a site shared with London Transport, another of these factories was located in Bristol. A third factory was in Oldbury in the Birmingham suburbs, we had a fourth factory in Hull, number five was located in Wigan and number six was located in Chorley Lancashire. Number seven was on London Road, Glasgow. These factories were completely self-sufficient and had their own management and staffing structures. There was also a central operation consisting of a Finance Director and his staff, a personnel manager and myself and my PA. The Bristol, Hull and Glasgow factories were responsible for servicing and maintaining trucks and selling spare parts. The other factories also provided these services but had additional responsibilities, the Aldenham site produced agricultural tractors under licence, and adapted truck specifications for export markets. The Wigan site was solely involved in producing re-furbished engines, the Chorley site and the Oldbury site provided specialist conversions of Leyland trucks for the home market, in addition to providing service and parts support. This was a successful business and for the most part the people running each operation were experienced, competent men, although there was one exception to this, the London business. Importantly most of the General Managers had an entrepreneurial streak, understood their customers and knew how to turn a profit. In 1981 my mini Group was turning over about £15 million per annum and returning a profit of £2million but there was a time bomb waiting for me.

Two years before I took over the management of the group, my predecessor had implemented a two-year wage deal which included individual Productivity Schemes in each of the factories. These schemes sought to reward the employees by sharing business growth as measured by output, a nebulous concept in such varied operations, with limited costing structures to measure growth. Nonetheless to show goodwill there was a safety net of 4% guaranteed for two years. It was a poorly constructed proposal and one that could never have been successful. When I took up the post, the productivity agreement was about to run out and with it the 4% guaranteed safety net, which had been activated continually through the life of these schemes since not one of the schemes ever triggered a payment despite the growth in productivity and profitability. These schemes were so poorly structured that they would never pay the employees, who not unnaturally thought it was just one more con trick by management. My first task was to implement a new wage deal and I had very strict guidelines because an austerity programme had been announced by the company, and all increases would be limited to 2% across the board, with no exceptions. Oh dear! So my introduction to my new employees was to announce the removal of the guaranteed safety net of 4% and then implement an increase of 2%, in effect they would see their wages decrease by 2% unless I did something about it. Welcome to the Leyland Truck Service Group, Owen. Poison chalice or what?

As it happened there was one great skill I had and that was understanding the mechanics of productivity schemes, I had designed a very successful one at the Bathgate plant, in the immediate aftermath of the massive redundancy, this should be a cakewalk by comparison, shouldn't it? The Group was very profitable and had clear opportunities for growth so I set to work and came up with revised deals for each site, which I knew would benefit both employees and the company, which is after all, the aim of a productivity scheme. The initial reaction to my wage proposals was one of outrage, "Are you saying we will get a reduction of 2% in our earnings? Are you mad, expecting us to agree to that?" and they were right, yes I was expecting them to agree to that because I had absolutely no room to manoeuvre in the basic increase, none whatsoever. And as for the new productivity scheme proposals there was a universal response of "get stuffed", we've had one of those before and it did not work. But hey, I had wrestled with some tough union nuts at Bathgate these parochial guys were surely pussycats by comparison, weren't they?

They were such pussycats that I clocked up 40,000 miles that first year visiting each site and spending a lot of time, explaining my proposals in detail, and convincing them site by site that these would work and would result in increased earnings. These new schemes were good and I believed in them and when I believe passionately in something I can be very persuasive. My hard work paid off and site by site the employees accepted that I knew what I was talking about and that I could be believed. The first of the factories to agree to my proposals was Bristol where I spent a great deal of time and effort explaining to the local employees through individual meetings and mass meetings. Soon all the other factories reluctantly agreed to sign up for the new deal with one exception, the Glasgow factory. As hard as I tried I could not get the Glasgow site to accept my proposals and they went on strike. I tried everything to get them back to work and to accept my proposals I even had informal meetings down the pub, but nothing would persuade those men. There were two local stewards, the more senior man was sensible measured Hugh and then there was his sidekick, a bit of loose cannon called John but known as "the bear" by his friends (!). A real life version of the good cop, bad cop combination and unfortunately they had a full time official who I think was frightened of John "the bear" and who was as much use as a chocolate fireguard.

To make matters worse while I was trying to sell the 2% minus deal to the Glasgow team there was a press announcement that Michael Edwardes, the Leyland Group MD had just received a salary increase of £40,000 per annum, just what I needed. At one meeting down the pub, "the bear" decided to try and rough me up a bit and said to me, "Listen pal, just because you think you have a local accent and come from across the other side of the Clyde in Cam'slang, don't think you're one of us. Coming up here with your shiny arsed suit and trying to reduce our wages." I laughed and said he had a quaint way with words which didn't actually help as he continued mumping quietly to himself but I had been insulted by experts and the bear just didn't cut the mustard.

By now the Productivity Schemes were working well on all of the other six sites and paying decent bonuses. I knew that the Glasgow guys talked regularly to their colleagues in other parts of the country but I still could not get through to them. There were a few things at play in the Glasgow factory, while on strike, most of the guys were working in the black economy for cash jobs and with no tax or other deductions, they were probably earning as much as they would have done in our factory. Secondly they loathed my predecessor for his perceived arrogance and refusal to meet with them to discuss the useless productivity scheme. Thirdly they had a sense of grievance at having been sold a pup with the last scheme, and this offended the two stewards greatly, since they were seen by other union members as being taken for fools by the management. And that is a hard place to be for a union official or indeed for any of us.

After seven weeks on strike I was getting some pressure to resolve the issue and so I tried a desperate gamble. I spoke to my brother who had some strong relationships within the union movement and I told him the facts. The Glasgow lads had been shafted by the previous agreement but I had no room for movement on the new proposed basic increase, even though in the circumstances it was unfair, illogical and punitive. The 2% increase was a sticking point for the Corporation and there was no way I would be allowed to break this principle for a small factory when it was applied strictly across the entire UK workforce, the car plants, the truck & bus plants and all the associated businesses, a workforce still close to 200,000 at that point. On the other hand, the productivity scheme I was proposing had the same fundamental principles as the ones in place on the other six sites and these were all paying bonuses. And if the carrot doesn't work, there was a stick, there was real chance I would be forced to close the site with the loss of 130 jobs.

A few days later I received a call from a man called Jimmy Airlie a very senior and high profile, full time union official. He told me he was calling me because the normal official was on holiday and he was covering for him and he wanted to meet with me. We had a formal meeting together with the local stewards. Jimmy Airlie was quite a man, I was very impressed with his grasp of the situation and he simply asked me to explain to him why I thought this was a good deal. When I finished speaking he told me that he thought it was disgraceful that any company should expect its employees to accept a 2% wage cut in these desperate times. He asked me a few questions about my proposals, how they would work, how much did I expect they would pay to the employees and why was I not prepared to put a safety net guarantee in place as had been the case previously. All great questions that went right to the heart of the matter but which I was able to deal with because I knew my stuff as well. After about an hour's discussion we had a recess during which time Mr Airlie spoke to his colleagues for another hour and then they all returned to the room. By the look on the local guys faces it must have been a tough meeting but I could not tell anything from Mr Airlie's face, he looked exactly the same as before. When he came back into the room, he said he was prepared to accept my word that the new scheme was an improvement on the previous one and would result in increased earnings for his members. On that basis he said he was prepared to call a meeting of the members and propose a return to work and acceptance of the proposals. The following morning there was a meeting in the factory, a very stormy meeting and Mr Airlie managed to convince his members to come back to work. What a relief and while there was some unhappiness at first, it soon became evident that the decision was the right one because employee earnings climbed immediately and the Glasgow scheme proved to be one of the best in the entire group. I will forever be grateful to Mr Jimmy Airlie, a tough but fair and very astute man. Following the initial pyrotechnics, the Service Group settled down and we got on with building the group, its product offerings and its profitability, and this was a very enjoyable post for the two years I was General Manager.

While all this stuff was going on with the wage negotiations I was getting on with running the group, in my spare time. There were plenty of other issues trying to get my attention. One of the most important was that my predecessor had provisionally ordered a computer system to link all the Service Centres to the Head Office. This had been fully approved and all the documentation was in place to get started on it, as the Finance Director explained to me. In addition, the computer company was anxious to get the deal finalised, but I was hesitant because I knew that many people saw computers as some kind of magic wand back then and thought that the simple purchase of shiny equipment would solve all of a company's problems. I did not subscribe to that philosophy. I asked for the documentation submitted in support of the capital expenditure approval, which I read over the weekend. A couple of things struck me, firstly there was no supporting documentation from our Central Purchasing team, which I would have expected for a project of around £2.5 million. There was nothing in that document I could see showing that a new computer would increase the profitability of the Group, nor could I see if we had carried out a proper comparison with solutions from other manufacturers, to demonstrate this was the best value option. I was not happy and I would not proceed with the purchase until I could satisfy myself on these points, I was suspicious that because the Service Group was so profitable and because the purchase was only for £2.5 million that it had been given an easy passage through Central Finance approvals system.

I asked the Finance Director to work with the General Managers of each of the Service Centres, to provide me with a justification for this project based on increased profitability for the Group. I asked the Group Purchasing Director for some help in determining if we would get value for money if we went ahead with this purchase. The Finance Director started his investigation after telling me that he had not really been involved in this submission until now, since it was my predecessors own flagship project.

Dearie me, that sounds a bit ominous, what would I find? I got a call from a Purchasing manager called Paul Nolan saying he was on the case and could he come and talk to me about the Computer project. Paul was a top professional and one of the shining lights of the Leyland organisation. We met in my office and I conveyed my doubts and suspicions to him as we chatted through the details of the proposed purchase. After a few days Paul got back to me and told me we were being skinned on this deal and that if we really wanted to buy a computer system we should start again. My Finance Director came back with similar sentiments and added that the General Managers of each of the Service Centres were dead against this purchase because they believed it would bring an increased workload as well as chaos during implementation for no discernible benefit. We canned the project, kept our money in the bank and the lesson was simple, 'because you can does not mean you should.' From that encounter, Paul Nolan and I became life-long friends.

Being General Manager of the Service Group was a great learning and growing experience, I was the CEO of a small conglomerate of companies, geographically spread across the country but with a commonality of activity. I was responsible for all Profit and Loss matters and ensuring the business serviced a wide range of customers including some in house business with the Leyland Bus and Truck factories. I enjoyed the breadth of my responsibility and the freedom I enjoyed in setting the direction of the business, developing new markets and making reasonable profits and managing a diverse group in pursuit of common goals. The job brought some interesting surprises but none more so than becoming involved in the visit to the UK by the Holy Father Pope John Paul ll.

THE LEYLAND POPEMOBILE

In the summer of 1982 His Holiness Pope John Paul II travelled to Great Britain for an historic six-day tour that saw him greet and bless hundreds of thousands of people at 16 different venues. It was the first time that a pope had visited our country in over 400 years, since before the Reformation and his kissing of the ground on arrival at Gatwick airport on the 28th May was a moving start to the occasion.

The Holy Father & Archbishop Derek Worlock

This was an event the Catholic Church had been planning for several years and our group Chairman Sir Michael Edwardes was deeply involved in those high level discussions. As a consequence of Sir Michel's talks, Leyland Trucks designed and built the first and (to my mind, at least) the most impressive Pope mobile ever built. The Holy Father's truck was based on our 3-

axle Constructor truck; in fact, we built two of those vehicles. The Pope mobile was unique, it had armour plating to withstand a bomb blast, bulletproof glass and a host of other security features. It also had running boards along each side, which allowed the Holy Father's bodyguards to be near and to keep an eye on proceedings when the vehicle was moving through large crowds, as it often did. I had two roles in the Papal visit, the first as the provider of the transport logistics, the maintenance and servicing support and the relief drivers. The plan was simple the Holy Father would fly to his destination climb in the Popemobile and make his visits then he would head off by aeroplane or helicopter to his next destination, to find the second Popemobile waiting, while number one vehicle would be driven to the next location. When the Popemobiles were being moved between locations, a team of drivers recruited from the workforce in our Service Centre in Chorley would be driving. Then the Holy Father's personal driver would take over when he was on board. The Chorley Service centre also supplied drivers for two coaches that had teams of mechanics and every possible spare part on board to ensure that there were no mechanical mishaps to interrupt the Holy Father's progress. The whole logistics plan worked beautifully and the relief drivers had an audience with the Holy Father at which he thanked them for all their hard work. Although not all of them were Catholics they were thrilled. For his efforts Sir Michael Edwardes received a Papal Knighthood and I got a nice letter from Sir Michael.

My second role in the Papal visit was as a steward on the streets of Liverpool where, on Sunday 30 May 1982, a million people lined the route to welcome the Holy Father into the city, following a helicopter journey from Coventry to Liverpool Speke Airport. His Holiness briefly visited Liverpool Cathedral to say The Lord's Prayer before making his way to celebrate Mass at the Metropolitan Cathedral of Christ the King. David Shephard the Anglican Bishop of Liverpool at the time and the Catholic Archbishop Derek Worlock worked closely together to further the interests of their flocks and this friendship led to the invitation to Pope John Paul to visit the Anglican Cathedral. The local newspaper had a wonderful article on this part of the visit and the headline ran "Two Cathedrals linked by a Street called Hope." For the Papal visit my beat was in Toxteth and having only recently arrived in the North West I did not realise that Toxteth had a reputation for being a tough area. My colleague Jim Troop, the HR manager for the Service Group and I volunteered through my Church St Patrick's in Southport, and we controlled the crowds in Toxteth together. As we marched from our base to take up our posts Jim gave me a bit of an update on the area's reputation. Despite the poor opinion some people had of the area, I had the most wonderful time in Toxteth where I found the locals to be kind, considerate and generous. They were Liverpudlians so they were also funny and I was kept amused as I patrolled the streets of this great city for over six hours.

There was one funny interlude where a group of young boys came out to have some fun with these blokes in their strange yellow crimplene berets. Initially they were teasing one of their own friends and calling "him a "woolly back". When I asked why they called him this they replied because he came from Wigan and that was the outback, sheep country. Wigan is a town with a population of over 100,000 so it's hardly the outback unless you are a city dweller I guess. When they heard my Scottish accent they went into overdrive, because the day before England had beaten Scotland 1-0 at Hampden Park, Glasgow. So I had to endure some good-natured ribbing and chants of one nil, one nil, one nil. The kids were lively and bright and it was all good fun. One lady brought me a chair from her home and I had a constant supply of tea and biscuits. I have very fond memories of my afternoon spent with the residents of Toxteth. The Holy Father's visit was a brilliant time to be a Catholic, particularly in Scotland where the reception at Murrayfield in Edinburgh and Bellahouston in Glasgow were remarkable spectacles. These events contributed greatly to Scottish Catholics emerging into the front of national life after centuries of living with a siege mentality. The singing of "He's Got the Whole World in His Hands" by Scottish catholic youth still brings gooseflesh when I think of it, and I only saw it on TV.

After the visit there was something of a conundrum of what to do with the Popemobiles, the Catholic Church owned one and they took possession of it for use on further visits overseas.

Leyland Trucks owned the other vehicle, which we placed in the showroom at our head office "Lancaster House" in the town of Leyland, and it was a great draw. My Parish of St Patrick's in Churchtown, Southport was holding its annual garden fete in July 1982 and I was part of the planning committee. In early June the organising committee was having a meeting and discussing how we could "pep" up the event. I casually suggested that I could bring down the Popemobile if they thought it would help. Total, utter and complete silence followed and everybody turned to me and looked at me and for a moment I thought they were going to cry. But they just looked at me and then Father Hickey said, "Could you really do that?" I replied that since I was in charge of it there was nothing to stop me, we would just have to put some insurance in place and I could organise it to be driven down and then returned. The place erupted and now they really were close to tears. I suppose I might have become a wee bit blasé about the whole thing having been so deeply involved but my colleagues on the committee were devout Catholics and for them to get this close to the Popemobile was a big thing. We advertised through the local churches, (all the churches not just the Catholic ones) that the Popemobile would be on display. On the day of the fete we could hardly cope with the numbers that turned up, our greatest turnout ever. We were swamped with people at the fete and I was astonished at the reaction, people approached this vehicle with respect bordering on awe. It was very touching, this simplicity of faith and reverence. We allowed some people to climb aboard and to stand where the Holy Father had stood and even to sit on the leather shooting stick he used for support and it was evident that they thought they were close to something very holy. And of course now we know that they were because Pope John Paul II is now Saint John Paul the Great.

Five-year old Nicholas posing on the Popemobile (note the halo)

After the success of the Popemobile at the Church Fete, I talked to my dealers and suggested that they might want to use it at their open days, which most of them did and again with great success. At one of these events, at our dealers Woodward's of Formby, I took my then five-year-old son Nicholas to see the great machine. I took a Polaroid photo of Nick and was surprised to see my saintly son crowned by a halo. The Pope mobile made a huge impact on the imagination of the people in the North of England in the spring and summer of 1982.

Many years later when I had left Leyland and the so-called merger with DAF was completed there was an incident which might have become unsavoury but for divine intervention. The merger was of course a take-over and tiny DAF absorbed giant Leyland in the UK, and naturally the DAF personnel triumphed in the allocation of jobs, resulting in some people operating with considerably more responsibility than had been the case heretofore. One particular beneficiary of this was the DAF marketing manager who found himself as the keeper of the Popemobile. He was at a loss as to what to do with this wonderful machine so he came up with the bright idea of repainting the vehicle in the orange colours of the Dutch Royal House, and using it for beauty pageants around Europe!! He then submitted a proposal to this effect to DAF HQ in Eindhoven. The city of Eindhoven is a Catholic enclave in Protestant Holland and the recipients of this request were horrified at the proposed desecration of the Holy Father's vehicle and immediately took possession of the vehicle themselves. The Popemobile then found a new lease of life touring the world's Catholic countries as part of a DAF initiative.

As GM of the Service Group there was one aspect of my post that I found highly amusing and that was the monthly board meetings I attended. The Service Group was a separate but wholly owned entity within Leyland, and bizarrely I reported to the Sales and Marketing Director, himself a board member of Leyland Truck & Bus. At the monthly board meetings of the S&M dept. these flower arrangers loved talking about concepts, deals, market share, shows and other exciting stuff. When I started to talk about "business", P&L accounts, balance sheet ratios and cash flows, I could see their eyes glaze over. The making of profit seems to be an alien concept to some of the flower arranging fraternity. There were some very clever and some very experienced men in the S&M organisation (I know these initials have another connotation and the significance was not lost on me then or now) but somehow they got lost in their own rhetoric. I always had the sense that they were addressing the peripherals and not getting to the heart of the issues, which was declining market share. I enjoyed listening to their waffle, nevertheless. Meantime, in my own little corner of the Corporation, the Truck Service Group's revenue continued to expand and we grew the business to £17 million revenue and just over £3 million bottom line, it was a good little business. It was also hard going running a business with seven factories so widely dispersed and I came to understand that the only way to keep the business moving forward was to have a presence in each of the factories on a regular basis. This meant a lot of travelling and in my first year with all the wage negotiation ongoing I clocked up 40, 000 miles over the calendar year, in three different cars. I was cementing my reputation as a man who got things done, and the company had endless capacity for testing me with new challenges like the Manchester Business Game. Thanks to the Managing Director's personal initiative.

YOU CAN'T BUY US, YOU'RE BUST

Les Wharton was an excellent Managing Director and extremely good at his job through a difficult period in the company's history. Les had a calm way of going about his business and was a practical, plain spoken Lancashire man. Les looked like an aesthete, he was long and lean and smoked like a chimney but he was actually a warm individual, he was deeply respected by the entire company. And uniquely for the hard headed, unsympathetic automotive industry our Managing director was known as Uncle Les to his immediate team. (Not to his face of course). He called me into his office one day and said to me, "Right lad, I've got a job for you, it's a good job and I am trusting you to do well." "Sounds good to me, Boss what is it?" "It's The Manchester University Business Game, I'm entering a team and you are going to be the MD and the leader. I'm not paying good money to finish second, I want you to win this game, ok?" "Right-o, who will I have in the team, Boss?" I asked tentatively. "I am trusting you with my best and brightest, the best of the best, Alex from Engineering, Colin from IT, Stuart from HR and Tony from Finance, every one of them a superstar. I want you to look after them and make sure they learn about the wider aspects of business from this. And I want you to win this game."
"Ok, Mr Wharton, sir I understand you want to win this, and so do

I." Les arched his eyebrow at my formal address, he knew bullshit when he smelt it. For my part I had become so comfortable in the company of our Managing Director that I allowed myself a little indulgence in irony.

We then looked over the papers, so I could understand the rules and work out a strategy to play and win this game. That done, Les called my new team up to his office so he could give them the same pep talk he had just given me. Of my new colleagues I knew Stuart and Tony pretty well and I knew them to be top operators for whom I had great respect, but I had never met Alex from Engineering nor Colin from IT. With the briefing over we adjourned to have our own meeting and to work out the details. The game was scheduled to last for ten rounds over ten weeks with weekly submissions from teams, which the judges reviewed and passed judgement on. The basic thrust of the game was that each team would be a company and should trade its products with the single view of increasing its share value. Each company had a bunch of assets which defined production capacities, a product range and budgets to be allocated to production, marketing, sales and overheads. Teams were able to allocate their budgets as they saw fit in an attempt to influence their supply lines and in order to stimulate demand in the markets they chose to operate in. The verbiage issued by the organisers suggested that teams should follow strategies that would result in them strengthening their company's bottom line. From there your asset base, profitability and market success would be used to assess your share value at the end of each round. The game organisers had an algorithm which evaluated share price based on the effect of the actions taken by the team. Ranking was strictly by share value and total turnover or asset value did not count towards position on the league table.

We decided to meet once a week on a Thursday night after work, have a meal together and then spend the night reviewing progress and compiling our next submission, which was sent off each Friday. After round 1, we were in second place, after round two we were first and after round three we were first again. My team members were great and we had a terrific time on this game, Alex and Colin worked out very quickly how the game worked and how to influence the results and we were very focussed on our objectives. Round four is when the interesting stuff started because that was when you could mount a takeover bid which would give you more capacity than you would be able to achieve through vertical growth. It was only possible to make a takeover bid if you were able to fund the bid 100% from your funds on hand, which of course meant that you had to have a pot of dough to fund the bid which in turn meant you had to sacrifice other strategies. We had been watching and tracking our competitors very carefully and decided that we would take over the British Telecom Team, (this was before the Post Office and BT split to go their separate ways). The protocol was that you should work out an appropriate share value then phone the Chairman of your targeted company and offer him a friendly deal, if he refused then you had to call the game organisers with a hostile bid. The organisers would then call the takeover target and tell them that unless they could somehow improve their share value to a better price than the bid price then the takeover became de facto. My two geniuses had worked out the best share value that our target company could achieve by liquidating everything and so we went a bit higher with our bid, just to be sure. The guy at British Telecom was appalled and deeply offended and said to me, "But you are British Leyland, you can't buy us, you're bust. The Government owns you." I replied, "Not in this game buster and in case you hadn't noticed the Government owns you as well, I will now call the organisers with a hostile bid." I called the organisers and they were also horrified and said "It's only the first open round they haven't even had a chance to play the game properly yet. Nobody's ever made a takeover in this round before, are you sure you really want to do this?" Trendsetters! The organisers phoned me back a few days later to say that our bid had been unsuccessful because the British Telecom team had liquidated all their assets and had managed to improve their share price to a fraction of a penny better than the bid price. We knew that not to be true, because we knew very well what their best outcome could be and it was much less than they achieved but I guess that the organisers wanted this company to submit a team each year. I was later to get some background on the BT team from my next door neighbour, who was Marketing Director of that organisation and he told me it had caused a lot of chat in the company. Apparently the guy who was head of their team took it really badly, he was the Finance Director and regarded this as a personal slight. To make matters even worse he had to settle for last place in the overall rankings while we soared to victory and a crystal thingamabob for Les Wharton. There was a big awards ceremony in Manchester and surprisingly the British Telecom team did not send anyone to the bash. Back at Leyland Les was beaming and proudly displayed his Waterford thingamabob on the Boardroom table. This was an enjoyable interlude.

ARE YOU A SALESMAN?

British Leyland was a dynamic organisation and changes were once more afoot, and it seems that two things were now constants in my career at British Leyland. One was that when the organisation changed, I would be changing my job and the other was that once more I would be involved in some fundamental re-structuring of a department. The Sales and Marketing Department were struggling to achieve the necessary market share and it was decided to have a bit of a clear out and to inject some new talent into the department. In addition to personnel changes the structure was altered to reflect a regional bias and focus. I was recruited to become General Manager, Sales and Service for the North of England and North Wales. Having witnessed the goings on from inside the Sales structure and not been overly impressed by those who had gone before it was now down to me to grasp this particular nettle.

Once again I was being drafted into fight forest fires. First at National, then at HQ, followed by MLVD, and Bathgate, then the Service Group and now Sales. I was a company doctor in all but name, and I was enjoying my career immensely, how lucky can a boy from the Halfway be? I called my Mum to say that I had received another promotion and I would be getting huge increase in my salary. My Mum asked me what the title of my new job was and when I told her I was General Manager for Sales and Service the phone went quiet. I asked my Mum if she was ok and she replied, "Did you say Sales?" I said, "Yes Mum, General Manager Sales and Service." "Does that mean you will be a salesman?" My Mum asked. "Well yes, I suppose so, "I said wondering what she was thinking. So I said, "Don't you think that's good, Mum?" She said simply, "Are you going to be a salesman after all that education?" I burst out laughing and then I spent half an hour trying to explain to my Mum that I would not be taking a case full of samples around various garages, trying to flog a few fan belts or spark plugs, which is what she thought being a salesman for Leyland might entail.

To get the new organisation rolling we had a resourcing meeting to form a series of sales teams, who would now be organised into four main teams based in the Glasgow Service Centre, The Aldenham Service Centre, The Oldbury Service Centre while my own team would be based at HQ in Lancaster House and I had responsibility for the remaining Service Centres. My team included a number of managers who were considerably older than I was and it seems that most of the men regarded as "old soldiers" (a euphemism for elderly trouble makers) within the sales and service teams found their way into my organisation, funny that. I called my team together for the first briefing and introduced myself because I did not know a single person in my team. They were a bit surprised to hear me talking about business and efficiency and how I expected the team to run.

This was a new approach to sales but I was determined we would be successful. Being completely new to the Sales function I gave a lot of thought about what I would say to my new team, especially since I had a number of very experienced operators in the group. I wanted to buy myself some time to get my feet under the table and to work out what I expected of them and what they could expect of me. When I finished the briefing, I said "There is something I should tell you and that is that I have a photographic memory and total recall. If you are ever thinking of telling me a fib, then I suggest you write it down and keep it safe because you will forget your indiscretion but you can be sure that I WILL remember. They were subdued as they left the room. Thank you Bill Monaghan and his speech to my 19 years old self.

My new job was a challenging role because I was so far out of my comfort zone. In all my previous roles I was in control of my own destiny and stood or fell by my own efforts, now it felt really strange that my success would be dependent on the reflected success of third party companies in the form of the Dealer

Network. This was a new experience for me. It transpired that in addition to having all the old soldiers in my team I had all the old soldiers in the dealer network as well. Three of the most senior dealer principals in the whole of the dealer network were in my patch, and I was going to have to work hard to make any headway with those men. I would learn that these senior dealer principals were vastly experienced and knew exactly what they were doing and were frustrated at some of the 'wet behind the ears' corporate men who tried to lay down the law to them. Salaried employees in large corporations should know their skill sets and know how to help those who can help themselves. The main part of the role was to develop the sales of trucks through the dealer network by ensuring that the production from the various factories was taken up by dealers, as it rolled off the end of the production line. This was a bit like quadrilateral equations, on the one hand the dealers were out selling and trying to get those units delivered as quickly as possible. At the same time, the factories were planning production out into the future with a six month firm programme and a soft plan of a further three months. It was unusual for dealers to know six months in advance what they would be selling so there was a lot of second guessing made by the production planning teams. When the trucks were produced sometimes they met the dealer requirements but often this was not the case.

To make sure we were not left with surplus stock at the factories, the company sales personnel would seek to wholesale all stock to the dealers. We had some carrots to help us in this process like a vehicle stocking policy which allowed dealers to carry truck stock free of charge for a period before they had to pay. We also had incentive programmes focusing on certain products that needed help to be more competitive. The Leyland sales team would work with the dealers own personnel and sponsor factory visits, product workshops, and vehicle demonstrations. To make sure all the product was placed in the market we might have to persuade dealers to take stock they did not really want and that's when good relationships came to the fore. On the odd occasion this did happen there was always a quid pro quo, friendships are good but business is business.

Once I wrapped my head round the different nature of this role, I really enjoyed the experience and I formed strong relationships with dealer principals and in the process I learned a great deal from some of them about the art of the deal and about making dough. This was especially true of Sam Newton who was the Chairman of the Leyland Truck Dealers Association and principal of the Group's most profitable and highest selling dealership. Sam told me that I was cut from a different cloth than the normal type of manager at Leyland and said that most of the ones he had known over the years were more concerned about their careers than their company. He then offered me an interesting piece of advice, saying "If the Leyland Marketing News asks to do a profile on you, tell them to bugger off." When I asked him why I should steer clear of the newspaper, Sam replied, "Because everybody who lets their face appear on the front page of that dreadful newspaper ends up losing the plot. They believe what the newspaper says and lose sight of what they should be doing, and go off the rails." Sam then ran through a list of people who were former employees of Leyland, often leaving under a cloud, I had known some of them. I took his advice and refused to allow the paper do a profile on me.

A Cartoon showing me controlling the dealers, the artist had a mistaken view of how I did business.

As I started to organise my team, I talked through the roles with each individual because I was keen to find out their own thoughts on effective organisation. It quickly became clear that some of these experienced managers had developed very bad habits and I concluded they were coasting and not really thinking about their jobs. No wonder we had been losing market share.

When I asked one manager how he would describe success, I was surprised by his response. He told me that as a sales manager trying to generate sales through a third party dealer body that his role was really hard to quantify. I burst out laughing and said "You are kidding, right? Sales is the most easily quantified and measured role in the world."

While he blushed (slightly) he nevertheless insisted that he had no real measures by which he could judge if he was effective or not, beyond the number of vehicles sold by others. I asked him, "Would they still sell these vehicles even if you were not there?" "They probably would," he replied. "Then why should I employ you?" he seemed genuinely surprised at this question and was even more embarrassed that he did not have an answer to my question.

I then asked him to describe his average day only to be told there was no such thing as an average day, that his days were dictated by the needs of the dealers. It seems that at least some members of the Leyland Truck Sales Team had been a superfluous appendage to the company. No plans beyond the last phone call. So that was an easy one to fix, and pretty soon everybody had a planned diary with clear objectives to garner intelligence and to assist the sales effort of our dealers. It's not hard, just a few changes in personnel encouraged the others to lift their game. It took a bit of time and some head butting but eventually we had a close knit team who were hard working but more important they were well organised and knew what they were doing and what was expected of them. We were, by a wide margin the most successful of the Sales regions, in each of the three years I held that job, it was probably just coincidence but all the other teams were staffed by people who had only ever worked in the Sales Department. I'm just saying!!

Fire engines order goes to Leyland

A Signing Ceremony with Mrs. Louise Ellman

While sales through dealers was the main thrust of our business I also had responsibility for developing sales through Local Government and through the Military and these were both substantial elements of our business. In fact, the single biggest one-off deal I completed in my time in this post was a deal for Fire Engines with Lancashire County Council's Fire Authority. Leyland Trucks had not been involved in the sale of Fire Engines for many years and I was convinced there were real opportunities in that sector. My colleague Tony Diss, who had responsibility for Local Government Sales worked hard and long with the Fire Authority to nail down detailed specifications and then he and I worked with our Design Engineering colleagues to create a demonstration model. We then invited the Fire Authorities to come and test the vehicle in our development centre where we had a full size circuit with off road, urban and race track capability. The vehicle passed with flying colours and we signed an order worth £700,000. In this deal we were greatly encouraged by the leader of Lancashire County Council Mrs. Louise Ellman, a young and dynamic politician who went on to achieve much greater things, as Chair of the Transport Select Committee in the National Parliament.

The company's massive investment programme had come to fruition and it seemed we were launching a new truck every few months. As I settled into the job I found my role being expanded, I was involved in the truck launch events, which was very demanding but very exhilarating. Sir Michael Edwardes, as he now was, decided we needed to go on a charm offensive and I was nominated to go round various bodies telling them how wonderful Leyland was. I visited chambers of Commerce, Lions Clubs, Rotary Clubs, Women's Institute clubs, dealer events and anybody else who would have me. The marketing department arranged my diary and for one year I was making three speeches a week pushing company propaganda.

Leyland was a great supporter of continuous professional development and tried hard to keep its managers up to speed with current management thinking and techniques. As a result, we were regularly sent off on courses and this was even more the case within the sales organisation. One day I was asked to attend a sales course organised by Mercuri Goldman in Birmingham. I was to assess this course for its appropriateness to roll out to the sales personnel in our dealer network

MIKE'S MIND GAMES

This sales course was due to last for a whole week and I wasn't really happy about going because I was busy and it meant I had to postpone some actions I was anxious to complete. There were 16 delegates on the course including three from one of our sister companies, Freight Rover. We sat in a large room in a horseshoe layout and the course leader introduced himself. "Good morning, my name is Mike Higgins, I am a French National, I live for 50% of the year in Florida USA and the other 50% in Switzerland."

Mike was of medium height, dark haired and had a certain Gallic charm despite his obviously Irish name, and good English, albeit in a Mid-Atlantic drawl, using every clichéd American word and phrase which was in vogue at that time. Having introduced himself Mike then asked each of us to introduce ourselves, name, company and position. And so he went round the horseshoe and we all dutifully responded, with Mike staring intently at each one of us as we spoke. When the last person finished, Mike paused and then went back to the start and repeated back to each of us the same biopic we had recited, word for word, most impressive. The course itself was interesting but I had reservations about Mike, because I thought he was bit of a conman, but he had highly tuned senses and he obviously felt my reserve and watched me closely. There was a strict routine and we did everything together starting with breakfast at 8:00am and finishing with dinner at 8:00pm, it was the same each day.

Before we broke up that first day, Mike asked each of us to prepare a ten-minute presentation on a subject of our own choosing for the following day. For my presentation I spoke about fostering which Isobel and I were involved in at that time. Most people talked about work related items. As the week progressed Mike became more and more intrigued by me and kept niggling me to get some reaction. The truth is I did not like him very much because I thought he really was a conman who blatantly manipulated the attendees into sharing his own point of view, although they seemed happy enough to be manipulated if I'm honest. I decided that if he could transfer that skill to our dealers' sales teams then it would be a worthwhile investment and would be relevant to what we were trying to do with our dealers, but he did not know that. And so he carried on niggling me. On the second last day he handed out a sheet and told us this was a light-hearted exercise. The sheet informed us that we had been flying a spacecraft above the surface of the moon but on the dark side, and out of radio contact. The craft had crashed leaving us stranded far from moon base and we had to make our way back to our colleagues. In order to do so we had to pick from the crash site those pieces of equipment we would find helpful in getting back safely. Among the many items able to be salvaged was a sledge, various food items, bottles of oxygen and a lot of silly things including a box of matches. We had a weight limit and so we were not able to carry everything that was available. After 30 minutes we were asked to read out what we had chosen and of course there was a number of people who had taken the matches and when anyone admitted to taking the matches, there was lot of name calling and a great deal of hilarity.

Mike then handed out a form in which we were asked to assess the course and the course presenter. I bridled at this blatant ploy, imagine asking for a form to be filled in when everybody was full of the joys of a dopey exercise. He was hardly likely to get any criticism, apart from me that is. I sat for a few moments collecting my thoughts before filling in the form, aware that I was being watched. The grading categories on this form were all multiple choice, ranging from unsatisfactory through satisfactory, to good, very good and excellent. I graded the course and the presenter with a "satisfactory" in all categories. The chap sat next to me looked over and saw my completed form and asked, "Have you not enjoyed the course?" I told him I had enjoyed it but I thought it was better to make an assessment when I returned to the office rather than after playing a game. He didn't say anything, but grimaced and looked pensively at his own form. This was the last night and we were due to depart at 3:00pm the following day, and Mike held us in the lecture room until after 8:00pm that night. Before we left the room he asked me if I would do another presentation in the morning, again on any subject of my choosing. I nodded and said, "Sure, Mike" smiling as I knew that he knew that I knew he had read my assessment form. Such pettiness.

After dinner we had a pint at the bar to finish off our last night, there was a lot of chat and Mike was in the middle of it until 11:00 pm until he decided he was off to bed. As he passed me he said, "You will remember that presentation in the morning, won't you?" I reassured him that I had not forgotten and he left the bar, not very happy with me. It took me until 2:00am to finish my presentation, which took as its theme the first five minutes of a sales interview in three languages. The first language was the lingua franca of my childhood, Glaswegian, the second was estuarine English and the third was the Mid-Atlantic accented smart arsed bullshit which Mike spoke. The presentation was in three columns alongside each other and I opened in Glaswegian and then offered the translation into English before confusing everyone with the spuriousness of bullshit. Of course the third column, (Mike's bullshit way of speaking) was about four times longer than the other two columns. Mr. Higgins was a devout believer in not using one word when ten would suffice.

The room was in hysterics at my presentation, I was the only Scotsman on the course and my English colleagues thought my Glaswegian patter was funny and completely unintelligible when spoken but displayed on the overhead slides they got the gist. While they were laughing they missed the point of the presentation but Mike did not miss the point he knew exactly what I was getting at and he was spitting blood. His silly wee game and his pettiness had rebounded on him, even if it was only him and me that knew that.

We parted the best of enemies and I went back and wrote a report that we should adopt the Mercuri Goldman course for our dealer sales personnel. Mike and his boss were summoned to Lancaster House to a meeting and Mike was flabbergasted when he saw me in the room and hastened to tell me how much he had enjoyed having me on the course.

Lying bastard.

CHAPTER FIVE

WHEN IRISH EYES ARE SMILING

Leyland had a strange business relationship with the Republic of Ireland in the early 1980's. As a lead in to full membership of the EEC, Ireland was allowed to maintain certain trade barriers for a number of years. In the case of Leyland Trucks this meant that if we wished to sell trucks in Ireland we either had to assemble the trucks in Ireland or pay import duty on all trucks imported into the country. We had tried assembling trucks in a factory on the banks of the river Liffy in Dublin but there were so many quality problems that we abandoned that idea. As an alternative to paying import duty it was decided to maintain the factory with a minimum employment level which was both cheaper than import duty and cheaper than the cost of quality problems incurred on locally assembled products. As the trade barrier was due to come down in 18 months, I was dispatched to Ireland to assess the market and to write a report on my findings, so that the company could decide how we should service the Irish market in the future. Together with some colleagues from International Sales, I developed a plan for my visit. I would speak to all our dealers, to the trade bodies, an official from the department of transport, a number of customers and also to some competitors' dealers.

But first I went to Dublin to speak to my colleagues and there I was re-united with the elegant and civilised John Battersby, who had been my first boss at Leyland when he was MD of Leyland National. The Dublin factory was a dismal affair and effectively operated on a one week on and one week off basis, on full pay. The only real production was the manufacture of lightweight trailers for cars. That aside, Leyland Ireland was a spare parts operation, ordering, storing and delivering parts, it was very depressing, and John was most unhappy. One thing I was trying to assess was how effective and substantial the dealers were and whether we could build on the back of one of them. After speaking to the Irish team I decided that it would be useful to have one of my colleagues from the UK Business Development Department come over and join me. I wanted to complete this part of the role as quickly as possible so it would be helpful to have someone else collect and review the dealer performance data while I got to grips with the dynamics of the market.

YOU MEAN OLIVER CROMWELL?

John Baldwin arrived to help me to assess our dealers in Ireland. We met at Dublin airport and he and I and the Irish Director of Sales, Tom King set off for Cork City. As Tom drove, I briefed John on what I was looking for, I had worked with John before and I knew him to be a good guy, he was head of Business Development for the UK. John Baldwin always seemed to be hungry and was complaining that he had only had a coffee on the plane across, so we stopped about an hour out of Dublin to grab a sandwich in a small pub, which was deserted apart from the three of us. The barman organised some sandwiches and then poured three pints of Guinness. As he was pouring the pints John commented on a large rusty piece of iron that was mounted on the wall behind the barman. He asked the barman what it was and the barman replied that it was a souvenir left behind by Mr Cromwell as he was passing through. John then said, "Do you mean Oliver Cromwell?"

"That'll be the fella'," said the Irish barman. "Oliver Cromwell is one of my heroes, "John said as I was busily kicking him, to no effect. The bold John in his wonderful English isolation continued, "Oliver Cromwell was one of the great Englishmen, the father of modern parliament," he continued oblivious to the pain in his shins. "Ah sure there's not many in these parts would agree with that," the barman was being very polite but I think he just regarded John as one more cretin with no knowledge of Irish history. John then realised that I was kicking him for a reason and shut up.

We ate our sandwiches and left before the local battalion of the bould IRA arrived to kneecap us. Tom went back to explain to the barman that the Englishman was an eejit but he and I were ok. We got John in the car and Tom and I gave him a quick lesson on Irish history and warned him within an inch of his life about expounding any further on any of his heroes, especially Cromwell. In Cork we met with Mr Noel Buckley who was the first ever Leyland dealer in the whole of Ireland and who was a great supporter of the company and its products. Noel was a gentleman and had lovely soft Irish brogue, he gave us a quick oversight of the market in Ireland and the needs of the dealer network. We talked about the market for new trucks and Noel said it had never been huge but it was pretty awful at that time, and very few new trucks were being sold. Noel said that many people would go "across the water" and buy a second hand vehicle. He said that the only new vehicles being sold in any quantity were Hino trucks, through their idiosyncratic Irish dealer Pino Harris. Noel had a broad business base within the auto industry and it was just as well, because he would not have been able to make a living on the proceeds of new truck sales. Noel was happy to provide John Baldwin with details of his business for John to take back with him. The idea being that we could then work out what kind of dealership could survive in this difficult market. For manufacturers to have a long term position in a market place it is vital to have a profitable dealer network, if the dealers can't make money they won't hang around long. Ireland was a small market in terms of volumes but relatively large in terms of geography, with small pockets of activity dispersed around the country. At the time of my visit we were trying to sell in Ireland based on the UK model, with dealers in every major population centre. It had already become clear to me that the UK model was inappropriate for the Irish market. From what Noel was telling us, we were going to have to think outside the box to create a long term presence in this country. That is if we thought we should have a long term presence.

Back at the hotel we had a long talk about what we had learned from Noel and I asked Tom King to put this in context for me within the overall market. Tom was clear that Noel Buckley was the best and the most successful dealer Leyland had, but he was sure he did not make much money from his Leyland Franchise. An honest but not a great assessment by Tom. At this point we concluded that the information we had gleaned from Noel was as much as were likely to get on our tour. While our service handbook looked good with a rash of dealers across Ireland, these were really micro businesses, whom Tom reckoned would be unable to provide us with hard marketing intelligence or even dealer performance data since they kept only the bare minimum in terms of paperwork. Armed with a bundle of information from Noel, John returned to England the land of his great hero.

The next day we had short trip to Clonmel in County Tipperary to talk to a man called Barney Canavan, a car dealer who had been talking to Tom about taking a light truck dealership. He was a very nice man, and he seemed to be doing quite well but our discussions did not add much to my knowledge of the Irish market but at least it was another view. That night Tom had booked us into a really interesting hotel, on the outskirts of Clonmel, this had formerly been an English mansion and was sat on the banks of the river Suir, which marked the boundary between the counties of Waterford and Tipperary. After a nice dinner in town we came back to the hotel and ended up speaking to the owner a man called Dennis English.

Mr English was a larger than life character, who dabbled in many things including vintage cars and he had a huge collection, or so he told me. As we got chatting he told us about the history of his old house and what a history. The manor house had been built originally by a man who had come to Ireland with Oliver Cromwell as a Colonel in the New Model Army. (Poor John, now that he was back in England he was missing out on this gem about his great hero). After Irish independence the family gradually severed their links with Ireland and the house lay empty for a while until Mr English came along and snapped it up. He used most of the house as a hotel but he retained the central block as his own family home and offered to show us round. The entrance to the house was very grand with a beautiful sweeping staircase that rose to a balustraded upper hall and ran both left and right around the central core of the building. It was breathtakingly beautiful. Mr English had decorated the hallway with period artefacts and furniture and it looked magnificent, somebody had good taste.

There was only one incongruous aspect to this magnificent spectacle, at the foot of the sweeping staircase there were two pillars where once upon a time there had stood two large statues perhaps Greek or Roman deities or maybe even John's hero, warty nosed Oliver Cromwell. On top of these two pillars Mr English had installed two magnificent, ten-feet tall, brightly coloured statues. One statue was the representation of the Sacred Heart of Jesus and the other was of His mother, the Blessed Virgin Mary. Oliver Cromwell and his estate building Colonel would be whirling in their devoutly Protestant graves at the effrontery of it all. The things you see when you haven't got a camera! Next morning, we set off straight after breakfast, having been regaled by more stories from the loquacious Mr English, a truly remarkable man.

We set off to the pretty town of Limerick to meet with our dealer there, Ray Kelly, another character in a land full of them. Ray was also full of chat, an open and very endearing man, who ran a haulage business as well as a Leyland dealership. He told me he loved Leyland trucks especially the Marathon maximum weight tractor, even though it had nearly killed him. When I asked how that had happened, Ray said, "It broke its back when I was hauling a load up to Dublin and the front pitched forward onto the road. I got out safely all right but I got a fright." I was horrified, and I asked Ray what the story was and he said, "It was my own fault, really, the truck was a wee bit overloaded." I said, "All our trucks are over-engineered to allow for some slight overloading, were you much overloaded?" "I was grossing out at 40 tonnes, or thereabouts." Said Ray. "But it was only plated at 32 tonnes" I said aghast. "I know, I know", said Ray, "it was my own fault but I had often carried that weight and it had never broken before."

Oh really?

I told Ray that was very naughty and he was lucky to have survived but this was another lesson in life, Irish truckers disregard plated weights and take crazy risks with their own lives and those of other road users. Ray asked me when I was taking over as MD, and before I could put him right he carried on with a piece of advice about how I should conduct myself when I did take over. "Always remember, Owen that Ireland is a village and if you fart in Limerick they will smell it in Dublin right away." I wasn't quite sure what to make of that advice but I think it was well meant We left Limerick and the irrepressible Ray Kelly, chock full of anecdotes and headed for Galway for another meeting with a dealer, Michael Joyce. Mr Joyce was a quiet, sober man, who was critical of the lack of support from Leyland over many years. He told me that Ireland was a difficult market and it was hard to earn any decent money from the truck business. It seemed to Mr Joyce that Leyland blew hot and cold about Ireland and he could not see any real commitment to the country. I pointed out that we had a substantial factory employing many people in Ireland and we had a sales team which was there to support him and the other dealers. when I asked him what more he thought we could do, he suggested we reduce the price of our vehicles by about 30%. I replied that would be difficult to do and anyway our truck prices were very competitive with the other manufacturers' offerings. It was really a conversation with nowhere to go but it did highlight the frustrations of at least one dealer within a stagnant market.

The future was not bright, Ireland was in an economic trough, and there was no hint that this situation would change any time soon. The total market for trucks was at an all-time low, dealers were not making money, manufacturers were not investing in their networks, all in all a pretty bleak outlook for anyone involved in the truck business. If you took all the annual business done in Ireland together it was no more than that of a small town in the UK. It was going to be hard to make a case for Leyland to maintain an in-house presence of any significance, in this country.

That night we stayed in a hotel overlooking Galway Bay and Tom and I had a long chat about what we had learned so far. Tom was not a fool and he understood the importance of my visit to the future of our business and to his own future, and he kept trying to be positive about the future. After dinner in the hotel we took a seat in the lounge and ordered a nightcap. We were joined in the lounge by a party of young people from the Irish Blood Transfusion Service, who were staying at the hotel, while they persuaded the locals to come and donate blood. We had seen a number of their mobile transfusion units in the hotel car park, as we pulled into the hotel. A number of young women broke away from the main party and sat at some tables near where Tom and I were discussing trucks and dealers. They were girls in their twenties and they commenced an animated discussion about the merits of the Legion of Mary. It seemed an odd conversation for otherwise thoroughly modern looking women but it was obviously important to them, and they spent the rest of the evening on this subject, although it did not interfere with their drinking. I could not imagine a similar group of young women having such a serious conversation about religion in a hotel in the UK. It was impossible to ignore their conversation since they were so close to us and I had trouble listening to Tom, so we stopped our serious chat about trucks and Tom told me about the Rose of Tralee Festival which included a singing competition, in which he competed every year. Tom was an accomplished tenor and loved singing and did so on a semi-professional basis, but his passion was that contest, which he told me attracted some great singers from all over the world, including Tom

YOU'RE A FINE BIG FELLA

As I travelled around the country word was clearly going ahead and everybody seemed to be aware of not only who I had been meeting with but what the content of our discussions were. Everybody commented on how Irish my name was, in fact it was more Irish than most of the people I had been meeting with, and I now understood that they all thought I was going to be the new MD of Ireland. I knew differently.

Next stop on our Grand Tour of Ireland was the dealer in Athlone. Tom did all the driving on this trip and as we drove to our appointment that morning Tom told me that if I thought I had met characters up to this point then I was mistaken, this next guy was the real deal when it came to characters. I was due to meet Pat Jennings whom Tom told me was one of a kind, very energetic, very opinionated and extremely unconventional. And in truth Pat Jennings turned out to be all of that and more. We arrived at the dealer's premises at 8:00am, to be greeted by an empty car park and as I stood assessing this post-modern concrete box, there was a screeching of wheels as four black cars made a striking entrance into the car park. Three black Mercedes were followed by a black Porsche. The Porsche was Pat's and the Mercs belonged to the other directors. Pat had red curly hair and was quite short of stature but big on personality, and full of bonhomie, I liked him immediately, he was full of chat and talked at a thousand miles an hour and I guessed he was a dangerous man that would need careful watching.

He led me through his very ordinary workshops and up the stair to his office, and what a surprise that was. The post-modern concrete castle all of a sudden became a renaissance Prince's opulent, luxurious hideaway. There was ornate, carved wood paneling on every wall, large velvet drapes behind Pat's desk and what a desk, it matched the ornate paneling and was vast. There was an amazing assortment of knick-knacks in that office, statues (not religious), lamps, thingamabobs and trinkets of every sort. All of the bits and pieces were tasteful on an individual basis but together they formed a remarkable mish mash of eras and genres, it was all too much. It was the most vulgar over-the –top office I have ever seen in my entire life but it seemed to fit with Pat and his amazing persona and I loved it, even if I could not have lived with it. This was going to be good.

Pat asked me to take a seat and went round the other side of his massive desk, whereupon he grew about two feet and was suddenly towering over me and all that he surveyed from his perch. He must have had some sort of platform behind his massive Monastery refectory hall table with drawers, that passed for a desk. Pat sat on his throne and glowed. "Will you have a drink, sur?" asked the bold Patrick. Tom had prepared me and even though it was just after eight o'clock in the morning, I said, "Yes please." Pat reached into one side of his desk and produced two Waterford crystal goblets that resembled pudding basins. It seemed only Pat and I were drinking.

"What's your poison, Owen?" asked Pat

"Vodka, please." The truth is I was not a drinker and I thought that vodka might do my body the least amount of damage at this early hour. Pat reached into another compartment in his desk and produced a bottle of chilled vodka, which he started pouring in large quantities into the deep recesses of this huge goblet, and I said, "whoa that's fine, Pat thank you." "Ah sure you're a fine big fella and you'll be having a fine big drink", replied Pat.

So holding a gallon of vodka in one hand and wondering at the sheer volume of alcohol in this mighty glass, we settled down to talk about business, while my head was clear enough to make sense. Pat was an engaging man with very firm opinions about everything but he was a successful truck dealer and as such had a right to his opinions on trucks and truck sales. Once the niceties were over Pat launched into what I came to realise was his favourite subject, himself and his ability to sell anything to anyone, anytime for a large dollop of dough. He started off by telling me that he would let me into a big, big secret, which was that Truck Manufacturers only got in the way of the dealers selling trucks to the buying public. When I asked him how we did that, he said, "You confuse customers by letting them know what they can have, instead of telling them what they need. You see all these sheets do you want to know what I do with them?" At this he reached into a drawer in his cavernous desk and pulled out a pile of Leyland Truck product specification sheets and began tearing them up into small pieces. Very theatrical, but these sheets took a great deal of effort to produce and to keep up to date and we were all rather fond of them back at the farm. Pat then said "Here's what I use," and from the same drawer pulled out a huge photo album, Pat might have been short in stature but everything he did, every gesture was big, very big. He then regaled me with the stories behind each photo, how he persuaded a reluctant customer to buy the truck that he had in stock and to pay top dollar for the privilege. "There's no point in selling if you can't make a bob or two," opined the bold Patrick and I couldn't disagree with that. "And I'll tell you another secret," said Pat, "The best incentive for a fella to buy a truck is envy." This is going to be good I thought. "If you tell a fella that the biggest trucker in the town has just bought one of your Trucks, sure he'll be desperate to have one himself, he'll bite your hand off for the same thing. 'If it's good enough for the best guy in the whole of the district, then it's good enough for me'. Sure that's what they all think." (Not only was Pat a salesman but a psychologist as well, and I have often found that the best salesmen understand the human psyche very well.)

"And that's where the photo album is a sure winner, Pat continued, "I always take me photos with me when I want to sell. Now, Owen you've got a fine Irish name and sure I've taken a liking to ya, so I'm going to tell you another secret." This really was my lucky day, three secrets and I've only been here for half an hour and still 99% of my gallon of vodka to drink.

"There are photographs in this album of Trucks that are a wee bit more than they seem. You see this one here? This is Tom Dunphy's Truck, look it says so on the front in big letters, see?" and sure enough in bold lettering on the front and side of the truck is said Tom Dunphy Haulage. "Well let me tell you, sur, that was never Tom Dunphy's truck, no, never. You see yer man always bought from Mercedes, but he was the most influential man in the business, he's a big powerful man is Tom Dunphy. So I goes to see him and I says, "Tom you're an awful stubborn man, why is it you've never bought a truck from me?"

Your man Dunphy says, "Pat, I like your craic but you're a gobshite, and anyway I like that old German star on the front of me trucks."

"So I says to yer man Dunphy, look I am going to do you a favour, I am going to have the newest truck in the range tarted up in your colours and with your name in big bold letters. And I am going to put it right in the centre of the Galway show. It'll stand in that show for the week and the whole of Ireland will see it. At the end of the week if you like the truck then I'll give you a good price on it, but if you don't like it then I'll take it back to my shop, no questions asked. What do you think about that?" "I know you Patrick Jennings, you'll not be doing nothing for nothing, sure you'll be screwing me for money somewhere. Will you be wanting some money up front?" said Dunphy. "Not a farthing do I want up front from you, Tom Dunphy" says Pat. Dunphy was a successful haulier, and he would have had dealings with Pat in the past and was rightly wary when he saw Pat in full sales mode, he undoubtedly knew him for what he was, a horse trader. So with more than a hint of suspicion he said, "You say not a farthing, Pat Jennings are you telling me the truth?" "I am indeed", says Pat. "Ok, you're on." Says Dunphy. Then Pat said to me, "And tell me Owen, do you think Tom Dunphy bought that truck?" "How could he resist?" I asked. "Well he never did buy that old truck, "said Pat "and I never expected him to. But I sold four trucks on the back of that truck with Dunphy's name on it, because everybody comes to that show, and I told them all of them "If it's good enough for Tom Dunphy then it must be a good truck". And I promised every one of them the same deal that Dunphy got. And do you know something? Not one of them asked to see a product specification sheet, because they don't need all that rubbish."

I left Pat's post mediaeval Vodka Palace a wiser man than when I arrived, and just slightly woozy headed having taken only a few sips from my breakfast cocktail. This had been the last of my planned trips and we had now completed the tour of Irish dealers. The tour started in Dublin and we travelled down the east coast to Cork before moving inland to Clonmel and then heading west to Limerick. We then headed northwards to Galway and finally concluding with Pat in Athlone, the centre of the country and handy for the trip back to Dublin. After my lesson at the feet of Pat Jennings on how to manage (manipulate) customers, we returned to Dublin. I discussed my findings with John Battersby before heading back to the UK, to file my report. It was all very straightforward, with the market predictions it would have been madness to continue with our investment in a stand-alone operation, having a wholly owned importer did not make sense. We should select one main dealer through whom we could import the products, distribute spare parts and create a service network to support the in-field products. That dealer should be Pat Jennings and then we could appoint a number of secondary dealers, including Noel Buckley, Ray Kelly and Michael Joyce, and that would be as much as the size of the market justified.

HERMANN & THE MEN FROM HARVARD

Life back home in the UK seemed tame after the collision of cultures in Ireland, but I had a bundle of stories to dine out on. In early 1985 I was asked to go on a management course, a high powered and very expensive course. I had been the fortunate recipient of a great deal of education and improvement by the company and I regularly went on management courses. The HR department was very pro-active in management training and readying us for promotion, but they excelled themselves with this course it was an outstanding experience and was easily the best I have ever attended. The course was held in Basle, led by a German national named Hermann Hoffer and a group of Professors, moonlighting from their day jobs at Harvard. There were 12 attendees from across Europe and I was the only Brit present but thankfully the course was entirely in English.

The attendees on this course were all Director level, and included people from Pharmaceuticals, the Oil Industry, Banking, Insurance, Consumer Goods, Auto Industry, Food and Education. A mixed lot and a very dynamic group of people. All sessions were video-taped, replayed and analysed to death to ensure we were equipped to deal with anything the world of business could throw at us. We dealt with a wide range of cases studies covering Marketing, HR, Investment, Engineering and Production. With those eleven delegates from different European countries I was beneficiary of the collective experience of a group of Harvard professors who took us through the topics in considerable depth. I learned a great deal from the moonlighting professors as we acted out role plays and then analysed the results on video playback to reinforce the good habits and get rid of the bad ones. The days were long and challenging but very stimulating. I was there for a week and learned a lot and grew in confidence and made some good contacts.

There were a couple of incidents on that course that made me sit up a little straighter and take notice of what was going on. In one role play, I was the managing Director of a company whose leading salesman's performance had slumped. After being an outstanding performer for a number of years this man's sales had dropped through the floor and after counselling and a warning there had been no improvement, now he was on the point of being sacked. That was as much of a brief as I had and I'm sure the salesman's was no fuller than mine. There wasn't much to go on and so when the man came to my office I welcomed him, offered him a cup of coffee and I asked him how the family was. This is my own natural way of dealing with people, just helping them to get comfortable but on this occasion the response was entirely unforeseen, the poor chap broke down and started crying. He then told me a very sad story about his wife's serious illness and how much difficulty he had coping with his young children, while trying to look after his client base. (I later discovered that the salesman had been briefed to react to any mention of his family by disclosing details of his wife's illness.) We had been told our role play would last between 5 and 7 minutes but we continued to discuss the issues raised by the salesman's problems until we were asked to bring it to a conclusion. I summed up our meeting by telling him he would keep his job and we would work with him to create a support programme that would allow him the work / life balance he needed to be with his wife. I told him we would also arrange for him to have support in looking after his clients' needs.

After this exercise was over, we came together as a group to analyse the six interviews on the video playback, picking up on each person's interview technique both the interviewer and the interviewee. Everyone was surprised at the reason for the salesman's poor performance, it just does not seem to be part of the European psyche to consider the wider familial aspects of a man's performance. We were encouraged to be honest in our critique of each other, and there were some very pointed remarks, by my colleagues, most of whom were harsh on themselves for not getting to the heart of the problem. The other European nationals were a wee bit more forthright than I was and one German Engineering Director was quite blunt about a particular interview. Of the six interviews that had taken place, five resulted in the salesman being fired, and only one saw the man being retained. It just shows what a kind word can produce.

Another session involved us doing an exercise where we had to judge a range of business situations on a prepared schedule with a series of options requiring us to tick the most appropriate box. We were allowed half an hour to complete the exercise which was a mixture of serious and light-hearted. The timing was always very precise and the papers were collected bang on the half hour mark and then we were formed into groups of four selected by Hermann the German and told to repeat the exercise, only this time we had an hour to finish. I found myself in a group with a Danish lady, Else a chemist with a large European Pharmaceutical company, a very tall Dutchman from the oil industry, whose name was Cor and Nils a Swedish banker. After a bit of banter, we got around to some serious horse trading and eventually we managed to complete the document with Else volunteering to be the group scribe. We handed in the group paper, once again bang on time, Hermann was very insistent on punctuality. Then we moved onto the next part of the course work.

Later that evening I met Hermann in the bar and he asked me to meet with him and Chris, who was a professor of psychology and who had set the last exercise. Hermann and I went into an office where Chris was waiting, looking thoughtfully at a bunch of papers in front of him and Hermann said, "Owen there is something I want to show you. This is the paper you completed earlier today and this is the one your group completed. Do you notice anything, unusual?" I was taken aback, what could he be driving at, was there something wrong? Anyway I picked up the two papers, initially looking for evidence of forgery or some such, until it dawned on me that the answers in both papers were the same. So I said, "The responses in both papers look very similar, is that what you mean?" Hermann and Chris laughed and Hermann said, "Owen they are not similar they are identical, exactly the same. Chris pointed this out to me".

Chris took over and said, "The point of the exercise is to judge levels of persuadability, who is a persuader and who can be persuaded. When I realised these two papers were the same I went back to check the individual papers completed by the other members of your group and they were markedly different from yours in some areas, so it's not as if you all went into the group session with the same opinions on these questions. Could I ask if you forced your opinion on the others or if there was much conflict in coming to an agreed common response?" I looked hard at them both and said, "Not at all, there was no conflict, if anything it was a light hearted session, we were very much at ease with each other. We simply discussed each of the questions, we all had opinions which we voiced before coming to an agreement and then Else completed the form, it was all very pleasant and quite straightforward." Chris then said, "Owen I have been doing this exercise all over the world for many years and I have seen papers that were similar but I have never seen this, two identical papers. How would you interpret this?" Now it was my turn to laugh, and I told them the story about my Dad's formation classes with my brother and myself, how he got us to prepare for Saturday night debates by reading everything we could find on his chosen subject. I told Chris this meant we could be quite opinionated and we learned to ferociously defend our points of view in those debates. Chris said to me, "Your Dad has done a pretty good job but it can be something of a double edged sword. You have an amazing ability to persuade bright, talented people to your point of view and that is great when you are right but you might not be right every time. So, although it is a great strength, you need to be careful you don't dominate situations for the sake of it and you must let other people express themselves." Wow, congratulated and told off in the same sentence, I wasn't quite sure what to think, when Hermann piped up and said "Owen I think you will need all your powers of persuasion in your next job," with an enigmatic little smile. What did he know that I didn't?

I have never enjoyed being educated as much as I did in Basle, the days were long but very stimulating, the attendees were impressive people, and the course leaders were top drawer. I was there for a week and learned a lot and I was able to extend my network of contacts with some high calibre people. One subject on the course had really caught my imagination and that was Transactional Analysis, I had not been introduced to this subject until Basle and now I wanted to know as much as I could about it. I bought the book, "I'm ok, You're ok" by Thomas Harris MD, and I have read it many times over the years. I then practiced using the technique in conversations with colleagues, customers and even with my friends. I calmed down eventually but TA has remained an intrinsic part of my tool kit.

A few weeks after returning from that course I was invited to a meeting with the Managing Director, Les Wharton and during that meeting he told me I was likely to be on the move again because Leyland International wanted me to go to France to run our European Truck Operations. He said he did not know any of the details but invited me to dinner with Isobel and his wife together with the Chairman of Leyland International, Chris W... and his wife, at the founder's house the following night. I was very familiar with the Founder's House, known as the 'Lodge' and my MD would certainly have known that it had been my de facto private dining room, for the previous three years.

The Founder's House

The founder's house had been the private home of Sir Henry Spurrier and was used as a hospitality venue for our customers' and being the local senior sales guy I used it extensively, especially with difficult customers who felt the need to complain or even shout. It was a sumptuous environment with two separate lounges, two dining rooms, and five bedrooms. The founder had thought of future generations by building a spacious snooker room with a full size snooker table together with a seating area for spectators and shelves to hold drinks.

Sir Henry Spurrier (16/06/1898 to 17/06/1964)

President of the Leyland Motors Corporation, last of three generations to head the Company

If a customer was upset (and some were) then this was a place where they could blow off steam without the embarrassment of being in a public place. The place was managed by an elegant and efficient Italian hospitality professional, named Giovanni, who looked after my guests very well and made them feel like a million dollars. On one occasion I had a meeting with a man whose specialist trucks had been delayed for three months and I wanted to re-assure him that we knew what we were doing so I arranged a visit to our Engineering and Research centre followed by a ride on the test track, an interview with our Chief Designer and then lunch with me in the Founder's House. The morning had gone very well and my customer was a lot more relaxed than when we had spoken on the phone to arrange this programme. When I arrived at our lunch venue, Giovanni was very excited and told me privately that he had discovered a long forgotten area of the Wine Cellar which contained exquisite wines. He offered me one for lunch and I was delighted to accept. The lunch was the time when we got down to the brass tacks of the delays and the impact on his business. It was a difficult discussion because my guest was rightly upset with the delays and he let me know of his displeasure. When the sweet was served Giovanni asked if we would like a port at which my guest's ears pricked and he told me was something of a port expert. Giovanni beamed and said he had a most excellent something or other from 1927. My guest, replied, "No you don't because there are only two cases of that vintage left and I have one of them." Unflappable Giovanni said, "That is interesting because I have a case here in my cellar, I will bring a bottle." While Giovanni was away my guest, who had become animated, treated me to an interesting lecture on the merits of this particular vintage. Giovanni arrived proudly displaying his bottle of port and my guest's jaw dropped and he marveled at the story of the forgotten room and the treasures it contained. We drank the entire bottle and then I arranged for the company chauffeurs to take my guest and his car home and then return for me. That customer became a staunch supporter of the company, and it wasn't necessarily the vintage of the port which made the difference but it does show there are many ways to cement relationships.

I had the great good fortune to welcome many customers to the Lodge and not all of them were unhappy with my company when they arrived, in fact some were utterly thrilled to be a customer of British Leyland Trucks. Through the 1980's we were updating our product range and it seemed like we had a conveyor belt of new trucks being introduced to the market. It was a wonderfully exciting time, replacing old, tired products with new market leading vehicles. We introduced a wonderful new truck to our product range called the Roadrunner, aiming to sell it in very high volumes. I was part of the team that took the heavily disguised truck on test drives around the county of Lancashire, during the development programme. Having spent the morning going through a mock delivery programme in the hill towns of east Lancashire I was making my way back to Leyland HQ via Liverpool and the coast. As I was passing through Southport, I called in at my home at 3:30 pm and picked up Nick and took him for a spin around the town. Nick proudly told all of his friends he was the first boy to ever ride in the Roadrunner. It was a beautiful truck, easy to drive, excellent visibility, a comfortable driving position and it looked great. I was also part of the team presenting the truck at its carnival of a launch. We had one show a day for a week for all of our dealers, followed by lunch and a chance to chat about the vehicle. That was followed by a shorter launch of the truck to all 28,000 employees on the Leyland/Chorley sites, with seven shows per day. The launch was a spectacular success in a specially constructed 300 seat theatre in our Engineering Centre, the climax being the massive truck emerging from the floor of the stage.

The press release and film footage was embargoed for one week until we had shown the truck to our dealers, but BBC blew that plan by showing all the details on its 6 o'clock news programme on Monday night. They even broadcast our unique TV advert showing the truck driving on two wheels along an airstrip in the deserts of central Spain, an advert which caused a sensation when it was aired, and contributed to the truck breaking all records for sales. The morning after the BBC broadcast, I received a phone call from a man in Middlesex who had seen the show and said he was very impressed by what he had seen and heard on the BBC news. He went on to tell me that he was about to place an order for 150 trucks with another manufacturer but liked the look of our Roadrunner, could he please drive one before making up his mind.

This was a problem because although we had plenty of demo trucks available for the launch they too were on embargo until after the dealer launch was complete, four days hence. So I took his number and promised to call him back within the hour. I called my team together and we set a plan in motion to collect this man from his home and bring him to Leyland, show him the vehicle, let him drive it around our extensive testing grounds, take him to lunch at the Founders House and then arrange for him to return home. It's amazing what you can achieve with a bit of imagination but I must confess this plan and its faultless execution was one of the highlights of my career. Frank Martin our Service Manager had a private pilot's licence and he was key to the plan. Frank and Bill Titmuss our sales manager rented an aircraft from Blackpool airport, Frank's home airfield then they flew to Biggin Hill where our customer was waiting for them having been transported there from his home, by a limo organised by our London office. The company chauffeur met him at Blackpool airport and brought him to Leyland HQ where I met him and after a coffee and a chat we took him to the Engineering Centre, to go through the features of the vehicle, he then drove the truck for half an hour and loved it. After some more chat we went for lunch, to the Lodge (of course), where Giovanni greeted our guest by name and explained the menu and the accompanying wines. I think the poor man was quite overwhelmed by all this attention. Aeroplanes, company chauffeur, test drives, and now a magnificent lunch. Over lunch he signed an order and we toasted the future success of a great product and he got the kudos in all the marketing as the first deal for the new truck, (embargoed for a week naturally). The whole exercise cost about £200 and the time of several employees but the prize was fantastic, and that man went home knowing he had done a brilliant deal and knowing he really had received the red carpet treatment.

I loved dining at the Sir Henry's home, and now Isobel and I were heading there to talk about the next stage in our journey together. I had not applied for this job, I had not even asked for a move but the watchers had decided that it was time for me to take on a new challenge, and here I was being offered this important job running our commercial operations in the European mainland. It's how things work, I had come to understand. When we arrived we were warmly greeted by Giovanni who led us through to the main lounge, where Les and Chris and their wives were already seated. I knew Chris very well but this was the first time Isobel had met him and his wife. The dinner was very relaxed and we kept away from any of the details of the job itself, in deference to the ladies, we talked instead about Paris, shopping, the attractions, where we would live and about schools for the children. Both Les and Chris had lived abroad with their families and were happy to pass on some of their own experiences. Les and Chris were interested to get our thoughts on how we would adapt as a family, and in particular to know how Isobel felt about the posting. Isobel was in sparkling form and said simply, "we are a team, we have moved several times already so we are used to it. And anyway when Owen is fixing Europe I will ensure everything else is in place. The children will see it as a great adventure. I don't speak French but I'm sure I will learn quickly enough." She could not have been better if we had rehearsed the replies (which we didn't) and I was immensely proud of her.

After dinner the ladies retired to the lounge for a chat and Chris, Les and I went off to the snooker room for a couple of frames. Before playing Chris wanted to give me some background on the recent history of our European business. He said, "Prior to 1980 our product range was not good enough and as a result we had a hard time competing. We had some good dealers who were prepared to support us while we introduced our new models and we had some very good employees, who soldiered on waiting for better times. The business wasn't very profitable, but we had kept our head above water. With the first models in the new product range including European models being introduced in 1979, we decided it was time to improve the resourcing in Europe because we believed that with some imagination and effort we could make real gains in terms of market share. In 1980 we appointed a new President of Europe, and I know that you knew him well. You will also know that he had a very strong record of success with the company both in UK and overseas and we were confident of success. He took an experienced group with him and we had a plan to expand the number of dealers and to secure 5% market share across all the main European markets, France, Germany, Italy and Benelux. Not only did we put in top human resource, but we backed the team with substantial budgets, to develop a strong dealer network, that was the plan in a nutshell."

Chris continued, "Things started very well, we created a business development team with the target of finding new dealers, and we made some good appointments in important locations. We also appointed some new sales and marketing personnel and by 1981 we had Benelux back up and running and France was improving steadily, we had not made progress in Germany or Italy but that was ok. In late 1982 things started to go haywire and I was becoming more and more concerned as results stalled and at Board meetings there was not much confidence coming across, to the point where I had to have a private chat with the President. He told me that he and his wife were having problems, she could not speak French and she was having trouble coming to terms with life in Paris. Things had got so bad that his wife was threatening to go back to the UK and take their kids with her. He added that he was trying hard to keep the impetus in the business while trying to save his marriage. I agreed that he needed to secure his marriage and suggested that he should take some time out with his wife to resolve the issues and I would arrange for someone to come and hold down the post pro tem. But he said that wouldn't be necessary that he and his wife had already planned a short holiday back in the UK and he was confident things would improve after that. What I didn't know at that time and only learned much later was that he had taken up with a French woman, and eventually left his wife. The woman was his French language tutor. Things never improved, and I started to get rumblings from the dealers and allegations that made me very worried. I had an open and frank discussion with him, which I would prefer not to discuss except to say there was plenty of evidence, to support the stories I had heard and in summary he admitted he had lost his way and offered his resignation, which I accepted."

I actually knew something of this tale already, it's impossible to stop the scuttlebutt and there is always some kind soul who is prepared to make sure everybody is up to speed with scandals, and salacious gossip. It came as a great surprise to everyone who knew that man, because he was always such a devoted family man and a bit of a workaholic.

Chris resumed his narrative, "The present incumbent whom you also know very well, was appointed at short notice and I asked him to go in and steady the ship. I needed someone that I could totally trust to put a stop to some of the excesses, to rein back on some of the wild spending on supposed dealer activities, where we seemed to have been throwing money at some dealers without any sign of improvement. I am very suspicious about some of the things that went on, especially in France. That's nearly two years ago and while I am confident the jiggery pokery that was going on has been halted I am sorry to say that we have made absolutely no progress on the plan of achieving 5% market share across the main markets. Worse than that I think some of the controls now in place are actually stifling sales. We have not been selling at the target level and we have large stocks of unsold vehicles at our dealers' premises, but we still own them. Let me be clear the present man has done what I wanted him to do and I am confident you will not find anything irregular, but he had to clear up a real mess. He has been there for nearly two years, he does not speak any European language and he and his family are keen to return to the UK. After that tale are you still up for it?"

I replied "Well it is quite a tale of intrigue and it sounds like we have a bit of a mountain to climb in terms of repairing our reputation with our dealers. You did not tell me too much about the business but if we have not been selling why not and exactly how much stock do we have at dealers?" "That's the heart of the matter" said Chris, "Under the previous regime we were at least selling on a consistent basis and we were very confident that, as the new models came on line that sales would increase. But instead they have now gone backwards, there is a big problem with the sales team, I'm afraid. The stock can be measured in months, probably many months given the low level of sales at the moment. At least we have now turned off the tap, no more will be delivered until you say so, but moving the existing stock is our top priority. We have some good people in the French HQ but I'm not sure about the personnel in the other countries because I have never met any of them? So back to my question are you still up for the job after hearing this sorry tale?"

"Yes, I am up for it, and look forward to working with you" I replied. "This sounds exactly my kind of job I have been fixing broken departments and companies for the whole of my career with Leyland, and it's what I enjoy. I think I'm pretty good with people and good at building teams, and for me that is the essence of getting things done, good as you are as an individual, you live or die by your team. My ability to speak French is pretty basic but I do have Scottish Highers in French and Spanish, my French vocabulary is decent and I can read and write French to a reasonable standard. With a bit of support, I will get my conversation up to an acceptable level. I have good experience across all the areas of the business, with Leyland and before that with Singer and ITT.

As you know my background was finance, but I have run Sales, Service and Engineering Departments as well and of course I had complete balance sheet responsibility with as General Manager of the Service Group. To be honest it seems pretty similar types of problems to those I encountered in the Service Group role. In all of these roles I had to face up to tricky situations and had to be creative in finding solutions. And one thing I think I am very good at is facing up to hard decisions, and getting the job done. In the Service Group, I had to sell a wage deal of minus 2%, Les challenged me to win that Business Game, I had to drink vodka for breakfast to make sense of Ireland and I have planned and organised redundancies that went like clockwork. I had the most demanding and hard-headed group of dealers in the whole of the UK to deal with and they became the top performers in the country, year after year. My record shows I can effectively manage the business side of the company as well as creating sensible marketing initiatives to drive up the sales." "I am familiar with your CV, Owen, but it's nice to hear this first hand, I am sure you will enjoy this challenge. I know I am going to enjoy watching you sort out our European Operations." Chris was gracious.

Before we started our game of snooker Les Wharton brought me up to speed on the political issues that I needed to know about. He told me that Mrs Thatcher's Government was adamant that the Group would be disposed of, come what may, and it could either go as a complete package or it could go in chunks but one thing was certain, go it would. He told me that discussions with both Fiat of Italy and Renault of France had failed to progress and now we were deep in discussions with General Motors of America, and these discussions looked very positive. Everybody understood that state owned businesses were anathema to the Conservative Government of Mrs Thatcher, since a fundamental plank of Conservative thinking was a free market economy and to them state owned meant socialism and that would never do. It was something of a surprise to learn just how determined the Government was to get rid of us, because the results of those years of investment in facilities and products were only beginning to be seen and the company was in a pretty good place to take advantage of all that support.

When I asked what the deal was with GM they told me it was for the entire operation, absolutely everything, cars, trucks buses, specialist vehicles, Land Rover everything. The idea was to create an auto group that would compete on a world-wide basis (now where did I hear that before?) He then added, of course it will be called a merger but it will really be a takeover and we are the ones being taken over. Chris then added that naturally the merger/purchase would see both companies come together as a force on mainland Europe, and there was no way of telling how the cards would fall, at this stage. He went onto say that my job might be a short term posting. When he asked me how I felt about that, I replied that I had worked for large American Corporations in the past and I enjoyed my time there, so let's go for it and see where it leads. He was relieved that I took that attitude. This was sensitive news because the stakes were high for British Leyland, and I was sworn to secrecy.

PARIS J'ARRIVE

I lost that game of snooker for several reasons the first being that I am a lousy snooker player, the second reason was that my head was full of the implications of this job and the enormity of what might eventuate, and also I could hardly contain myself to get to a phone and tell my Mum, that her first born was about to become President of Europe, to be based in Paris. On the drive home I kept pinching myself to make sure I wasn't dreaming, the Halfway and its coal bings and steel works was a long way from the beautiful City of light that is the capital of France. When we got home, I called my Mum and my brothers and sister and Isobel's parents. Everyone was delighted for us and wanted to know when they could come and stay with us to sample life in Paris. Over breakfast the following morning we told Nick and Carrie about our imminent move and they were wild with excitement at going to live in Paris. The very name sent a thrill through me and the prospect of living and working in that great city was something I relished. But first we had a holiday planned and we were all looking forward to the break away from all the hustle and bustle of life. We were going to spend two weeks in a Gite in Southern Brittany and we would drive to the Gite, which we had booked a year earlier. We had been holidaying in France for a couple of years and we enjoyed the country and the culture and I enjoyed the chance to practice my very rusty French, and now we were within a short time of actually living in the country, destiny at work, I suppose.

I told Isobel that I would take two days out of our holiday and drive to Paris for a meeting with my new colleagues and she was ok with that. In the meantime, we had a holiday to get on with and two excited children who could not wait to get to France, we had developed a certain pattern to our French holidays, morning we were up early and off having fun with the kids, we were a beach family, swimming, diving off rocks, chasing crabs with tickling sticks, playing games and kicking balls around, and for a few days forgetting all about business and new jobs. Both Nick and Carrie were strong swimmers and loved the sea, but they also enjoyed scrabbling over the rocks and exploring the dunes for little creatures. Nick was very keen to see the standing stones at Carnac and we spent a day there, and what a sight, more than 3,000 of these huge stones stretch for many kilometres, a veritable motorway to Stonehenge's roundabout. The children were now at an age where they enjoyed these visits almost as much as they enjoyed the beach (almost), and we organised a couple of outings to take in a bit of culture and a few church visits just to get bit of balance. I disappeared for two days, did what I needed to do in Paris and returned. I would be taking up my post full time one week after we returned from holiday, but for now we were in Brittany for fun and frolics with the kids, and that is what we did, for the rest of the holiday.

When I left Brittany, for the meeting with my new team in Paris, I knew we needed a substantial presence in Europe for many reasons, for the revenue it would bring of course, to increase our negotiating leverage in future merger talks and to make sure we were competitive in terms of product, price, features and strategies in the market place. If we continued to flounder on the European mainland how could we compete with the growing presence of the Europeans in our own domestic market? Translated that meant we had to sell and sell lots, especially the fields of trucks my predecessor had allowed to build up. As everyone knows selling is all about capturing hearts and minds and we believed if we captured the French hearts and minds of the French, we could roll out from there. That is why I would be based in France and why most of my energy would go into conquesting French hearts and minds. As I drove through the quiet countryside I reflected on this momentous year, which was rushing past at a rate of knots. The Irish experience was still very much in my mind, especially my meeting with Pat Jennings in his mock mediaeval palace where he dispensed vodka in Waterford pudding basins, and wisdom in pearls of insight. Then there was that amazing course I had attended in February, in Switzerland, and I wondered if Hermann Hoffer did know that I was about to be offered the job as President of European Operations, back in February, months before I knew myself. Whether he knew or not didn't matter, what did matter is that his course was a good preparation for what I was about to embark upon.

I was looking forward to this job so much, and as well as being President of Leyland Europe I would hold a string of job titles, I was President Directeur Generale of Leyland Vehicules Industriels based in Paris, I was Chairman of Deutsch Leyland, based in Augsburg, I was Managing Director of Leyland Belgium, Managing Director of Leyland Nederlands, and Managing Director of Leyland Luxembourg, all based in Mechelen, Belgium. These were the countries where Leyland had tried to establish their business over many decades, often in a half-hearted way.

Driving through the quiet villages, I ran over the information I had on the key players in my new team and I was impressed with what I read but on the other hand this business was massively underperforming. As I drove I laughed quietly because I could not get the image of my home village out of my head and its difference from the capital city of France. That little self-effacing village with its coal bings, mines and steel works was a long way away from Paris, a wonderful city of light with its beautiful, wide boulevards and elegant boulevardiers, its chic restaurants and its high opinion of itself, its culture, its history and its place in the world. Now I was on a journey from Halfway to Paris, and to be honest on my previous visits to the city I had felt more at home in Paris and less overwhelmed by its scale than I had been in any of the UK cities where I had lived or indeed in any of the cities of the world I had visited.

My new HQ was in the town of Gonesse, near Roissy airport in the northern Banlieu of Paris. I made the visit to the head office, on the morning following the European Cup Final between Liverpool and Juventus in Heysel Stadium, Brussels. I drove from Brittany, in my UK registered vehicle, to my new office unaware of the dreadful tragedy the day before when disturbances among the fans caused a wall to collapse, resulting in the deaths of 39 Italian fans and injuring hundreds more. The traffic was very heavy and it was mostly Italian registered cars and I wondered why they were so subdued, believing they must have lost the final. I got some strange looks on that stretch of motorway, and I hadn't a clue about what happened until I reached my new office and was informed of the goings on the day before.

I had asked for all the senior personnel, from the various countries, to be in Paris when I arrived so that I could have a chance to meet and greet as many as possible. Before leaving my office in Lancaster House, I had collected and read every piece of information I could get my hands on concerning our historical performance in the European markets. Over the decades the Group had invested right across the mainland of Europe and although our biggest investment in terms of bricks and mortar was in Belgium, the prize was always France, win France and you win Europe was pretty much my thinking at the time. When I met with my new colleagues I was clued in as much as was possible, and I understood there was an ambivalence in France towards the UK. Perhaps more correctly there was a frisson between the English and the French, there were those who loved some aspects of English life, and those who despised all things English, those who saw England as a staunch ally in times of war and those who found it difficult that they had to turn to England twice in the 20th century for assistance, these things I knew before I left.

The meeting went well and I listened to what they had to tell me as we talked about the products, our people and structures, the various European markets, our dealers and on the company's performance, financial as well as commercial. I also asked for a briefing on the problems they were facing. There is a great question which gets everybody talking and it is this, "If I had a magic wand and could change just one thing for you, what would that be?" This allowed my new colleagues to venture opinions they may otherwise have kept to themselves and their responses gave me a flavour of some of the problems they had been dealing with. My first impression of my new colleagues was positive, we had an interesting range of European nationals who were as committed to the Leyland cause as I was. What I found confirmed Chris' opinion offered over that game of snooker, in the Founder's house. I was delighted with what I saw and heard but why were such an impressive group of people performing so dismally, and why was the mood in the room subdued to the point of being gloomy? There was much to think about.

My new job was to revitalise a company that in truth had not been vital for a very long time but which had managed to plumb new depths in recent years with poor performances. Not to worry, that was 'mon metier', it's what I did, I fixed things that were broken as I had been doing my whole career. From the moment I arrived at Leyland National in Workington I was watched and monitored and given ever-tougher challenges to see how I coped. I steadily rose through the ranks taking on bigger and bigger roles within the Finance function. By 1979 I knew what I really wanted to do was to run companies and have responsibility for the whole of the business. I was too interested in making the 'whole' tick to remain content as an historian recording that which had already happened or as a prophet forecasting that which may or may not happen. I wanted to make a difference in real time in the real world and fortunately, I was trusted with bigger and bigger tasks. The Group MD asked me to review our Irish business and to recommend how we should invest in the future of that market. I had been sent to rebuild departments and businesses broken by incompetence and inefficiency. When the company decided I should be educated a little more I attended expensive management courses in the UK, the USA and mainland Europe. At the time of our much heralded renaissance under Sir Michael Edwardes I was tasked with taking the message of my Company's renewal to the press and to pressure groups around the UK, I was exposed to the highest level of negotiations with the unions, I was even challenged to win a prestigious Business Game. Remarkably only six years and three jobs after leaving the safety of my Finance comfort blanket I had become President of Leyland Europe.

When the holiday was over and we returned to the UK it was all systems go as we prepared for my imminent departure, Isobel and the children would stay in the UK until the school term finished and then join me in France. Since my contract was for two years we had decided we would keep our house in the UK and rent a property in France, and Isobel was clear she wanted a house with a garden and not an apartment in one of the chic Arrondissements of Paris. My dear wife would arrange all the details at the UK end and I would do likewise in France and then we would exchange our quiet suburban lives in sleepy Southport for the glamour and excitement of Paris. When Nick and Carrie realised they would be going to a French school they were very happy and went around telling everyone they knew and feeling very grand and international. That left the small matter of saying goodbye to everyone, back at Leyland Trucks the members of my team were disappointed that we were breaking up a good team but were happy for me, and I told them that any success that I had was because of their own success, and I meant it, I had a good team of people. At my going away party, my colleagues had a wee surprise for me, at the beginning of the evening, I was made to wear a striped shirt, a beret and a string of onions. Talk about stereotyping, we Brits have a very narrow view of the average Frenchman.

I was also presented with the most garish, over the top trophy I have ever seen, it consisted variously of a marble base, a plastic golden crown with plastic red velvet lining and atop this monstrosity was a plastic golden figure of an athlete holding a plastic golden laurel wreath aloft. Vulgar does not do justice to this plastic obscenity, but it did have one redeeming feature, the faux gold, brass inscription which read "To Owen Quinn, King of Total Recall." This was a lovely touch, recalling that first briefing and not letting me forget that I did not have total recall. Thank you, once more to Bill Monaghan, my mentor at The Singer Corporation, for giving me one of my favourite quips. We also had a party for our friends and neighbours in Southport and then another for our family back in Scotland, with many people inviting themselves to come and stay with us in the great city.

Now I was ready to commit myself body and soul to the resuscitation of my company, to take the fight for market share to our competitors on their own patch and to capture a meaningful share of the truck markets across the whole of mainland Europe. I was looking forward to re-energising our companies and our dealer networks, to motivating my colleagues to be the best they could be. That meeting I had with my new colleagues in Paris, was very interesting. On the one hand I had met an impressive group of people, bright, purposeful, erudite and linguistically gifted, knowledgeable about their business and their markets but on the other hand they were so gloomy and the business was performing so badly. These attitudes needed to change and I needed to change them.

On a personal level, I was delighted that as well as being a chance for me to develop as a businessman, this was an opportunity for Isobel, Nicholas, Carrie and me to grow as people and to take advantage of living in the very heart of one of the world's great cultures.

CHAPTER SIX

A DEALER IN HOPE

There was a lot of arrangements to put in place after I had accepted the new job, I would be in France while Isobel and the children would need to remain in Southport until school finished, or until I could find us a home, whichever was later. This meant Isobel was left with the job of closing the Southport home and securing it for the duration of our stay in Paris but at least she wasn't pregnant as she had been on the last two big moves, I was delegated to find a home in France and to organise the schools for the children.

My role in Europe was twofold, firstly fix a broken company which although never hugely successful had declined dramatically in the previous three years and secondly to grow the business as quickly as possible to increase our attractiveness to potential partners. It had been made clear to me that we were deep in negotiations with a US giant to merge our commercial business with theirs worldwide and that was the Group's preferred option, but if that did not happen then my two-year tenure would be extended. When I arrived at European HQ in the spring of 1985, business was for me the most exciting thing in the world and here

I was in this beautiful city where I felt completely at home. I was the boss of Leyland, one of the UK's largest companies, certainly its most notorious at that time, and I had the opportunity to make my mark on the business world in a significant way. Also I had the opportunity to give my family an unmatchable and unforgettable experience as we lived, laughed and grew up together in this most beautiful of European capital cities, and I was determined we would experience all the city had to offer- well most of what the city had to offer.

On the brink of the biggest job of my career so far, I was all too aware of the fact that I had inherited a group of people who had been crushed and left dispirited by the events of recent years. I was impressed by some of the people I had met but I could also see wariness in the eyes of my new team. Reflecting on the sombre tones of my colleagues I knew I was going to have to think very hard about how to get them fired up, and who better to get a Frenchman fired up than the great Emperor himself, so I decided to adopt one of Napoleon's own sayings as my banner motto: *A Leader is a Dealer in Hope."* By creating a vison for this business and by defining clearly where we were going, I would bring hope to the Leyland Europeans. With Napoleon on my side I'll do ok.

The first three weeks in France were scheduled to be spent at the Berlitz language college, where I was booked on a total immersion course, to brush up my proficiency in French. This was a very good course where I spoke with people with different accents on a range of subjects for 10 hours and then took my homework back to my hotel.

After a week and a half of the three week course I had to cut it short to take a press conference – in French. The deal with GM had collapsed and I only discovered the real reasons much later. General Motors had been insistent that if this deal was to fly then they must have Land Rover included in the package. Remarkably for a government that wanted no part of a state owned enterprise and could not wait to get shot of BL, it seemed there were some old colonels within the Tory party who could not bear to think of their beloved Land Rovers and Range Rovers being owned by some jumped up colonial outfit. Apparently Mrs Thatcher felt a need appease these dimwits and so she refused to allow Land Rover to be sold. The GM negotiators were most unimpressed at this turn of events, believing that this was the best part of the deal and for them the whole thing would stand or fall on this and when it was clear Land Rover was not in the deal, they walked. No deal.

The news of the collapse of the deal was going public so someone needed to front the Press Conference in Paris and that someone was me with my week and a half practicing the beautiful French language. That was a trial, we had TV and radio reporters as well as the national press and the trade press, to whom we spun some line of bullshit about being unable to reach a mutually satisfactory conclusion. It seems I acquitted myself well enough and I had François sat alongside me just to make sure I didn't say anything dopey. After taking a press conference it seemed a bit pointless going back to Berlitz so the following day I started the rebuilding of Leyland Europe.

My first day I had a review of business performance with the senior members of my group, just to get a feel for where we were. I soon realised that things were much worse than the folk back in the UK believed, and I would have a major job on my hands bringing this operation up to the level that the Corporation expected. My colleagues were very downbeat, leaving me in no doubt of the scale of the job in front of me, and I was disappointed to learn what had been happening or rather not happening in the various European markets for quite a long time. Performance all round was lousy, but it seems they were in line with expectations and nobody seemed to be too upset, nor were there any suggestions as to how we could improve. Listening to the views expressed around that table I don't think my new colleagues were expecting too much in the way of change or that they could even make change happen. Had they never read Sartre, did they not understand what man is capable of?

> *"Man is condemned to be free; because once thrown into the world, he is responsible for everything he does. It is up to you to give [life] a meaning."* © Jean-Paul Sartre

Were these guys even French? Over coffee after that meeting I concluded that there was probably not too much expected of me, even back at the farm.

For a the first few weeks I stayed in a hotel in Paris and my days always started with an exciting ride on the choc-a-bloc Periferique and despite initial misgivings I came to enjoy this journey and the adrenalin rush it gave me, I was always buzzing by the time I reached the safety of my office. The morning rituals were lovely, lots of kisses and handshakes and literally everyone had to be greeted, my new secretary Ann Lesgourges set the ball rolling with a cheery "Bonjour, Patron" and a kiss on both cheeks. I think I might enjoy these French customs. After greeting everyone I returned to my office to find a large cup of thick black coffee awaiting me, thank you Ann.

In the first few days, I pored over the financial accounts and the business performance statistics, the local versions not the fairy stories they had been sending back to head office. My next task was to meet as many of the people in the company as possible, a gentle interview process to gauge what I had and assess how they were suited to what lay ahead. Then I needed to take stock of the assets and get out to visit our dealers across Europe, inspect the fields of parked trucks, examine systems procedures and protocols. After three weeks, I had established the scale of the challenges facing me and just how far this brilliant company had been allowed to slip behind the competition. Well that's ok because this is what I do, I fix things, and I had Lacoste and Napoleon on my side. But where to start?

Where to start? Here you are in a company that is struggling badly and has been for a number of years, everybody is depressed, there is a distinct lack of energy, you can see that an awful lot needs to be done so where do you start? Well my watchword is 'cash is king' and a good place to start would be to spend my time on nailing down the cash position to ensure we were not insolvent, I wouldn't want to end up in the Bastille, that would not be nice. It's always reassuring to know you have enough cash to meet your obligations and minimal aspirations, like making it through to the weekend.

My European group consisted of a series of separate legal entities, registered in each of the European countries in which they operated, but we enjoyed the support of the corporate treasury to provide liquidity and I had organised a guaranteed credit line, until I got a handle on what was happening, so most unusually cash was not top priority at that moment. So secure that the cash was ok for the moment I could start by looking at my people, who have we got in the team and what are they capable of? I have developed a way of identifying people which is quick and which is very seldom wrong. Start by getting out into the heart of the organisation and talk to everyone you can, this is not necessarily a formal interview but it is an interview. A few simple questions let you know as much as you need to know.

What is your job?

What tasks do you undertake each day?

Where does your job and your duties fit into the organisation?

What do you count as success in your job?

There are other questions of course that you must wrap around for the purpose of conversation and so as not to scare anyone but for me these are the key ones. With this simple technique I classify everyone in the organisation into one of three categories: Warrior, terrorist or pacifist.

So let the profiling begin, and in a period of intense activity, I quickly found out the entire population was dispirited and alienated. The Sales team weren't selling, the dealers were going broke, the admin people were overworked shuffling paper, there was no pizazz, no plan, just kicks and rubber ears. But some of these people were exceptional, really exceptional, smart, clever, hard-working, dignified and professional. Francois Lacoste is one of the most impressive people I have ever met in or out of business, an outstanding mind, great negotiator, hard-working, charismatic and very professional, Alain Gignoux was another man with a fine mind, Don MacIntosh a great sales negotiator with enormous charisma and a great favourite of the dealer network, Michel Boudier, a strong and very professional dealer manager who prided himself on doing things correctly, Patrick Hagenaars another fine man who spoke five languages fluently (and who could make himself understood in every European language with the exception of Basque and Finnish), Marc Lories, General manager of Benelux and the Finance Director, John Hollis who accompanied me from the UK

John Hollis apart, these talented men had endured a succession of British nationals as President of European

Operations, mostly men with little or no language skills and no feel for anything beyond their own advancement. They did not seem to care about the "team", the dealers or the customers. I felt sorry for the senior members of my new team I am certain that at least one member of the team, Lacoste was better qualified to run this operation than some of the people he had reported to in the past. These Frenchmen, Belgians and Germans were strong people but I guess they had one big flaw, they were "Johnny Foreigners".

Even the Brits who had been employed locally were regarded no better at HQ than their continental colleagues. This was a British company and things had always been done the British way and they had all come to understand the rules and had no real input to the way the business was run. Such foolishness! While at first I wondered about the fortitude of the team I had inherited I was to learn later that it had been made clear to the senior members of the team that local initiatives were not welcome, so oftentimes shaking their head at daftness going on. they had learned to keep their own counsel, conditioned to await instructions and as Pavlov's dogs had learned to salivate at the ringing of a bell, these people had learned to respond to their masters' voices from across the channel, and follow commands issued no matter their own thoughts, what a waste. There was no joy evident in anything that was going on, everything seemed so serious around the place. Meantime everyone was wondering what the new guy was like and whether or not he would be able to order himself a coffee without assistance. I knew I had some great people and if I could get past the gloom and show them a believable vision of our future then I was sure I could create a great team. It was up to me do that and to make use of their talents, it was for me to redress that situation and I was determined to do just that.

While I was still coming to terms with all the issues, I established weekly management meetings for the French operation, with the heads of each department. These were run to an agenda and managed against formal minutes with action points and dates for completion, and all attendees were accountable. These meetings allowed me to establish with my team my modus operandi and to let them all know what I expected of and from them, the agenda was in French covering finance, sales, marketing service, parts, personnel, and IT. We conducted these meeting mostly in French, allowing for regular translations for me. The first meeting also included an in-depth review of our products and their strengths and weaknesses, to ensure that they were both legally compliant and in line with customer needs. I needed to know if the products were the reason we had fields full of trucks. I learned that some products had to be "finessed" when we received them to comply with the needs of the various European markets. My colleagues told me the products were good but we needed some 'tweaks' to be able to satisfy the needs of certain market sectors, and we had been unable to get the required support from the central engineering team to ensure the vehicles arrived in Europe fully compliant. Quite a bit of work needed to be done with engineering, who were more focussed on developing and improving products for the UK market and the African markets, because that is where the corporation made the bulk of its sales. It seems my predecessors had failed to make the case strongly enough for mainland Europe's needs in terms of product specifications. Engineering departments have learned through bitter experience to be wary of requests to make product changes from sales operations. Valuable resource can be burned on useless and pointless development based on whim or fancy, if you are not careful.

At least we had quantified the technical needs and although we had a long to do list, I was confident I had a strong enough relationship with the corporate engineering team to convince them of the need to get these upgrades into the system. In the meantime, within the European Operations team we had the wherewithal to adapt and improve the vehicles as they arrived. It seemed that my new team had a lot of confidence in the basic quality and features of the products. That meeting provided me with valuable insights and it was clear that, historically BL had paid scant regard to our European Operations being too absorbed in all the razzmatazz and politics in which our corporation was embroiled in the UK. We had treated the European business as a holding operation but as we started to lose significant market share to European imports in the UK, we had a wake-up call and now was the time to do something about it. But in mainland Europe and particularly in France, Leyland was just another importer competing in an overcrowded marketplace where the competition had first rate products and support.

So what was so bad about the European Operation? Actually there was quite a lot wrong but the most obvious problem when I arrived was the demoralised people working in the business, there was no energy no desire just a fatalistic acceptance that life was garbage. The dealers were no better, and they too had just about given up on us and some were seeking an exit to other manufacturers. But the biggest problem I had was as a direct consequence of those issues, our sales volumes had dropped through the floor and we now had a massive overstocking problem, which the industry and customers would be aware of. The 14-ton lorry named the Freighter had the equivalent of 4 years' sales lying in the Green Fields of France. Stocks of the rest of the range were not much better. How could this be? This was a brand new range of products, the newest and I would argue among the best commercial vehicles available at that time in Europe. The UK factories had always programmed truck output to manage their own issues and to balance production efficiency and this had continued in face of declining sales by my companies.

My predecessor seemed paralysed and incapable of turning off the tap and so as sales were plummeting, trucks poured across the channel to find a home in the fields of rural France. French farmers found yet another source of income to supplement the largesse of the EU. Normally, when you have a large overstocking problem then you must work at creating a demand

and there are tried and trusted techniques for doing this. It's called moving the metal. Marketing the product is usually one of the first things a company will try, creating an expectation is always good, a bit of advertising often helps, product placement can be useful, courting customers has been known to work.

The only marketing being done was on the skinniest shoestring by a couple of really bright but besieged Frenchmen and it was very low key due to lack of funding, and consisted mainly of schmoozing the trade mags and blagging free copy. These guys were doing a pretty good job in pitiful circumstances. If you choose not to market your products, then there are other things you can do to drive up sales such as incentivising your sales force. The sales force, I found, had been provided with a unique incentive plan to help move all this stock.

The cars for the sales team had been changed to mini metros, the most basic car available in the corporation's product range. It is a well-known fact that sales personnel are peacocks who like to strut their stuff and show how successful they are to their friends, so giving them a tiny car was ok!

The number of salesmen was reduced to save costs, which meant that those who were left after the cull were expected to cover a truly massive territory. Each of the sales guys had a patch not far short of the English land mass. With such a large territory and with a low volume of sales, customers and leads tended to be widespread and so the sales team had to travel far and wide to reach existing and potential customers.

In the past the sale team had a package of expenses, which was not generous but which allowed them an overnight stay, to cover the sales territory and work the market. But as part of the incentive package this too was reduced to a derisory level where the sales team could opt for a cheap meal or a cheap bed in a cheap hotel but could not stretch to both.

This part of the cost reduction package was extremely successful, since it wiped out overnight stays, thus saving money but unfortunately this was offset by the increased cost of fuel, since the sale guys went to one call per day, they left in the early morning and drove back at night.

The worst aspect of this policy was that the fact that our sales team only managed to get in one visit per day. So who should they choose to get the valuable visit, a dealer, an established customer, a potential customer, someone with a problem? Being inventive, when possible they invited a customer to the dealers' premises and so managed two visits for the price of one. Success was managing two visits in one day.

One other unintended consequence of this mental policy was that the mini metros very quickly racked up high mileage and in 9 months some had 50,000 kms on the clock and needed to be replaced.

Since these were basic models it would seem a straightforward matter to replace these well-worn vehicles. Not so. The car could be replaced only when the salesman sold the vehicle he was presently driving, and here's the catch, he had to sell his mini metro at a price determined by my predecessor the cost-cutter. Since the price he set for these vehicles was considerably in excess of the actual market value of a clapped out mini metro, you can imagine that the vehicles took a long time to shift. Not many people were looking for an over-priced, low prestige, high mileage foreign car. My sales managers spent an inordinate amount of time trying to flog their old cars so they could get a new one. And guess what? Sales slumped as a consequence – Genius – not hard to see that one coming. If you don't feel the need to incentivise your sales team, at least don't work hard at dis-incentivising them.

Those are the main reasons that I inherited a gloomy, disenchanted sales team and fields full of vehicles, but I saw enough among these men to believe we could build something better, remarkably they cared about their products and their company and most of all they cared about their customers.

The sales team were not being motivated but conventional wisdom says if you don't want to incentivise your own sales personnel, you will incentivise your dealers instead, right? Wrong! These were people putting their own money into this venture and they were left to it, with products that had no presence or image in the market place.

The previous leader of the pack had taken his brief to an extreme level and in reacting to the excesses of the team in place before him, he had gone to the other end of the spectrum, defying logic in the process. He had decided the only way forward for the Group in Europe was to contain the cost base and all the actions he had taken were to that end. While this was undoubtedly required to bring the business back under control at the beginning of his tenure and to ensure that we were only spending on programmes that brought about improvements it had carried on too long. When he should have been releasing the reins of over-control, he was unable to do so and seemed unable to change tack when it was needed. He found himself locked into a policy which was the exact opposite of what needed to be done. He had found the perfect way to make a bad situation much worse and it wasn't even part of an overall plan, it was firing from the hip stuff, and it was in effect an anti-sales strategy.

The guy in post before me, wasn't a stupid person but he was at heart an arch conservative and a cost cutter and when sales started to decline, (because of his policies) instead of addressing the marketing issues he reverted to type, battened down the hatches and slashed and burned. He did not speak very much French and maybe he felt a bit isolated in the job but the evidence was that apart from the swingeing cuts he had no other weapons in his arsenal. Why in the name of the wee man had nobody intervened to stop this madness?

Oh dear, never mind I'm here to do that now.

WHAT'S THE PLAN?

Now I must find a solution to fields full of trucks, dealers thinking of defecting, a dispirited top team and an alienated sales force dedicated to selling mini metros rather than heavy trucks. Before leaving the UK it was made clear the task was about expanding our presence in the major markets of mainland Europe, with a target of a not-impossible 5% share which would be a huge improvement from the miserly 1% we currently managed. The idea was that we should establish a front line to take on the Europeans in their own backyard, to learn what it takes to sell in Europe and to be better able to resist the diminishing of our UK market share by European manufacturers. Having listed the things that I could see were wrong with the business I could now sit down and start the process of creating a strategy that would address all of these points, in as short a time as possible, and re-energise the people and the company.

In my hotel in Paris, I would have a light meal and then head back to my room to burn the midnight oil, trying to get my thoughts together and to define what I thought could be achieved in this market. I had formed the view that I would make the French market my number one target and the other markets would piggy-back on the French initiatives. Whatever was successful in France would be adapted and rolled out into the other markets, I did not have enough time in my day to run parallel programmes for the others. I needed some quick gains and this is how I would achieve them. Conventional thinking says you should always start at the beginning when creating a plan, but I decided that the solution to the problems of my company meant I should start at the end.

Start with what you expect, define your future business, the market share you expect and the sales volumes needed to achieve that share. From this simple beginning you can structure a plan or at least you have the bones of what you need. I sketched out what I wanted my business to look like and I wanted this strategy to be in place within six months. With that done I needed to bring my team on board, convince them I would back them to achieve this plan and allow them to put flesh on those bones. I would give them hope. After all, a leader is a dealer in hope! Napoleon said so.

When I was ready to unroll my strategy I decided to be as matter of fact about what I was doing as possible so rather than convene a special meeting, I would make it an agenda item on our regular weekly management meeting. My thinking was that if I introduced my plans in a low key way my colleagues might not be overwhelmed by what I was aiming for, given their dismal performances in recent years. At the next Monday meeting I shared my thoughts on where I thought we should be heading, I identified target market share by product types, showed a scale of pricing I thought was achievable, took them through the profit and loss implications and demonstrated the size of budget we could afford to underpin the targets. The initial reaction was, as expected a wee bit guarded but I persisted and kept pushing the points I felt were important and insisting we would only be limited by our imagination and energy. Lacoste said, "Why not? We can do this it is really a small share, there are other importers who take a bigger share of the market than this, but they also spend more money than we do." "Not any more they won't" I answered, "we will do what we need to do to motivate the sales team and our dealers. I am ashamed, and you should be as well, that our trucks are lying in fields in France and the only people who are making money are the farmers. We have the responsibility to let the farmers' nice French cows get their fields back."

Frenchmen are very proud and the 'ashamed' comment hit the mark.

By the end of the meeting the team were on board, maybe Hermann the German was onto something when he spoke to me in Basle about my powers of persuasion. The targets I was setting were not outlandish they were practical and probably that and the fact that for the first time in a while they had actually talked about taking the business forward rather than backwards, helped persuade my colleagues. Also they would no longer be hunkering down under siege in their bunkers waiting for something to happen, they would be active and having a go. After the main meeting I had a follow up with the Sales Director, the Finance Director and the Marketing Manager on how to take this project forward. So what do we want to achieve and how do we resource it? We had lots of market intelligence so we had a basis to plan our way forward. We knew how big the market was, we knew the split of sales by marque, by dealer area and by product type. We knew in which sectors we could be competitive and we knew the pricing levels. This team with fields full of product actually had all the information to hand in order to create both a marketing plan and make a real impact on the European market. We would use that intelligence and French truckers would get to buy our lovely trucks and French cows would get back their nice green fields. From that meeting our Sales Plan evolved, and here is what we did to begin the renaissance.

1. We changed the sales organisation, created regional offices, recruited two additional sales personnel
2. We upgraded the sales team's cars to a better spec and a more prestigious model, with a GT badge, giving the sales team some sense of self-worth and some bragging rights
3. We put in place a sales commission scheme based on numbers sold and profit retained
4. We created an expenses package that allowed the sales personnel to visit the dealer and customer base in a civilised manner
5. We created a dealer motivation programme, with a team of psychologists led by a formidable lady who favoured white boots and straight talking. Boy was I in for some surprises!
6. We started to develop a marketing plan which included dealer support, pricing initiatives, specific branding of certain products

7. One other initiative that they came up with was to support the Truck Grand Prix Circuit that was starting to take off in Europe. This was avoided by most of the manufacturers including our UK colleagues for fear of us being tarnished as boy racers. But it proved to be an outstanding initiative in our drive to re-establish the brand.
8. We created an advertising plan with the aid of Professor LeSouer from the Sorbonne who looked a bit like Ronnie Corbett in haute couture, complete with a classy man-bag The marketing plan had two objectives the first of which was to re-launch the company and to let Europe know we were serious about our presence in the market for trucks on the mainland. Secondly we had lots of trucks waiting to be sold. The campaign needed to address both issues. I told Professor Ronnie that in my view we needed to distinguish ourselves in a crowded market place. My final thought for the dinky professor was that he must not return with any "Me too" suggestions for this campaign. The players in the market all seemed to have an identical approach to marketing and advertising. So "pas moi aussi" it was. The good professor would not disappoint.
9. Patrick Hagenaars, the Service Manager, lobbied to improve the service network because we had major gaps across Europe and as truck routes expanded we could not support our products across large swathes of Europe. Patrick was a big fan of the DKV independent, Europe

wide service dealer network and we resolved to open up discussion with that company

10. We started a dealer recruitment plan to fill vacant territories and to provide Europe wide service cover. We would get out and about to meet the press, the customers, suppliers and the other movers and shakers to try and get a feel for the market, and do a tour of all the dealers for a meet and greet and just to let them know that we knew they were there. We would also attend every exhibition around the country. France at least would know we were on the march.

After two months of hard, hard slog we were ready to roll out the plan and start the wheels rolling, especially the wheels of all those trucks lying in the green fields of France. The sales team were on fire, buzzing around, organising local shows, visiting customers we hadn't seen for years and generally creating a stir. Dealers, however were keeping their powder dry and waiting to see, there were still whispers of potential defections and general unrest. So we moved the dealer motivation programme to the top of the agenda.

One other interesting initiative came from Francois and Alain who invented something called Le Cercle d'Or Leyland, this was a club with a special credit card that brought benefits to truck drivers rather than owners or fleet managers, a bit of a revolutionary idea at the time. Francois reckoned, correctly as it turned out, that having drivers onside could help the sales effort

La Carte 'Le Cercle d'Or Leyland – for truck drivers

NICOLE TAIEB

Alain Gignoux had the idea of getting inside the dealers' heads to convince them that they could be successful and he and Francois looked for a company who could carry out such a mission. They found a lady with white boots and a big personality, the mighty Nicole Taieb who ran a company of qualified psychologists who, she reckoned, specialised in lifting people out of the gloom and helping them to find their inner tiger. We needed someone who could turn our dealers from the wary group they were at present to a highly committed sales organisation, and Nicole convinced me she was that person. Francois and I had several meetings with Nicole in her quirky offices on Le Boulevard des Malesherbes, in the 8th arrondissement.

These meetings proved to be very interesting occasions because Nicole had a unique office and a unique style. The meeting area in Nicole's office was like a sunken bath that you had to climb into, and her favourite lunch dish was steak tartare, with very hot pimiento peppers, which she ate straight from a jar. I had to pinch myself frequently when I was in Nicole's company she was like no other person I have ever met, a real one of a kind. Nicole did not do anything just for the sake of it and eating raw meat in those meetings had a deeper meaning, and was intended to point to where our dealers, our salesmen and our company needed to be, (inner tigers) and somehow it all seemed to make sense. She was a mighty woman was Nicole Taieb. As she rolled out her ideas to me, I was impressed, Nicole motivated me and I thought she would make a great impression on the dealers, I certainly hoped she would. I dreaded to think what my colleagues in the UK might think about using this remarkable lady to motivate the dealer network, it would have been too much for the refined tastes of the Anglo Saxon, I think.

Nicole quickly had her team in place and her strategy established for re-invigorating the dealer network. We arranged for a weekend retreat in Deauville, a classy town and this was meant to mark a change in thinking as well as direction. Nicole said, "It is important to know that success is generous and outreaching, it does not 'garde les sous'', Owen. Success smells of success." Well I suppose success has to smell of something and it may as well smell of success as anything else, but this worldly advice was costing me a packet, I needed it to deliver, big time. We issued invitations to the weekend in Deauville and all the dealers accepted, good start. We had our sales team there as well and some service and engineering personnel. Our dealers were organised into groups and a psychologist was allocated to each group, each session would start with "Degonfler" which Nicole meant as a way for dealers to get things off their chest. Let them have their moans but in a controlled environment, then take those very issues and use them to develop the dealer wish list, which we could then work into our marketing strategy. Very simple in theory but it is a plan that needs careful managing, in Nicole we had a pro!!

This was a big deal for me and I spent my time fretting and checking in with all of the psychologists to see how things were going, I was committed to this process but I kept thinking what Sir Michael Edwardes would think if he walked in on this weekend. He would probably have sacked me for wasting time and money even although he himself was a big fan of the more traditional psychological assessment. I wanted to keep an eye on what was going on so I dropped in to each of the rooms as the sessions were in progress, stayed at the back and watched proceedings before quietly leaving again. When I went into Nicole's group I almost walked straight back out again when I saw what she was doing. She was lying on the floor, listening intently to our most senior dealer giving forth on the issues he was most concerned about. She was lying with one leg crossed over the other, her head supported on one arm looking for all the world as though she were attending a Roman feast (or orgy) and utterly relaxed and at ease with herself and the world. And her white boots were shining like beacons in a dark sky. As I looked around at these very important and very wealthy men I could not believe my eyes, they seemed to accept this as the most natural thing in the world.

Nicole was very unconventional in the way she went about things, the way she dressed (and not just the white boots) and the way she spoke. She also had a gift which I have been privileged to witness on other occasions in different countries, where a person speaks and they immediately have their audience in thrall, even if an outsider cannot understand what is going on or worse thinks what is being said is nonsense. It seems to me that this has less to do with the words used as the way in which the words are spoken. I have listened to a person start out on what I believed was a rambling rant, only to look around the table and see others (part of the same cultural group) listening intently almost spellbound. I think this must be some sort of unspoken national consciousness, a sense of oneness which outsiders cannot fathom but which has some profound impact on others with a common understanding of that culture. There is a way in which some people can tap into an emotion or a sense of place and time, to which like-minded people can relate. Such was Nicole Taieb, mighty Nicole.

"Please don't let Sir Michael find out about this", I was thinking as I beat a hasty retreat, a little embarrassed, oh we repressed Anglo-Saxons and Celts have so much baggage to let go.

After each session the delegates had time to enjoy the facilities of the hotel, while we reviewed the issues raised and discussed the implications and how to stitch them into a coherent market strategy. Dinner that night was brilliant, lots of enthusiasm and a great feeling around the tables and these very sophisticated Europeans were right up for this new way of doing things, Nicole was a huge hit and I was enjoying the reflected glory. By Saturday lunchtime we had completed the "Degonfler" and we spent the rest of Saturday and Sunday morning putting together the bones of our new approach to marketing our trucks and supporting our dealer network in conquering new markets. There were many important points raised in these sessions, (commercial, financial and marketing) which found their way into our everyday practices, proving once again that "Those who are hit hardest by problems often have the solution to those problems in their own hands. Even if they do not know this themselves." It takes awareness, sensitivity, the ability to listen and experience to coax these issues out and to recognise them for what they are. That was where Nicole was truly mighty.

Perhaps the single most significant issue raised proved to be on product positioning related to the T45 truck, maximum weight tractor and the flagship vehicle of our product offering. This truck came with two engine options, our own in-house Leyland engine the TL 12-litre engine, and an alternative 12 litre engine manufactured by Perkins but badged as a Rolls Royce engine. Perkins had acquired the commercial vehicle operations of Rolls Royce when that company was being broken up by the British Government. In the UK this engine was badged as a Perkins in line with the sale agreement between Perkins and Rolls Royce, but on the continent we had a ten-year grace period where we were able to use the famous RR badge in our marketing efforts.

The dealers were pretty vociferous in demanding that we should only offer the Rolls Royce engine and display the badge much more prominently in our advertising. Since we were not in contravention of any agreements we did as the dealers asked and we pushed the RR connection with our flagship truck. This single initiative had a profound impact on the European psyche especially in France where truck drivers began to believe they were driving a "Rolls Royce" truck, despite the prominent Leyland badge on the front of the cab. That advice really helped and we sold a lot of trucks as a result, with the whole range benefitting from a 'pull through' effect of the RR branding. This seems such an obvious thing to do but then many great ideas seem obvious with the benefit of hindsight, or even with the benefit of 'Degonfler'.

As we concluded the round up everyone was in good humour and there was a genuine sense among the dealers that they were being taken seriously and their opinions had some weight with the manufacturer – at long last!! Lunch was relaxed and enjoyable with a sense of expectation as to what the final session would bring. Nobody was disappointed as we or rather Lacoste, revealed our dealer incentive package which covered a six-month period with individual targets and various support tools, including a pricing package, demonstration vehicles, customer events and a promise of a yet to be revealed continent-wide advertising package from the Ronnie Corbett of the Sorbonne. (Our good Professor was presently holding clinics around the continent and gathering information on buying patterns and motives in several countries). At the end of the six-month period every dealer who met his agreed target would be rewarded with a trip for him and his partner to Thailand all expenses paid. And these sophisticated men were reassured and excited that there was energy in the brand, it had taken long enough.

THE PROFESSOR TACKLES CHURCHILL

So the sales team were on board, the dealers were on board, the senior team were on board, and the budgets were in place. We were ready to go. Our dear Professor LeSouer (still looking like the Ronnie Corbett of haute couture) came back with the results of his clinics and reported his statistics which effectively said:

In France 50% of truck buyers love all things British, especially lady Di, Rolls Royce (yippee) and Range Rover and the Iron Lady (really?)

The other 50% would not buy British if it was the last product on earth

In Germany 90% of all truck buyers will buy any truck as long as it is good quality, good value for money and has a three pointed star on the front.

The other 10% of German truck buyers like MAN trucks

In Italy they believe in buying macho trucks and they think the British trucks are very feminine (!!) with their curvy lines

In Belgium all truck buyers are interested in quality and value and will buy from any European Manufacturer. Good Europeans that they are.

Dutch buyers loved DAF trucks and Scandinavian trucks.

So that was good to know.

Professor LeSouer then said that based on this research he had prepared some images for consideration in the clinics. The way he had done this was to bring in a range of people to review magazines and then to question them on what they remembered from the magazines and on their level of retention of various images. Before taking us through the results he showed us the images and copy he had used in the clinics. At first he teased me with some advertising images that were exactly the same as every other truck maker in the market place, a truck in glorious technicolour, with lots of shiny bits, roaring across the page of a magazine. The strap line on this was simply a Great Truck for Great Truckers. His second image was one of the very few photos of Winston Churchill available for use in advertising. This one was a sepia image showing the great man (this was absolutely not my Grandmother's opinion) with his hair akimbo, a flyaway collar flying away and a large cigar in his left hand, with billows of smoke wafting upwards. With this image he had included a quote from Churchill "Je suis un homme de goûts simples, mais j'aime ce que j'aime." I am a man of simple tastes but I like what I like.

The third image nearly knocked my socks off, this was a black and white image washed through in deep blue, of a young couple locked in a tender embrace. The young man had his naked back to the camera and the young woman was resting her head on his shoulder and her beautifully sculpted nails were placed delicately on his back.

A bewitching image.

The strap line was "the future is near". This was absolutely not "me too" and wee Ronnie Corbett of the Sorbonne had really taken me at my word and gone to the extremities of the spectrum to match my wishes. This was definitely out of left field and I wondered how it would be received in the macho, big bellied world of heavy trucks. It was the most striking piece of advertising I had ever seen, it was more like an image to be used in a gentler, more refined industry than trucks. But I had trouble convincing myself that it was something that I wanted for my company or even that it had any relevance in the truck market. Wee Ronnie had served me a curve ball, alright.

Having silenced the room with his final image the good Professor was ready to go through his analysis of reaction and you can be sure he had our full attention, we were hanging on his every word. The first image of the big truck laden with shiny bits like a Christmas tree, was invisible and Professor LeSouer told me that my sense of not me too was absolutely right, this sort of image did nothing for the company's profile nor would it make it easier for dealers to convince the buying public to plump for British trucks. One down two to go. The second image we talked about for a long time. This image of Churchill was remembered by everyone and loved and loathed in equal measure, there was no middle ground. The good Professor took us through a whole lot of demographics and lots of reasons why the results were as they were. But in the end there was no way we could go with a campaign that divided the continent. Two down and only the canoodling couple left.

The striking third image and its strap line, got positive responses right across the board and there were no negatives associated with this image. Among the responses were:

This is a company that believes in quality

This is a company that thinks of the future (obvious)

This is a family oriented company

This is a company that loves its customers

This is a company that cares about the environment (ahead of its time that one)

This is a company I would deal with

Professor LeSouer finished off his presentation and the room was pretty silent, he had given us a lot to think about. He looked around and said "well what do you think?" I didn't know what to think except images one and two were absolute no goers, being ignored or polarising the continent into two camps was not going to help us empty the fields of trucks. As for image three, wow that was something else! Now I had some big decisions to make, if I was worried about how Sir Michael would react to Nicole and her white boots I was doubly concerned about his reaction to Ronnie Corbett's soft porn advertising. I needed some space to think this through.

There were some people I wanted to talk to, a couple of fleet owners, self-made no nonsense men and some sophisticated dealers and there were two trade magazine owners I knew to be on side especially if there was a scoop to be had. There was one group of people I would definitely not be speaking to and that was my colleagues back in the UK both inside and outside my company. There was no way they would be on side with the image of the young couple. Some things just don't translate and my buddies back home would think I had contracted the worst of all diseases – that I had gone native!

So I asked the Professor to give me some time to review his proposals and arranged to pick up with him again in two weeks. That arranged, the Professor took his haute couture back to the Sorbonne and I needed a strong black coffee. I also wanted some time by myself to think about all that we had accomplished in the last few weeks and to ensure I was actually in control of this process AND that I knew where we were going with all this. I arranged a meeting with my senior guys for 10:00 am the following morning and settled down in the cavernous office I had inherited, alone with my thoughts and my black coffee.

It's not easy being a revolutionary.

CHAPTER SEVEN

VAN GOGH & THE BONNIE LASS

There was an Englishman, an Irishman and a Frenchman who met a Scotsman for lunch one day in Paris. The venue was the Duc de Gascoigne, a restaurant on the Rue de Berri, a side street running from Boulevard Haussmann to Avenue Champs-Elysees, a discreet place for trysts and interviews, where the food was great, the wines top notch and there was an extraordinary selection of very fine Armagnacs in Methuselah bottles, ranked by type and vintage on rows of shelves.

To be completely accurate the Englishman was very English, even in his name, Rod England, the Irishman, however was half Irish and half Indian, Paddy Mannion, double honours and gold medal from Trinity and a towering figure in the European motor industry and the Scotsman had a fair dollop of Irish blood. The Frenchman, on the other hand was definitely French, 100% French, smooth, scented, sophisticated and attentive, very attentive. This was my first meeting with the amazing Jean Louis Courboisier or "Le Courboisier", the sobriquet he laboured under with some of my colleagues in Leyland HQ Paris, but that came later, today I was having lunch with a man who might be able to help me. A few weeks earlier my colleague and friend, Rod England had introduced me to Paddy Mannion and we talked about my ambitions for the company in Europe, Paddy had been around forever, was tremendously urbane, linguistically gifted and well connected. Although I had a very good team in place and I was happy with the way our plan was rolling out, I realised there was a large sector where we had absolutely zero impact and that was Government and Military customers in France and I was keen to make progress there. Everyone insisted it would not be possible for any foreign manufacturer to sell to the French Government, we had tried many times over the years but we could never get past first base, officials were polite but "non" was always the reply. We had never sold a single truck to the French Government and the Chairman of the Board had bet me a case of champagne that we could not sell to the French Government, what a challenge!

Paddy reckoned he knew someone with the right connections to help me sell trucks to a French Government department, and that person was M Courboisier. Now we were in the Duc de Gascoigne chatting and feeling each other out. Jean Louis had been around the truck game his entire life and was a mature "schmoozing" kind of salesman rather than a technocrat. So I let him tell me about himself and his career thus far and then I asked him how he would go about selling trucks to the Government and he gave one of those eloquent Gallic shrugs and made one of those duck lip-pursing gestures they all love that says nothing and implies everything and anything you think it ought to.

After the French gesturing, he said "It is not so difficult, it is a question of knocking on the right doors and making sure the right people are aware of you and your products." So far so good, but even in 1985 that was a reply straight out of book one, page one of the salesman's guide to interviews. "Ok Jean Louis who are the right people?" I asked. "In France," he said "the people who really matter are the politicians. They make all the real decisions, if you can convince them that you are an honourable man then they will listen to your propositions, and if what you say makes sense to them and helps the people of France they will buy. It is not so hard." "Do you know these politicians, Jean Louis?" I asked. "But of course, I am a politician, I am a member of the Gaullist party." Came the retort.

THE PRESIDENT OF PRESIDENTS

Jean Louis was indeed a politician, in more ways than one and produced his ID card which said he was a regional councillor, one of the lower rungs on the Political ladder. Paddy then added that Jean Louis was an active politician and a very active member of the Gaullist party and the political machine works up and down. This political structure means that people like Jean Louis have enormous influence and can open many doors. I was intrigued by the potential access he may bring for my company, while realising he was as different from Lacoste as it was possible to be, a completely different type of seller and a very different sort of man. Before we parted that afternoon Jean Louis invited my wife and I to dine with him and his wife in the French Senate, I accepted and the following week we not only dined at the Senate but we met a number of Senators and had a conducted tour of the Senate itself including Napoleon Bonaparte's office. I declined the opportunity to sit in the great man's magnificently ornate chair, who is worthy to sit in the place of the Emperor? Jean Louis really could open doors, literally. During that dinner meeting Jean Louis was at pains to tell me he was not a one trick pony and that he had many contacts in the commercial sector and we discussed some of the opportunities we might be able to pursue together. I offered him the job over an Armagnac and he accepted.

The following day I told Lacoste that I had employed a certain M Courboisier and he was aghast, Francois is not only one of the smartest guys I've ever met he is also one of the most truthful and straight talking blokes I have ever met. "Owen how could you employ that man, he is wriggly like the snake, he is only interested in his fine political friends, he is totally different from us. This Courboisier cannot be part of our team, he is a different type, this one" I guessed then that Francois did not like Jean Louis and Michel Boudier was no less outraged and said to me "Owen you have employed Le Courboisier? I do not believe this!" Don't mince your words guys tell me what you think. I wasn't entirely surprised which is why I had not involved my colleagues in the interview process, but I knew I needed something different to crack Government sales.

The old adage is so true, "If you always do what you've always done then you'll always get what you've always got". Jean

Louis would be staying. This was a personal project and he would report to me and take direction from me, I wanted government sales for a number of reasons, it gave us more of a foothold in the country, it gave our dealers a new target to think about and being part of the establishment is very useful for 'pull through' of other sales. My long term ambitions for Leyland Vehicules Societe Anonyme was for it to be properly integrated into the French business community, not to be regarded as a British importer or worse an English importer. In order to do that we needed to be able to sell into all sectors of the market. My French colleagues had suffered decades of conditioning by all my "Little Britain" predecessors and had developed a siege mentality and actually believed that some sectors were closed to us and not just government departments. Selling to a Government body would let them see that we could sell to anyone.

Jean Louis would be playing a key part in this strategy, and a month after joining us he had arranged a meeting with Senator Salvi, who chaired the Public Transport committee and who was "President of Presidents", this is a post unique to France. Each of the 100 French Departments has a President who coordinates Departmental activity within the Senate and the other organs of the state on behalf of the department for which he is responsible. These Departmental Presidents in turn have a Senate Committee representing their interests and Senator Salvi was the President of the Presidents Committee, this was a powerful post and he was an influential man. The meeting would be over lunch and was arranged in a discreet country restaurant in the Department of Val D'Oise. Senator Salvi turned up in his Government car and with a team of motorcycle outriders!! He entered the restaurant looking for all the world like a diffident aloof politician, cementing the impression when he announced "I am very pressed for time and I must be away in 50 minutes." This Senator was a man of substance and great presence and he looked directly at me with an unflinching gazer as Jean Louis did the introductions, after which we sat down to some small talk over ordering a meal, nothing too flash for the good Senator and only one glass of wine, nice wine though.

"So M. le President, how do you like working in France?" a nice touch from Senator Salvi, polite and very correct in observing protocol. I replied "my dear Senator Salvi, I love France and I have spent many holidays in this beautiful country. Of course, my race and the French have been friends for many centuries, in Scotland we call this the 'Auld Alliance'. Our greatest Queen was half French and as a child she was raised in the French court and was married to the Dauphin, who sadly died. Had the Dauphin lived then the course of European History may well have changed. When Mary Queen of Scots succeeded to the throne of Scotland then, had she still been married to the Dauphin we would undoubtedly have become a single country. This was of course at a fascinating point in European history being at the very start of the Reformation which swept through parts of Europe. I wonder how the English would have felt about Scotland and

France being a single country and a Catholic one at that?" I said. Senator Salvi pricked up his ears and replied "M. le President you are student of history and a Scotsman, how splendid." I could feel the Senator relaxing and when I asked him about his role in the Senate he was happy to describe the workings of the French State apparatus, and the conversation rolled along, prompted every now and then by my colleague Jean Louis, who obviously knew the Senator very well.

Two and a half hours later with the chauffeur and the outriders looking decidedly bored the good Senator took his farewells and went off to the business of the day. He said he had enjoyed our meeting, was impressed that we were investing in France and felt sure we could do business together. The whole time I was with this powerful man it did not occur to me that this was unusual, I simply took it for granted, and went along with the way things were playing out. On occasion I have reflected on the fact that back in the UK I would never have had access to senior mainstream politicians the way that I could do in France, thanks to Jean Louis. In the UK, only local MPs were readily accessible or at least some of them were but once they got beyond back bencher level the only time they were interested in talking to you or giving you some of their valuable time, was if there was a photo opportunity around election time. Here in France it was different, politicians were active in all sorts of areas of society, anywhere that they could make an impact for the greater good. That was impressive and I realised that I was greatly privileged in having men of status within the political community give me the time and opportunity to make my case.

My time in France was so very special, I felt completely at ease with myself and with the challenges before me, as a matter of fact things seemed to come very easily, of course we had our fair share of problems but we considered them and decided on a course of action and fixed them. If I thought that maybe we should chart a new course, we did and it worked for us, we grew and grew and it all seemed so natural. I was charmed, life was good and there was nothing beyond us, just about everything we tried worked out well, we were successful and we had fun, what a time to be the President of Leyland Europe.

But I was young and still in the first flush of youth, so maybe I can be excused.

CHRISTMAS IN PARIS

As the business started to flourish so did our social life, we had made a number of friends in the area, through the school our children attended. It had been our intention to send Nick and Carrie to the local Lycee in St Germain en Laye but unfortunately we applied too late and they ended up going to the British School of Paris. This turned out to be a great stroke of luck since the many expats living to the West of Paris also sent their kids to the BSP. There was a very active social committee attached to the school and we made many friends through the events at the school, friends we have to this day. The other great thing was that our friends had teenage daughters and we had an outstanding babysitter, Liz Finn, a mature sensible girl who was a great favourite of the kids and who gave us peace of mind to go socialising. Our first Christmas was terrific, we had my Mum and Isobel's Dad and step Mum come and spend Christmas with us. We all went along to the BSP Christmas social the highlight of which was an incredible drag act, "The Bristols" who did a Crystals routine miming to that group's records including, 'Then He Kissed Me' and 'Da, Doo Ron, Ron'. The three guys in the group were Liz Finn's Dad, the towering Les, Geoff Litchfield, who was over six-foot tall and the more diminutive but beautifully packaged Trevor Wilcock. Standing side by side was funny enough in itself but in their stage gear and make up they were an absolute riot. The guys wore long dark wigs and sophisticated, stylish floor length sequinned gowns, in shocking pink. They had a beautifully choreographed routine and had lip synced the lyrics perfectly. With their miming and two-step, crossover (!) dance routine and graceful arm gestures the Bristols brought the house down. The fact that Les was six foot seven tall and Trevor was five foot seven small, only heightened the comic aspect, what a great act. That was the first of many enjoyable nights at the BSP social evenings.

The following day I was on holiday so we decided to take our parents into the city, Isobel's step Mum was really looking forward to seeing the city for the first time since 1947, when she last visited the country with here late first husband. He had been part of the Lloyds of London reparations team and they spent a number of years in the occupied countries assessing the damage. She was delighted to be able to recognise much of the city and a bit surprised at how little it had changed. As we drove into the city Isobel's Dad, Jimmy was up front with me and the three ladies were in the back seat. We left the Periferique at Porte Maillot and drove up the Avenue de La Grande Armée to the Arc de Triomphe, an arresting sight. There was a gasp from the back seat and then my Mum exclaimed "Oh son how can you drive in this mad place?" I looked in my rear view mirror to see my Mum covering her eyes at the horror of the traffic.

The Place d'Etoile roundabout has 12 main avenues feeding onto it, and it is wide enough to accommodate about eight lanes of traffic. It is always very busy with people trying to cross the various lanes in order to enter or exit this moving maze, one of my colleagues described the traffic on this roundabout as being like an explosion in a spaghetti factory with everybody in a tangle. The local custom was to get on to the road and to head straight for the inside of the eight lanes, then when it was time to leave to drive straight as an arrow to your exit and the devil take the hindmost. Crazy as it sounds and despite most cars bearing the scars of bumps and prangs, I have never actually seen a crash at the Arc. I had become used to driving in Paris and took it for granted but my Mum was a debutante and was shocked at all these cars scrabbling and shunting their way across Paris.

In the meantime, good old Jean Louis was busy with his political manoeuvrings and arranged a meeting with Prince Poniatowski, "Le Petit Prince" all 6 feet 4 inches of him. This man was descended from Polish nobility and one of his forebears was a Marshal in Napoleon's Grand Army with his name on the Arc de Triomphe and a statue in the Louvre. The Prince had been a Minister in the Valery Giscard D'Estaing Government and was now the Mayor of a beautiful town in Val D'Oise. We met for lunch and then the Prince/Mayor gave us a conducted tour of his beautiful town of which he was very proud. I met this lovely man on a Saturday morning and his first words to me were "Vous etes bien cravate, Monsieur le President", I had picked my tie carefully before leaving. The meeting with Prince Poniatowski lasted for over three hours and for the first two and half hours we spoke in French. As we left his office to go on the tour of his town, the Prince asked me if I would mind speaking in English since he so seldom got an opportunity to speak English these days.

He spoke flawless English with a posh south east accent, I later learned he had a double first from Cambridge. And there was I butchering his beautiful language and he never batted an eyelid, a truly great man. The object of this meeting was to cement the progress made with Senator Salvi. It took some trials and a bit of effort but three months later we received an order for 20 trucks with hi-rise platforms to maintain the lights on the Parisian Periferique. In addition to these meetings Jean Louis and I had regular weekly meetings with various officials, chefs des Cabinets and the like, mostly around Paris or in the Assembly or Senate offices.

On one occasion we were meeting someone in the Concorde Lafayette at Port Maillot, we arrived and Jean Louis parked his car on the Ronde point, the massive roundabout which straddles the Periferique. This is an absolute no, no and I said to him you'll get booked. "Pas de problem, Patron." Was Jean Louis's confident reply. So off we went, had our meeting, and returned to find a meter maid writing out a ticket for Jean Louis's illegally parked car. Calmly and confidently he approached the bored and severe looking young woman and wagging his finger he said, "Non, Mademoiselle, non."

The young lady looked up momentarily and then carried on with her ticket writing, as she calmly replied "Mais oui, Monsieur, mais oui." I was a very amused spectator at this uniquely Gallic sport. As she continued to write Jean Louis produced his wallet which had his ID card on the right face and on the left a metal roundel in blue, white and red and bearing the initials RF. On seeing this the young lady shrugged her shoulders looked at Jean Louis with daggers, sighed loudly and tore up the ticket. Only in France.

AUBERGE RAVOUX

Initially Jean Louis concentrated on his political contacts and I could see he was trying his heart out to get an order from a government Department, but he was a professional salesman and he needed to sell, not least for the commission it would generate, although that was too vulgar a subject for discussion. Jean Louis was keen to show me that he had more than one string to his bow and decided to introduce me to a certain Monsieur Maurice Cleret who owned a fleet of heavy trucks. We met in M. Cleret's office, on the northern outskirts of the city. His office was a double deck portacabin arrangement in the middle of his large yard, with dozens of trucks parked in a circle like wagons in a western movie. It was dark when we arrived and we made our way upstairs to M Cleret's office, where he was seated behind a large desk, there was one other person in the room, the transport manager. Maurice told me that he considered himself to be "Monsieur Trou de Paris" since he dug the foundations for all the tower blocks built in the city and for most other major building projects. Maurice Cleret went through the same routine I had enjoyed with Pat Jennings in Athlone in Ireland.

With the introductions completed, M Cleret invited me to join him in a pastis and I readily agreed, having been briefed by Jean Louis on what to expect and how to respond. Anyway I liked pastis and since I was not going to be driving I may as well enjoy the ambiance. My car was left behind at the office and Jean Louis was driving as he knew exactly how the night would proceed if it was a successful visit and M Cleret and I hit it off. Like Pat Jennings, Maurice produced only 2 glasses, apparently the others were not invited, and we had a pastis with a dash of chilled water, we chatted for a while to get to know each other and had a good connection.

After two more glasses of pastis and iced water, Maurice invited me to dinner at his favourite restaurant which I accepted and off we went Maurice and I in his car and Jean Louis following in his own car, just the three of us were going to dinner. In the car Maurice explained to me that the restaurant was the Auberge Ravoux and was very famous in the area, because Vincent Van Gogh had lived here, in the last days of his life, and it was in this restaurant that he committed suicide by shooting himself. I was very impressed that I was to be going to this restaurant to dine because I love Vincent's work, (who doesn't?).

When we arrived at the restaurant unfortunately it was closed, it was Monday and most French restaurants close on Mondays to recover from the weekend exertions. But there was something Maurice wanted to show me, on the top floor of the building two floors above the restaurant, and he was determined I was going to see it even if the restaurant was closed. He kept knocking and calling until the restaurant owner opened an upstairs window and peeped out to see who was making all the noise. When he saw who was at his door the owner said "Hang on a minute, I'm coming down." Maurice had a bit of influence here, clearly. The restaurateur looked a bit sleepy headed when he arrived but he was very gracious and explained to Maurice that he was closed and it was not possible to have a meal but Maurice told him, that I was the President of British Leyland and I wanted to see Vincent's room and this nice man, shrugged his shoulders and said ok. So we trooped through the restaurant and up two floors to find this unprepossessing, tiny room which was sparsely furnished.

Vincent did not indulge himself

I took a step back as the owner opened the door to this tiny room in the attic of the building, a cold dreary place in winter, I suspect. I was familiar with Vincent's own painting of his room at Arles and this bedroom was spartan and absolutely identical in every detail. The floor was bare wood, the walls were a washed out shade of blue and it was sparsely furnished. There was a single bed pushed against one wall, it had a wooden frame, headboard and footboard, there was a chair with a wicker seat, a table with a bowl and a jug and some non-descript paintings on the wall. There was an antique looking window with small panes. It seems that Vincent was pretty consistent in his requirements for bedroom furnishings, or maybe not. Perhaps I am slightly cynical but looking at this piece of time warp I could not help feeling that I was not the only one familiar with Vincent Van Gogh's painting of his room in Arles, was this a case of life imitating art?

The sleepy restaurateur was now stirring from his slumbers and getting into tour guide mode as he told me this room attracted many visitors and that Vincent had indeed lived here for a period after leaving Arles. He then dropped a bombshell and said that this is the room where Vincent died after he committed suicide by shooting himself. Van Gogh was pretty hard on himself and never did things the easy way and when it came to his suicide he made things tough by shooting himself in the stomach. He really was a tragic character, and although I knew quite a bit about his life I had not realised that his suicide was by shooting in the stomach. That must have been horrendously painful.

Van Gogh lived with the Ravoux family from 20 May until his death on 29 July 1890, in a memoir the daughter of the house, Adeline described Vincent's last moments., *'Here is what I know on his death. That Sunday he went out immediately after lunch, which was unusual. At dusk he had not returned, which surprised us very much, for he was extremely correct in his relationship with us, he always kept regular meal hours. We were then all sitting out on the cafe terrace, for on Sunday the hustle was more tiring than on weekdays. When we saw Vincent arrive night had fallen, it must have been about nine o'clock. Vincent walked bent, holding his stomach, again exaggerating his habit of holding one shoulder higher than the other. Mother asked him: " M. Vincent, we were anxious, we are happy to see you to return; have you had a problem?" He replied in a suffering voice: "No, but I have..." he did not finish, crossed the hall, took the staircase and climbed to his bedroom.*

I was witness to this scene.

Vincent made on us such a strange impression that Father got up and went to the staircase to see if he could hear anything. He thought he could hear groans, went up quickly and found Vincent on his bed, laid down in a crooked position, knees up to the chin, moaning loudly: " What's the matter, "said Father," are you ill? Vincent then lifted his shirt and showed him a small wound in the region of the heart. Father cried: "Malheureaux, [unhappy man] what have you done?" "I have tried to kill myself," replied Van Gogh. These words are precise, our father retold them many times to my sister and I, because for our family the tragic death of Vincent Van Gogh has remained one of the most prominent events of our life. In his old age, Father became blind and gladly aired his memories, and the suicide of Vincent was the one that he told the most often and with great precision.'
©Adeline Ravoux Les Nouvelles Littéraires of 12 August 1954.

While living in Auvers at Auberge Ravoux, Vincent painted prodigiously, he created more than 80 works in 70 days, including the Portrait of Dr Gachet, the Woman in Blue, a portrait of Adeline, the daughter of M Ravoux, who was thirteen years old at the time. Later she was told that Vincent had painted her as the woman she would become rather than the girl she was. Vincent left the family with four paintings, the Blue Woman, The Town Hall of Auvers on 14 July, the Sandman and one other. The portrait of Dr Gachet sold for US $82.5 million or US $138 million at today's value. The family later sold these four painting, under duress, for forty francs, about US$ 200 in today's value. It's tragic to think that Vincent lived such a tragic and impoverished life and yet since his death many have become rich through trading his paintings, now recognised as the work of a genius and yet derided in his own lifetime. The story of Auberge Ravoux and its part in Vincent's life was known to only a few but it has now become a tourist attraction. The room occupied by Vincent, in which he died has been preserved, exactly as it was in his day and as it was in athe famous painting of the bed and chair (which was painted in Arles not Auvers).

As we trooped downstairs we stopped on the second floor which housed the gallery. The gallery itself was very impressive and had some outstanding works on display, mainly by local artists, who had a cooperative nearby. There were also prints of many of Vincent's works available for purchase in the gallery but the gallery was not open and the owner had no intention of opening so we had a quick look around but we could not buy anything. Having shown us the room and the gallery the owner was keen to return to whatever it was he was doing before being interrupted by Maurice Cleret, and ushered us to the front door. All in all, an amazing interlude. Maurice must be a regular customer and a good tipper. Good tipper or not, the owner was insistent the restaurant was closed and there was no chance of his eating here this night, so what to do about dinner? Maurice said no problem I'll phone the wife and have her make something, so he borrowed the sleepy restaurant owners phone to call his wife and organised a meal for him and his two guests. Firstly, he blagged some baguettes and milk from the restaurant then we drove to the next village, knocked up the butcher and got a box of meat from him and then we proceeded back to M Cleret's for a meal. All this time I was sat in Maurice's car thinking "this is most unusual, French people don't often invite you for a meal in their home, preferring to meet on the neutral territory of a restaurant."

We had a lovely meal with Maurice his wife, their son who was 13 years old, and their grown up daughter and her husband. The son in law, who was a producer with a television channel was a man of mischief and insisted in calling his father in law, his beau-pere, "Jolie Papa" much to everyone's amusement. Maurice, I am pretty sure put up with the son in law for the sake of his daughter whom he idolised but I suspect left to his own devices he might have given the son in law a slap or maybe even *'un coup de pied au cul'*, for being cheeky. As the night wore on we swapped stories and experiences and found we had much in common, Maurice and his wife were born and raised in Lorient in

Brittany and were Breton first and French second, and he was very happy that I was a Scot and a fellow Celt. Both Maurice and his wife were steeped in Celtic culture and we talked about the things we had in common, the seven Celtic kingdoms and the Folklorique festival in Lorient each year. The conversation rolled on and the wine kept flowing, we were all very much at ease in each other's company and I was really enjoying being in the heart of this lovely family. Maurice was relaxed and expansive surrounded by his family, of whom he was clearly very proud.

Posing with M Cleret's first Leyland in a hole in Paris

The conversation came back to trucks and we discussed the market place and which marques were doing well, and why. I said that I was surprised at how well Mercedes were doing, that I didn't realise that had such a large share of the French truck market. Maurice became a bit more serious and decided to share with me a very personal story. During the Second World War, in June 1944 after the D day landings in Normandy there was an uprising in Brittany, aimed at tying up Nazi resources to aid the invasion. There were many local Resistance groups, across Brittany and they attacked various installations controlled by the Nazis. After much bitter fighting the Nazis overcame the freedom fighters of Le Maquis and then set about making reprisal killings. Both Maurice's Father and his wife's Dad were part of those rounded up (both of them were deeply involved in the revolt) and both young men were summarily executed by the Nazis. As he was speaking it was clear that Maurice was back in 1944 although he was a very young child at the time, then said quietly that is why I will never buy German vehicles for my fleet. And then he added as an afterthought "If I did my wife would probably kill me." I felt privileged that Maurice was comfortable enough to open up in this personal way to me. It was a nice meal and a great night which finished after midnight, and Maurice Cleret and I became firm friends. We did a lot of business together and I valued his friendship.

Jean Louis was showing that he was far from a one trick pony and we were penetrating niches in the French Market that had been firmly closed to us before, we were more aggressive than we had ever been in penetrating other sectors, and of course the wider your customer base the greater the opportunities for growth. The whole business was growing as the sales force grew in confidence, we were going from strength to strength. We had faced up to and overcome some stiff challenges and now we were seeing some reward for all that hard work.

THE BONNIE LASS O'CORSICA

With our progress on the government front and his additional contact with builders we had a more balanced sales team and we started hunting down some of the larger fleets, in market sectors we had not tried to enter before. A fired up, confident sales team is a powerful thing to behold. As our profile was raised with our increased activity, the competition sat up and took notice because as we were increasing our sales others were naturally losing sales, that's the way it goes and they were not happy. This was most true of Renault Vehicules who regarded every sale lost to us as some sort of slight to their manhood (it is a macho business) and a slighted Frenchman is a dangerous opponent – and sneaky too, as it turned out. The French claim to be the greatest nation in the world at complying with each and every detail of regulation but I think sometimes they can play fast and loose with the spirit of legislation while complying with the letter of the law.

While we enjoyed success with the French government through the efforts of Jean Louis, the same Government was anxious to make sure national interest were looked after, much more so than any UK government, in my experience. They can be quite shameless at giving locals assistance against foreign competitors, they make no pretence when it comes to the national interest, you've got to love them for it even if it is hard to swallow at times. Take for example all those Japanese manufacturers desperate to sell electronic gadgets in the mid 1980's, they had conquered the rest of the world and were puzzled at their lack of success in La Belle France. Well it wasn't too hard to figure out the reason for their lack of success in the French market. In order to sell in France or any country your products must comply with local regulations, European wide legislations in the case of France and the rest of the EU. However, in order to comply your product needs to be inspected and in France the inspection is known as "Service des Mines" and it can be an onerous process as manufacturers of electronic gizmos in Japan discovered. The Service des Mines for electronic gadgetry was located in Toulouse and staffed by one wee fat bloke, the least competent in the whole of French officialdom and he was entitled to 4-hour lunch breaks. He was equipped with a pad and a pencil and a slide rule. (Of course, I exaggerate to make a point, or do I?)

You will understand that this wee, fat official had to check every single detail and he had a backlog of products that would take 100 years to catch up with, by which time technology would have moved on – especially French Technology. No less surprising regulations would also have changed and, as a consequence the products in the backlog would become non-compliant and could not be marketed in the country. The French will tell you that you can sell anything in France by simply complying, what they won't tell you is how bloody difficult it is to get things inspected in order to comply. It was slightly less difficult for Truck Manufacturers but even then we had a couple of engineers who practically lived at the Service des Mines and who walked our vehicles through the homologation process. You cannot accuse French officials of not doing all they can to assist indigenous manufacturers.

It's not only French officialdom that play games, French Manufacturers pull some stunts of their own, and one of the favourite one was to use financial clout to sway deals their way. This worked on two levels, firstly they had their own in-house finance company which gave them preferential rates, this edge was often enough to take a deal away from us, which is fair enough, business is business. At another level it was explained to unpatriotic purchasers of foreign trucks, that their own French customers would be disappointed when they heard that their goods would be hauled by an English wagon. These were pretty crude tactics but effective enough and if people were prepared to use this kind of tactic there was no way of responding to it. But the normal business edge provided by in-house financing, we could do something about. While we did not have the resource to launch an in-house finance company and a competitive Finance package I could go seek a partnership with a third party financier. I went looking for a partnership among the independent Financiers who might see the Truck companies own in-house finance companies as legitimate competitors, and be up for a share of the business. I prepared a review of the French Market as a pitch to Finance companies showing our growth potential and the likely benefits to a partner as well as to us. I then made some appointments.

The reaction by the first two companies to my pitch was a polite disinterest, they were not really interested in the truck industry, possibly because they did not really understand it. My third appointment was with a company called CECICO, this was the Finance arm of a major French Conglomerate which included the Strasbourg Brasseries among their daughter companies. The President of this company was a red headed native of Normandy, called Paul-Herve Buret, a gregarious, dynamic man, who listened to me and my proposal. We talked for a couple of hours and Paul-Herve told me he was intrigued by what I said and since he did not have a presence in this sector, he would think about what I had said, check with some of his colleagues and give me a call back. On leaving he said "We are mainly in major construction project funding, aeroplanes, main-frame computers and industrial equipment but I suppose a truck is just another piece of capital equipment."

Two weeks later I got a call from Paul-Herve, who said, "Have you ever been to Corsica?" when I replied in the negative he invited me saying "I am having a conference there in two weeks and all my senior regional and overseas people will be there as well as some of our agents, why not come and tell them what you told me?" I said that sounded great and I would love the opportunity to speak to his team, so that was it I was off to Corsica for four days in November. We left Paris on a Thursday afternoon in the cold and rain and arrived in sunny Corsica, what a difference. CECICO had taken over a rural hotel for the 70 delegates who would be attending the conference. After check in we had a registration process and then a run through by Paul-Herve and his senior people, we were given copies of the weekend agenda and two things leapt out at me, the first was I had a major spot on the agenda on Saturday morning from 10:00 am to 11:00 am to make my pitch to the team. The second thing that jumped out was we would only would be working in the mornings there was a fantastic programme arranged of swimming, sailing, water skiing and generally having fun.

Friday morning at the first session and Paul-Herve asked me to sit beside him on his right, and thereafter at lunch, dinner or in the sessions that is where he asked me to sit, and there were a number of raised eyebrows, who was this foreigner with the funny accent? The Boss obviously liked him. While we were sailing on Friday afternoon one of the delegates called Phillippe, struck up a conversation with me, he was the manager of the Paris operation and I learned that he, like me was a big fan of Bob Dylan. He and I had a right good chat but I was being weighed and assessed, and hoping not to be found wanting. This was an important gig for me and it would make a huge difference to our European sales effort if I could clinch a deal with this group. Phillippe told me that the Boss had paid me a great honour by inviting me to sit in "le siège de fils de Dieu". I replied that I felt very honoured. The sailing went well, we were in small catamarans and Paul-Herve had me hanging way out in the wind, all great fun and very exhilarating.

After a break for coffee we were off playing petanque, this was obviously a team building exercise that Paul-Herve had organised. For La Boule I was in a team of 4 and I bowled first or last, in the positions where I would create least havoc for my team, as directed by the team skipper. When I was asked if I played the game, I confess I was less than honest when I said I was very inexperienced, I loved the game and played frequently on holiday. My nine-year old son Nick was a petanque hustler which helped me hone my skills. Anyway I did as I was told and did not commit any monstrous faux pas, so that was good. At dinner in the hotel on Friday night, I was in my usual seat and we discussed the events of the day and my presentation the following morning. We went to bed late that night, preferring to spend some time fraternising in the bar; I was pleased with the way things were going. On Saturday morning I was up early for a quick run through of my presentation and a last check of my slides, I was well rehearsed and I had a list of potential questions, "Now's the day and now's the hour, see the front of battle lour", as Rabbie Burns might say.

I was second on, following Phillipe the Dylan fan, of all people. Phillipe was a very polished performer, quite theatrical and made very good use of his hands, making lots of dramatic gestures to underscore his points. I would buy finance from this man, he was good and believable. As I strode to the podium Phillippe gave me a great big smile, "Was this a competition, was he throwing down the gauntlet?" I spoke for 25 minutes, gave them a bit of background on British Leyland, our European Operations, the French Market, our ambitions and the upsides and opportunities for both companies. I took questions for about twenty minutes and then we had a coffee break. It was well received and I was pleased that I had done ok and made all the points I wanted to make, and anyway you can tell by the questions how it went. If the questions are polite and vague you bombed, if they are relevant and pointed you scored.

One of the difficulties I always find in making a speech in a foreign language is getting the emotion right, you can get sidetracked by overly focussing on pronunciation that you end up flat and monotonous. Both Paul-Herve and Phillipe were among my questioners. I am an avid people watcher and I particularly love observing group dynamics, it tells you so much about people and it was fascinating watching power plays and attempts at influencing/ingratiating among the various individuals. Phillipe was not number two in the group but he saw himself as heir apparent and others also saw him in that role.

One more presentation and it was time for play again, on Saturday afternoon we went for a tour of the island. We saw forests of oak trees and it was interesting to hear how they harvested the bark to supply corks to the wine industry. We visited the town of Ajaccio, the birthplace of Napoleon Bonaparte, who's chair I had declined to sit on when visiting his office in the Senate Building in Paris. There are some really interesting tenement buildings in Ajaccio with steep and narrow staircases that inspire vertigo. I could get used to this lifestyle, the weather in Corsica was glorious but Isobel and the kids were enduring wet, windy and cold weather back home in Paris.

Dinner on Saturday night was in a dockside restaurant in Bonifacio and the restaurant was given over to Paul-Herve's party, the doors and shutters were all open on a glorious evening, warm and glowing in the night. We assembled at the hotel and a fleet of taxis took us to the restaurant, as always I sat alongside Paul-Herve. At the restaurant we drank an innocuous rose wine – by the gallon and after an hour, at 9:00pm things started to happen a group of musicians were playing local folk songs and we took our place at the table, me in my usual place in "le siège de fils de Dieu". As we sat down with an accordion player at the end of our table Paul-Herve asked me in a matter of fact tone if I would like to sing a song from Scotland, I don't know whether it was the wine, the ambiance or that I that I thought he was kidding but to my horror I heard myself saying "yes of course I will."

What have I done? I'm tone deaf and a rubbish singer.

Anyway Paul-Herve said not just now because some of the French will sing first. Oh my God I am going to undo all the good work of yesterday and this morning, when I fluff the Corsica's Got Talent audition. A man from Marseille sang, and very good he was too, then a young woman sang a Beatles song in French and she was very good as well and then a few others got up and sang, oh my goodness these folk can actually sing. In the meantime, the starters appeared and the mood was getting more boisterous, everyone was having a lot of fun but I was scared stiff and my knees were knocking under the table. I thought how do I do this and that sobered me up a bit. Right I need to sing some kind of folk song, which ones do I know the words of? I thought about it and decided that a good old martial air was probably best, something that even a shouter could get away with, and I realised that I knew most of the words to an old song called the Bonnie Lass of Fyvie'o, a song about a troop of Irish Dragoons that came marching down through Fyvie, a village north of Aberdeen. The Captain of the Dragoons fell in love with a bonnie lass and asked his Colonel to delay leaving until he could ask the lass to marry him. The Colonel refused and the Dragoons marched off with the love sick Captain at their head. As so often happens in these songs the tragic hero pined away and died for love of the bonnie lass and the Irish Dragoons had to bury their Captain before they reached Aberdeen.

I loved this song which I regularly sang in the shower and I knew if it was belted out it would be capable of stirring the blood. That was it settled, I would sing the Bonnie Lass O Fyvie-o. I scribbled the words on my napkin and went over them in my head and when Paul-Herve turned to me I stood up and launched into my party piece. I had never sung in front of anyone in my life except on a very odd occasion at family parties but this was a business thing and so I got on with it. Amazingly I remembered all the words, in the right order as well and somehow I managed to hold the tune which really surprised me.

Now, I know I am not a good singer but that night, the warmth of the evening, the glow of the wine and a song in a foreign language cast a spell over the 70 people in that restaurant. When I finished my stomping and shouting, it was as though they had just witnessed a proper singer and all of my audience stood up and cheered and clapped. The men formed a line to shake my hand and the ladies rushed to give me a kiss, it was a spectacular success. Phillipe came up to me, grinning from ear to ear and said I know that song that is on Bob Dylan's first album, he calls it Pretty Peggy'o. Phillippe was absolutely right and I told him that like many British folk songs this one too had crossed the Atlantic and had the lyrics altered and were now claimed as authentic American ballads. Paul-Herve was beaming, I had made real progress that night, not because I am a good singer because I am definitely not but because I did what was expected of me. A lesson in life.

The night went beautifully we had a lovely meal and a lot of fun.

The following morning when I went to take my seat in the conference room I received another standing ovation, which was a very nice touch from my new friends in this terrific company. I know it's a cliché to tell someone they have to sing for their supper but it is something less of a cliché when you have to sing to clinch a deal with a finance company. But if that's what it takes. Nobody in the room had a problem with me sitting in the 'Siege de fils de Dieu' and Paul-Herve positively beamed when I came in. The rest of the morning went well and then at lunch time I left to catch a plane for Paris with a feeling that we might just have secured a strong ally in our bid to capture market share. The following day back in the office I contacted Phillippe with a proposal for a deal and that led to our first project with CECICO.

I wonder what would have happened if I had actually been able to sing?

CHAPTER EIGHT

TERROR COMES TO PARIS

I had been in the job for a year and things were going very well, our sales were the highest they had ever been and the sales team were on fire. The dealers were also fired up, and their trip to Thailand had been a great success, even if Monsieur Francis Million had been ripped off by being sold a piece of glass instead of a diamond, by a shady dealer in Bangkok. We were conquesting many new customers, aided greatly by our deal with CECICO, and the input of Professor LeSouer and Nicole, all in all there were lots of smiles around the place and much to be happy with. At a management meeting one Monday morning I picked up on a strained discussion between two of my colleagues Phillippe Saglio the Personnel Director and Jean-Pierre Hallet, who was Director of IT and Parts, a big job. Phillippe Saglio was a past master at upsetting people and Jean Pierre was quick to rise to any slight. Saglio had a very heightened sense of his own importance and made sure everyone knew he was from an important family, Grandma had a Chateau on the Loire and his ancestor was important enough to get his name on the Arc de Triomphe as part of Napoleon's all conquering Grande Armée. He had an unfortunate manner and came across as aloof and arrogant which led to him being most unpopular with his colleagues. On this occasion Saglio was snapping out the side of his mouth to Jean-Pierre and I was unhappy because I liked my meetings to be structured and focussed. I stopped the meeting and asked Saglio if he would like to share his thoughts with the rest of us, he was reluctant to say anything and I told him to share it or leave the room, so he told me the subject they had been discussing and I was shocked and furious in equal measure by what I heard.

Our French HQ was in the Banlieu, north of Paris in the town of Gonesse, close to Charles de Gaulle, Airport, in Roissy. In this small town there was a hostel for men from North Africa and we employed a number of these young men in our stores operation under Jean-Pierre. My two colleagues had been arguing about an incident where a young woman had come on to the premises to provide a personal service to some of the young men employed in the stores. I exploded, how could this be happening? We were allowing a bordello to be run on our premises. I was incensed and I shouted it's not a whorehouse, it's a warehouse, what's the matter with you people? I shouted and raved in English and I am sure that nobody really understood the words but they all got the message, that I was angry. Actually I was incandescent, why had I not been told of this before? When I calmed down I asked how long this had been going on and why nobody had put a stop to this. There were a lot of sheepish men sat around that table as I thundered at them, when Lacoste added his tuppensworth by saying "At least nowadays we do not have the girls on our company payroll as was once the case not so long ago, Patron."

If Lacoste was telling me this, then it was a fact and not an opinion. I was truly upset by this, life is hard enough without dealing with this kind of nonsense. I wanted to find out who else knew of this inside the company to be told that basically everybody knew. I asked my colleagues if they were not ashamed to allow this to continue, only to be met with a lot more expressive Gallic shoulder shrugging. I wrapped up the meeting and asked Phillippe, Francois and Jean-Pierre to stay behind. In that discussion I was told the reason that nobody had done anything was because they were basically frightened to confront the problem in case there were personal repercussions and so everyone turned a blind eye to the problem. Now that I knew about this there was no way I could or would ignore it, for my own standards but also because it's the sort of things that disgusts people, and if it became known in the UK the tabloid press would have a field day. At that stage of my career I had not yet read the management book on how to best avoid the pitfalls associated with the closing of a brothel. Come to think of it, I still haven't read it. So without the guidance of those with experience in this matter I had to make it up as I went along. Francois had told me that the forklift driver in the stores was the boss of the young north African men, a kind of village elder who kept them all in line. So I had a good think about this for a few days and then I sent for the forklift driver, a certain Monsieur Georges.

When he arrived he looked very apprehensive and told me he had never been in the Patron's office before. I poured him a coffee and asked him how long he had worked with the company and if he enjoyed working at Leyland. He told me he really liked the company and was pleased that the company was able to employ so many people in France including his "nice boys" from Algeria, Tunisia and Morocco. He told me the boys were hard workers and came to work every day, and I said I was pleased to hear that and I asked him if he was the union organiser for the stores area and he said he was. So I asked him if he would talk to his "nice boys" and ask them how they felt about things and if there were any improvements we could make to the way we shipped out our spare parts to the dealers. I asked Monsieur Georges to come back the following week when we could have a coffee and he could tell me what the "nice boys" thought. The following week M Georges came back and was giving me an update over coffee and when he finished I asked him if he could be honest with me, because I had something really important that I wanted to talk to him about. He replied that the Patron could depend on him.

I reminded him that I was Scottish not English and he said he knew that. Now it was time to get to the point and I told M. Georges I was very worried about the English because they wanted to close the parts warehouse in Paris and move all the parts from Paris to the company's central warehouse in Belgium in the town of Mechelen or Malines depending on your preference for

Flemish or French. Monsieur Georges was suitably shocked and asked what would happen to his "nice boys" and I think this was more than simple rhetoric, I believe he really considered himself as some sort of Godfather with a real responsibility for these men. I told him that the English could be a difficult race and were very insistent that they wanted to make this move and if we had to close then there would have to be redundancies in the warehouse. He was genuinely horrified and very, very concerned. He asked me if there was anything we could do to stop this.

I told him that I had heard that certain things had been going on in the stores and that girls were visiting the "nice boys" and that made me very unhappy. I added that if the English found out they would close all of the French business, not just the warehouse. He said he did not know about this but he would find out and let me know, so I said he should return tomorrow and let me know.

When he left Lacoste came in and said to me, "Owen I hope you know what you are doing, you must be careful with these men, life does not have the same meaning for guys like this, be very careful." I thanked him for the warning, and then I said, "How can you know what the right way is to deal with something like this? All I know is that this is wrong, these blokes are paid to work, they are not paid to sneak off into some dark corner with a girl. These girls should not be allowed onto our site and what if word of this gets back to England, what do you think they will do?" Lacoste looked at me in his laconic French manner, shrugged his shoulders and said, "Owen, it is the way of the world, these men have needs and the girls help them." I wasn't having any of that nonsense and told him so, if they have needs they can attend to them in their own time and elsewhere not on our site, that I will not tolerate." The next day I had coffee with the forklift Godfather, who told me that he was very sorry but the things I told him about had indeed been happening and he said he had given the boys a lecture and he could promise this would never happen again, and he would make sure of this. We finished our coffee and I thanked Monsieur Georges and I told him I thought he was an honourable man and I would depend on him to make sure things were correct in our warehouse. In the meantime, I would make sure the English forgot about the idea of transferring our parts warehouse to Belgium, and we might even have to employ two more people in the warehouse to cope with the extra work. This was not exactly a bribe but he probably had lost face over this and this would be his victory, he could tell the nice boys he had achieved this, and anyway we did need extra help. Monsieur Georges left and that was the last we heard of girls visiting the warehouse.

April is supposedly the month to visit Paris, it is the month for dreamers and romantics, according to songwriters and movie makers, at least. Certainly the weather is gentle, the trees are coming into leaf and it's the time when the boulevardiers start to strut their stuff, along the leafy, broad streets of the French Capital. By April 1986 the Quinn family had settled into life in France we lived near St-Germain-en-Laye, in a very nice house in an old apple orchard. We were about fifteen minutes from the city centre and made the most of our location, spending a lot of time exploring the city and its many sites, touristy and sacred. In April 1986 Paris was about to get a wake-up call and so was I.

GHADDAFI & THE GARDENER

Terrorism was in the news with a number of bombings and attempted bombings in Europe and the Middle East which were mainly aimed at Israeli nationals, institutions or sympathisers and allies. But in truth that April it all seemed to be far away from us in this civilised corner of the world. Paris carried on as normal and everything seemed set fair for the Quinn family. On Tuesday, 15 April 1986, while I was busily trying to persuade Europe to buy lots of shiny British trucks, second term President Ronald Reagan once again asserted his country's right to act as the world's policeman with the launch of Operation El Dorado Canyon against Libya. President Reagan ordered the US military to carry out a series of air strikes on an airfield at Tripoli, the Baab-al-Azizia barracks and at a naval academy, outside Tripoli. There were 40 reported Libyan casualties, and one U.S. plane was shot down. This raid was ostensibly in retaliation for the bombing of "La Belle" discotheque in Berlin by Libyan agents, in which more than 60 US military personnel were injured and one soldier was killed, a further 2 German nationals were killed and 170 injured. It is likely there were more reasons for this attack against Libya than the one offered, the bombing of a discotheque in Germany. This attack was widely interpreted in Europe as an act of war against a much smaller nation by the United States of America. The Leader of Libya, Colonel Ghaddafi was securely ensconced as the strong man of Libya and a leading voice of Arab discontent against the West in general and the USA in particular, and as such was a constant annoyance to the USA.

Colonel Ghaddafi was widely reviled in the West where he was regarded as an open and generous supporter of international terrorism and US spy satellites had found proof positive of a number of training camps for various terror groups thriving in his country. Britain was outraged when it found there was one camp supposedly dedicated to training IRA operatives, the USA was outraged because the CIA told Ronnie he should be outraged so Ronnie made a speech saying he was outraged. Whenever he got the chance Colonel Ghaddafi had a rant against the continued survival of the state of Israel and in 1986 he was anxious to forge a Pan-Arab alliance (of which he hoped to be the leader – Saddam Hussain harboured similar notions).

Also the Colonel had a lot of oil available to sell and to fund any operations which took his fancy. He was Public enemy number one as far as the CIA was concerned, at a time when they were still cuddling up with Saddam Hussain, who remained their best bet for getting revenge against Iran and the Ayatollah with whom they had been in conflict since the attack on the US embassy in 1979. While Operation El Dorado Canyon was totally a US initiative it was publicly supported by the United Kingdom in the form of our gentle Prime Minister, the well known pacifist,

Mrs. Margaret Thatcher. In addition to overtly supporting the position of the US with words we allowed them to use our sovereign soil as a base for the attacks with some of the bombers taking off from airfields in southern England. These attacks caused a shockwave and there were many protests across the continent of Europe and the Middle East, but that is a long way from Boisie Idaho, and besides this was a second term Presidency and re-election was not an issue for Ronnie boy.

Even though I was pretty much consumed with the affairs of my company, keeping up the pace of change, this attack cut through all of that, this was serious for us and I wondered what impact it would have among my warehouse colleagues, some of whom were Libyan by birth and pro Ghaddafi by instinct. The large North African population in the Paris area, and the many young men in my company became very subdued and were keeping their heads down, so we got on with business as though nothing had happened. At this time, I started to notice a new graffiti tag line appear around the city, 'Touche pas, mon pote' accompanied by a hand appearing to pat a distinctly African head. This meant hands of my little friend apparently, but I had to ask what it meant since I hadn't come across the word pote before.

Two days after the attacks, I had a guest in my office in Paris, Jim Thomas our Corporate Security advisor who spent the day with me briefing me on my personal security in the wake of the US action in Libya. Jim was a retired senior Police Detective and he and I knew each other from a previous investigation of fraud in which he and I were jointly involved, he was a real no nonsense type of man and good at his job. Now he was here to offer advice to me, my colleagues and my family.

He started his briefing by letting me read the latest security review notices. These were produced by different bodies concerned with matters of security relating to terror groups and available to men like Jim, for the cost of an annual subscription. It's amazing what you can subscribe to! These reviews showed that every terror group in the world had a branch office in Paris, and I read stories of the activities of the Baader-Meinhof Group or the Red Army Faction (until then I had thought these were two separate organisations), I read of atrocities attributed to the Palestinian Black September, I read what dastardly deeds the PLO were supposedly planning to unleash on an unsuspecting world and there was scrutiny of the activities of the IRA and many others and I was really surprised at how many terror groups existed and how many had a base in Paris. If you want to scare yourself or anyone else subscribe to Terror Monthly, it'll keep you awake at night.

Once I had scared myself silly reading these tomes about the world's most notorious groups and baddest people (I was actually surprised to learn that there were girls involved in these terror operations as well as men) Jim then turned to his task in hand, briefing me on how to stay safe. He started by walking round the Paris site, the workshops, the warehouse the offices, he asked about security arrangements and got the name of the company who provided our security. Our on-site security was in place when I arrived to take up my post and I must say I was very happy with the arrangements which consisted of armed guards with dogs, 24 hours a day 365 days a year, and alarms on all the main buildings centrally controlled by the security company. I don't know which of my predecessors had organised this or why but it was very efficient, even though I initially thought it was a wee bit over the top, especially the fat guard with the one eyed dog and a gun that would make Dirty Harry salivate. Jim was very impressed with our security protocols and said it was the best he had seen in any of the worldwide businesses of the corporation, praise indeed.

He went on to ask about our regional installations and how they operated and how often I visited, who knew in advance and all sorts of details about the day to day operations. He was particularly interested in the fact that we had a Hostel for North African men in the town and decided he would speak to the local prefect and get some background on that, so I arranged for Phillippe Saglio to make an appointment for some time in the future when Jim could come back to meet with this man. He spent a bit of time in the warehouse looking through narrowed eyes at the many Arabs working there, old habits die hard I suppose. If Jim had known what I knew about what had been going on in there in the past, he would have been horrified but I'm glad he didn't and I didn't make him any the wiser. Jim then asked me about my personal life, the things we did in Paris as a family, the places we went on a regular basis the people we met with and befriended, any sporting events we attended, the children's schools and their leisure pursuits, what Isobel did during the day, any charity work she did. This was real serious stuff and I paid close attention to what Jim was saying, even although at the back of my mind I could not help thinking "what value would I be to a terror group?"

He went through a lot of simple stuff, Jim told me to stay away from large groups, not to do the same things at the same time each week, not to go to places which were overtly American, (that meant a new church on Sunday from now on), always check under the car, before opening it, just to see if there was anything unusual, something that should not be there. All very straightforward and very sensible. Jim asked me about the routes I took to work, was it always the same one, did I always leave at the same time etc. And then he briefed me on how to determine if I was being followed by another car or cars. To which I said "Jim for goodness sake, this is beginning to sound like a Bond movie. I am only a boy from the Halfway." No nonsense Jim, my friend said, "Ok Owen, you may not have a very high opinion of yourself but you are the President of a large British Company and you would be of great value to a terror group, capturing you or killing you would certainly get attention. And these people are after attention, that's their life blood."

Jim really had my attention now. So he carried on "change your route to and from work each day, and be careful who you are talking to and be very careful making appointments with people you don't know." It makes life a bit more complicated but it could save your life. Then he told me that I needed to write a statement, and it needs to be written not typed or printed. He gave me this printed statement which I copied onto a prepared document then I made a note of any identifying scars and where they were on my body and then listed the jewelry that I normally wore. I made three copies of this by hand, one for the office safe back at HQ in Britain, one for the Personnel department in France and one for me which I popped into my briefcase and continued my conversation with Jim.

I can confess that I was alarmed by Jim's briefing and resolved to be very careful about my security. Later that evening I took Jim back to the airport and then headed home thinking about Jim's dire warnings and all the way home I kept a close look at the cars behind me, but it was starting to get dark and I was limited to what I could see. The journey home was nice and calm, notwithstanding the normal antics of Parisian motorists, who seem to need the adrenalin rush of motorway chaos to get through the day, that and tooting their horn for no obvious reason.

When I got home Isobel needed some help in the kitchen, so I forgot about terror groups, kidnappings and bombings and helped Isobel in preparing the dinner. After dinner I got on with my normal evening activities, baths followed by prayers and reading the children bedtime stories when Isobel called upstairs to ask if she could borrow my calculator. I told her it was in my briefcase and carried on with the stories for Nick and Carrie.

When I finished the stories we said our prayers together and then I went downstairs where I saw Isobel reading a document.

"What is this?" Isobel asked holding out the document Jim had me asked me to complete. It started off: - *"Dear Isobel, please don't worry about me, I am healthy and being looked after but I need you to read this carefully and follow the instructions exactly......,* "and so it continued.

It seemed quite reasonable when Jim explained to me that the format had been put together in order that my handwriting would be recognisable, even if I was under great strain. Now in the quiet of our lounge room in the suburbs of Paris it seemed very, very frightening to be telling my wife that I was ok and being well treated by persons' unknown. I had intended explaining all this when the children were in bed, I did not want to alarm my wife, but Isobel had beaten me to the punch. I tried to say that it was just precautionary and that we had nothing to worry about but in truth I was pretty shaken about the whole thing myself. We talked through the implications of what Jim had told me and what we should do to make sure we avoid any harm befalling us.

In the end we decided, we would start attending our local Parish Church for Sunday Mass in St Nom La Breteche, and we would not knowingly go where we knew there would be groups of Americans. This in itself was a victory for the terrorists and yet another unintended consequence of American Foreign Policy under Ronnie with his vision as Policeman of the world's oil deposits.

The following morning, at 6:50am I went into our garage beneath our house and before getting into my car I checked all around, including the underside of my car for foreign objects. My car was a Range Rover four-wheel drive, so checking the undercarriage was no great problem and satisfied that all was ok, I set off for the office 45 kilometers away via the motorway and the Parisian Periferique. Immediately on the motorway I was aware of a number of cars that were following me and they really were following me, a red Renault, a black Citroen, a white Volkswagen, a blue Renault, a silver car that kept quite far back but appeared with a regularity that had me worried. I speeded up when possible and slowed down when I could but still they appeared and disappeared. This pattern of cars appearing, dropping off and reappearing repeated itself all along the Periferique and onto the Autoroute du Nord to Roissy airport. By the time I left the Periferique I was really worried and when these same cars followed me onto the Autoroute I could hear my heart thumping in my chest and panic was taking hold.

Where would they ambush me? It would be easy on the motorway and once they had me they could be many miles away before help could get to me. It had been daft to take my normal route because "they" obviously knew that route, I should have taken another route or left at a different time at least, idiot that I am. As I was giving myself a talking to I came to the Autoroute exit before the one I normally took and so without signaling I left the motorway at the last minute. Crossing several lanes of traffic, I left the motorway to the accompaniment of the French motorists favourite instrument, the rasping, croaking honk of the car horn, or in this case several car horns. Cars had to swerve as people tried to avoid another dozy Frenchman driving like a crazy person. Nothing unusual in that, just another morning on the French motorway for everyone, except me!

To my great relief none of the cars that had been following me could be seen, but to be sure I turned a few corners in a big loop just to make sure I wasn't being followed. Secure that there was nobody following me I calmed down and proceeded through the streets of the town to my office. As I drove I was thinking that I was quite early because the motorway and the Periferique had only light traffic this morning and I was able to make good time. Probably my preoccupation with cars tailing me also made the journey pass more quickly but it was only 7:45 am and some mornings it could take two hours to make this trip. I was rudely interrupted in the middle of my musing on the journey time, when suddenly a canvas covered van came careening out of a side street and stuck on my tail. Every time I turned a corner so did he, I could see there was group of men in this vehicle and they were intent on following me, stupid me thinking I had shaken them off when all the time they had accomplices waiting in ambush. As I drove I was wondering how they knew to pick me up here. It's amazing what goes through your mind, here was I being pursued around the streets of our little town by a bunch of shadowy international terrorists and in mortal fear of my life and I was trying to work out what kind of communication system they had used to trigger the ambush.

The Range Rover has a four litre engine and has a useful turn of speed when required and so I put my boot down and went as fast as was possible through the early morning, suburban streets and at last the office and the factory came into sight. We had two car parks on the site one for head office staff and one for the factory and warehouse employees and then there was a special parking spot for the President. This VIP parking spot was located in a large quadrangle in front of the office and nobody else was allowed to park there. At that moment I was very glad to have this privilege, even if I had originally been dead against it. The quadrangle was covered with flinty pebbles and as I screeched to a halt I ignored the parking spot in order to get as close to the office door as possible.

I must have been really noisy because the fat security guard rushed out with his large, ominous looking pistol drawn from its holster and his one eyed, multi-scarred, cross bred Alsatian Doberman dog was howling like a wolf and slobbering. I was at the centre of quite a spectacular scene with my dramatic arrival and I was very grateful for the presence of this particular security guard whom I had previously thought of as a fat useless burden on the payroll, but he and his one eyed dog were now my best pals. I jumped out of my car and was stood with my briefcase in hand and the door open in a scene frozen in time and burned into my memory like a cattle brand, if that's not mixing too many figures of speech. There was I shouting I know not what but whatever it was, it was in English and the guard would not understand the words but he sure as heck got the message that I was frightened of something. The guard and his huge pistol and his one eyed dog, were trying to work out why the Patron was driving like Alain Prost and shouting like a big Mademoiselle when round the corner came this canvas covered van, which also screeched to a halt on the flinty pebbles and three large, swarthy men leapt out and started walking towards me. What to do now? I must have missed that class as well.

One thing that I found interesting was that although all this happened in a few short seconds, there seemed to be so much going on and time seemed to be going ever so slowly, giving the impression of a very long time. This scene will stay fresh in my mind for all time, and as I reflect on it I can see everything with astonishing clarity, I think abject fear also extends your peripheral vision and you take in absolutely everything in your immediate environment, every little detail. As the three international killers approached there was evidently a leader among these men and he advanced from the others, stopped, clicked his heels and bowed. I must have looked like an idiot standing with one hand on the door of my car and my briefcase in the other hand. The guard and his dog were watching closely, finger on the trigger and teeth at the ready. Then the leader of the assassins said "Monsieur le Président je vous demande de me pardonner d'être tellement informel et s'approcher de vous, mais votre voiture a reconnu ce matin. Je suis le jardinier en chef de notre ville et j'ai un ami qui veut acheter un camion et je lui ai dit que je connaissais le Président de British Leyland, qui font les camions meilleurs en France. J'ai dit à mon ami que je demanderai au Président si quelqu'un pouvait dire mon ami des camions Leyland." I was still thinking in English and so it took a moment for what he said to sink in and then I nearly passed out with relief, this lovely man was the chief gardener of the town and having recognised my car decided to tell me he had a mate who wanted to buy a truck. He and his two big mates weren't international assassins after all. They weren't trying to ambush me and hold me to ransom, they only wanted me to send someone to his mate to sell him a truck!

Stand down pistol, back off one eyed Alsatian Doberman dog, the President is safe, shaken but not stirred – well maybe just a little stirred. I invited the head gardener and his two mates inside for a coffee and a chat about the town and the public gardens. We even talked about Scotland and the long friendship over many centuries between our two countries, it's a subject dear to the hearts of many Frenchmen, it seems. The head gardener was a civilised, cultivated man in blue overalls and he was also an engaging conversationalist and we passed a happy half hour together. Then Francois arrived to take over and organise a visit to the head gardener's pal by a sales man and I settled down to collect myself and to try and calm down.

The vehicle of choice for international assassins and French gardeners.

The moral of the story, well actually there are two morals to this particular story, one is if you look for cars following you on crowded roads like the Periferique then you will surely see them. I also reminded myself, after my third coffee that red, white and blue are the most popular colours for cars, and that both Renault and Volkswagen had healthy shares of the car market. No surprise then I should see such cars appear and reappear on the roads to work in the morning. I think that made me feel better – eventually. The second moral of this story is that the bombing of countries has unintended consequences, not always considered by those who play war games in ivory towers or oval offices.

After I had recovered my equilibrium I called a meeting and I told my colleagues of my briefing from Jim and advised them they should exercise caution. I sheepishly told them of my being chased by the gardener much to the delight of the team. My colleagues were quite sanguine about the possible repercussions from the American raid on Libya and rightly so, but I still exercised caution for a few more weeks before everything went back to normal and I started worrying about the company again and not terrorist groups who may or may not be planning to ambush me.

TALKING TRUCKS AT THE TOWER

April became summer and thoughts of terrorists, kidnapping and ransom notes receded as the demands of life re-emerged and I was soon back to business as normal and the springtime nonsense was forgotten. Every day was a challenge, but in a good way and every day we took the business forward, thoughts of the GM collapse were behind us and to be honest, I never gave the future of the Corporation much thought as I was consumed by the here and now of my European Group. Paris wasn't all about hard work, Isobel and I found ourselves extremely popular with family and friends, all of whom were missing us so much they couldn't wait to visit us in our new home. We had some great times with our visitors and we developed a three day and a five-day tour programme to cram in as much as possible. These tours always included seeing the sights by day, climbing the Tower and if we were lucky to get one of the few clear days to see the magnificent panorama across the Marais, in which Paris sits. The Arc de Triomphe is always popular although most of our friends loved to simply stand and marvel at the craziness of French drivers as they weave through the chaos of the traffic on the Place d'Etoile. The Louvre was always popular and most people were happy to spend a few hours looking at the awesome art on display. Isobel perfected her own routine in the Louvre and could 'do' the great museum in 20 minutes by which time she would be safely ensconced in the café waiting for the rest of us with a magazine and a cup of tea. Everybody who visited Paris, wanted to sample the life of the boulevardier with a stroll along the Champs Elysees.

My French friends insisted that on the Champs Elysees, it was impossible to meet any one who was born in Paris, since everyone was a tourist, a foreigner or a country hick seeking to make their fortune on the gold paved pavements of Paris. We always took our friends to a nice restaurant by night, and it is not difficult to do that, since there are so many fine restaurants with every possible style of cuisine. But perhaps the highlight was a visit to the Tour Eiffel by night, especially in summer. When the night is warm and the lights are on, the Tower is almost magical, and everybody loves it, especially when the water fountains of the Trocadero are on.

One balmy night in August we took some friends into the city which was throbbing with activity and tourists and the Tower looked particularly impressive. There was so much excitement as people marvelled at the sheer extravagance of this monumental structure and queued for hours to ride the elevator to the viewing platforms. As we strolled around there was one family, Mum, Dad and two children taking photographs and I offered to take over from the father of the family so he could join the happy group in the snap. It turned out they were an English family and the Mum had a definite Lancashire accent. After the usual poses, smile for the camera and say cheese routine, and with the snaps safely in the camera we had a chat. During the chat the dad asked me if we were here on holiday as well, when I told him that I lived in Paris he said, "You are very lucky, how did you manage to do that?" I said to him "Well first you have to work for British Leyland for twelve years." To which he replied, "Ok, I've done that, then what?"

I started laughing when he told me he was an engineer with Leyland and worked at the Spurrier factory, named after our founder Sir Henry Spurrier, the pleasures of whose house I had enjoyed so much. We had a long chat about our company and he wanted to know how things were in Europe, as an engineer he wanted to know what trucks we were selling in Europe and about any changes we had to make to accommodate European regulations. As we chatted I could see a bit of a glaze come over his wife's eyes, which I recognised, men who work for Leyland can get passionate about their company. This poor girl had probably thought she had escaped shop talk for a wee while and probably the last things she expected on her visit to the Eiffel Tower was to hear her husband talking about Leyland Trucks. As a parting comment he gently reminded me that he hadn't seen all that many Leyland lorries on his travels through France, I diplomatically reminded him that France was a very large land mass which was four times the size of England, but he would probably see lots on his way to the channel ferries. I guess 5% market share does get lost in such a vast country. But I was with my own guests so I had to leave my UK colleague with a story to share back at the farm of how he had met the President of Leyland Europe at the Eiffel Tower in Paris. I returned to my own friends and family to continue our own tour of Paris.

MOONLIGHT ON THE SEINE

As summer gave way to autumn, it was time for reflection and for the annual exhibitions across the whole of the continental land mass. First up was a conference for our dealers from France, Belgium and Luxembourg. Francois and Alain Gignoux put together an extraordinary event. This would be a great chance to congratulate the network on a great performance, in 18 months the company and its fortunes had been completely turned round, things were going very well and the fields of trucks were now no more than a distant a memory and we were long since back to ordering new product from the UK factories. Although this conference was primarily for our dealers and our sales team we took the opportunity of inviting a sprinkling of customers and potential customers, to join the Leyland Family on this important occasion. The closer manufacturers can be to their customers the stronger are the silken threads that keep you bound together.

The conference would be held on the largest of the Bateaux-Mouches and we would sail up and down the Seine while taking the opportunity to review our first full year performance, unveil our new targets, incentives and opportunities for the next twelve months and schmooze with our friends. I would make a state of the nation speech and Francois and Alain would do a double act on Sales Targets and Incentives and Marketing Initiatives, one of our dealers would also speak. After the speeches it would be time for dinner and after dinner it would be time for dancing to the orchestra, it promised to be quite a night and I had invited some colleagues from the UK to see how dealer events should be done. I was very confident that my UK colleagues would be impressed, Francois and Alain were very good at this sort of thing.

So it was all in place and I had written my speech which I spent a lot of time rehearsing, because when speaking in a foreign language you can be so absorbed in getting the pronunciation right that you lose the emotion and the speech is "flat" as a consequence. Although I was competent in French and able to converse socially and in technical discussions I was desperately aware of my Scottish accent much more when speaking French than when speaking English. So I was now at the stage of practicing emotion and getting the timing and punch lines for my two jokes correct. There was one passage in the speech where my accent seemed to be getting in the way of what I was trying to get across. I was walking up and own in my ballroom of an office I had inherited when in a fit of frustration, I threw my speech to the ground, and at that very moment Francois Lacoste came into my office, just as my speech was bouncing across the floor. Francois, looked very surprised, I wasn't given to fits of temper being a pretty placid person, at least most of the time. He said "Owen what is wrong why are you angry with the papers?" Lacoste had a literal way of speaking and a great knack for articulating the ridiculous in a way that let you understand just how ridiculous it was. Of course I wasn't angry with the papers I was angry with myself or at least with the sound of my accent. "Francois", I said "I am butchering your beautiful, elegant language, with my thick Scottish tongue. Whenever I speak I can hear my Scottish accent sounding so strong. Nobody will get the message I am trying to get across."

At this Francois looked at me and smiled, and his smile was wicked, whenever we travelled together he had women spellbound with his Gallic charm, he is the quintessential French smoothie. So Francois, of the charming smile said, "But Owen, what do the English roses think when they hear a Frenchman speaking English with a French accent?" this was a rhetorical question to no one but himself, and without waiting for a response he went on "of course they think it is very sexy." He stood back and looked at me, and he had me smiling now at the silliness of it all and because I had a pretty good idea of what was coming next. "Patron, when the French Roses hear you speaking French with your fine Scottish accent *zey weel zink eet is verreeeee sexxxeee.*

Zeee French roses love the warrior cry that you Scoteeesh call speaking," he said in his best parody of a Franglais accent.

What he was really saying was that my accent was authentic, and that was more important than me trying to sound French, and anyway it was what my dealers would have expected of me when I spoke at the conference. What a man, he knew exactly how to change the mood and had me laughing and more importantly I was now secure with my Scottish accent when speaking French, a smart man. I felt better for that interlude and stopped worrying about how I sounded and concentrated on getting the emotion right. The dealer conference was a great success, the speeches were well received, the esprit de corps was enhanced, the feel good factor was soaring and my colleagues from the UK were pretty impressed with the way we Frenchies did things.

JEROME'S BARMITZVAH

After the dealer conference we had a brief respite before the hectic period of the Paris Motor Show, the famous Salon Mondial. But before that there was time to enjoy a charming interlude when we were invited to a very special celebration by one of our customers. One of the features of a professional sales team is the relationships forged with customers, if your clients know you are always prepared to go an extra yard to make sure their experience is top drawer you can build a relationship of trust, and we established those relationships. Such customers become your strongest advocates, your best ambassadors, and some can even become firm friends, and you get invited to share their special moments and when you are invited by a Frenchman to a family functions this is a sure sign of being accepted. One such customer was Transam, a parcel delivery company with a large fleet of 7.5 tonne Roadrunners, the truck in whose development and launch I had been so involved. This company had been won over by Don MacIntosh, Francois Lacoste's right hand man. Don was born in Yorkshire of Scottish parents and had spent his University years and much of his adult life, living and working in francophone countries. Don was one of the best, most intuitive salesmen I have ever met, he had a great grasp of the French language from the street to the boardroom and this skill allied to his charismatic personality and red hair and beard, contributed to his great success in selling trucks.

The owners of the Transam Company were two brothers, they were Jewish and had been born in Tunisia before moving to France and building a great business. The brothers trusted Don implicitly and as a result the two companies became very close and we worked hard to make sure they knew how much we appreciated them and their business. It was a good relationship thanks to Don, and I felt very honoured when he appeared in my office one day to tell me I would be getting an invitation to a very special occasion, the Bar Mitzvah of Jerome the eldest son of the older brother. The invitation included the whole family, Isobel, Nick and Carrie as well as me. Francois and his wife Marie were also invited but Don had declined to attend (I'm still not sure why) but insisted on briefing Francois and I on the protocol of the Bar Mitzvah. We both knew Don was not above a practical joke so we triangulated his briefing with advice from Alain Gignoux, since Alain was an orthordox Jew and his input was more secure. This was indeed a great honour on two levels, firstly to be invited into this sacred celebration which meant so much to the family and to Jerome, and secondly because it was one of the great social occasions on the Parisian Calendar that year and the paparazzi were out in force. The celebration was held in the Intercontinental hotel in Avenue Morceau in the 8th Arrondissement, one of the better hotels in Paris at the time, vying with the Bristol on Rue du Faubourg Saint-Honoré and the Georges Cinque, on the corner of the Champs-Élysees. It was a very nice hotel and no doubt an expensive location to celebrate with 200 guests. When we arrived we felt like celebrities as we walked across the red carpet laid out for the event, actually it wasn't really for us at all, it was for Jerome, still it was nice to walk on that red carpet.

Isobel looked stunning in a little French number, a yellow silk suit, quite ravishing. Nick was 10 years-old and he looked very French having been kitted out in the best that Galeries Lafayette had to offer. He was wearing black watch tartan trousers, black jacket, white shirt and tan leather tie, very grown up. Carrie at the age of 7 looked beautiful in her Alice-in-wonderland, inspired dress in white with red accessories, and her glorious long blonde hair shining in the evening light. I was extremely proud of my family, we scrubbed up well. We were greeted warmly by Jerome and his father then a waiter escorted Isobel and I to our table, Nicholas left with Jerome and found he was to be at the top table and the only boy at the top table who was not Jewish and not a native French speaker, but he conducted himself with great aplomb. Carrie was taken off to a table with other younger children in the care of two nurses who would be their chaperones for the evening and help them through the details of this religious ceremony and the accompanying celebrations.

Clan Quinn arriving to celebrate with Jerome

Isobel and I were at a table with Francois and Marie and the older of the two brothers, this was one more lovely gesture from the family. The organisation of this celebration was impeccable and I grew more impressed as the night wore on at the way this religious ceremony unfolded. After we had some starters and drinks the ceremony proper began and it was all captured on film and broadcast live on large screens around the ballroom. I had never been to a Bar Mitzvah and I was fascinated to learn more. The proceedings began with Jerome being called out, he entered the ballroom through a Huge Star of David, which parted to show billowing dry smoke and Jerome then stepped through wearing his prayer shawl. The format was that there would be a reading from the Torah, tailored to Jerome, who would then take the corner of his prayer shawl and kiss the scroll, he then said something which I could not follow. Then there would be a clip from the Hollywood movie, The Ten Commandments, starring Charlton Heston, the guests would then eat something, have a sip of their drink as we toasted Jerome.

After the toast we would get up and dance and sing songs which most guests seemed to know the words of, it was easy to spot the non-Jewish guests, they were the ones miming to the lyrics. As the night of dancing and singing progressed there was only one song that I knew the words to and that was Hava Ngila, which is no great feat since there are only seven words in the song. On one occasion when I was miming to yet another raucous song, a nice lady, clearly a Gentile who was beside me on the dance floor picked up on the lyrics of the song and began to sing in a beautiful voice, "C'est la Vie, C'est la vie" only to be told off by a slightly insulted Jewish guest who pointed out that the correct lyric was actually Tel Aviv, Tel Aviv – oops. The ceremony continued like this for almost two hours and it was a magnificent way for a young man to mark his progress in the ancient faith of his ancestors. Jerome's family had spared no expense to make it memorable for him and their two hundred guests in one of the best restaurants in one of the best cities in the world. The emotion in the room was palpable, this was an important and beautiful ceremony to mark Jerome's passage from childhood to adulthood and was laden with symbolism, it was very moving and many of the guest were moved to tears.

The meal itself was sensational but in the middle we had a minor crisis. While the children were being entertained by the nurses they had each been given one of those luminous bands that glow in the dark which at the time were very popular with the street sellers in Paris. These bands can be fastened around your head or your wrist or even your ankle but Carrie had decided to open her band to see what caused it to glow in the dark. The result was that she ended up getting the liquid in her eyes which started to sting, so the nurses came and informed us. While they were explaining what happened Marie Lacoste took matters into her own hands, she cleared a table and laid Carrie out on top of it, organised a bowl of water and some clean napkins and proceeded to bathe her eyes until she had removed the offending liquid. Marie is a very self-assured, super confident lady with a terrific no-nonsense approach to things. While the Bar Mitzvah was both a sacred and spectacular celebration it was also a very enjoyable evening for those present as well as Jerome and his family. In addition, it cemented the already strong bond that existed between our two businesses Transam SA and Leyland Vehicules Industriels SA.

Business is truly about more than mere profit and loss.

CHAPTER NINE

AU REVOIR ET A BIENTÔT

Jerome's Bar Mitzvah was a chance to relax after the high energy dealer conference, which was a signal to the world of trucks that we were serious about the business and we had reason to be trumpeting our success to the world. The first eighteen months had sped past but in that time we had made substantial progress across the entire market in France as well as within Benelux and our sales figures were the best they had ever been. We were no longer being excluded from deals on the basis of financing, CECICO had plugged that gap. We were visible at local shows and dealer exhibitions right across France, Belgium and Luxembourg. We sponsored the truck Grand Prix events, especially the French GP at Circuit Ricard in Marseilles, we were all over the mags with lots of copy and many featured stories placed by us. Alain Gignoux had secured the sponsorship of the Les Routiers Guide to dining and accommodation for truckers and tourists, which was a great way to get our truck range in front of every trucker that was looking for a place to have lunch. Our improved image and our sales success had some manufacturers concerned, especially the market leader. We had set out to create a much higher profile and I was very pleased with the results.

We had been working hard to re-establish a profile for our company because for far too long we had been an anonymous participant in the truck industry in Europe. That was not our intention, it was simply a result of our actions to contain costs and reverse the nonsense and extravagance of earlier regimes. My predecessor was a good man but he had a fixed attitude toward what was needed in the business, coloured by the wild excesses of the regime before him, where in an attempt to woo dealers, money was being thrown at projects, with little to show in return for such 'investment'. He was not alone in this assessment, at the conference on the Bateau, our dealer in Normandy told me that one of the Business Development managers in the old regime was known as 'Pere Noel' because of his largesse.

While at the start of his tenure it was necessary for strict controls, he allowed the austerity to carry on far too long. In trying to steady the ship and curb the excesses his actions resulted in us literally becoming anonymous, we withdrew from shows, exhibitions, advertising and any kind of profiling activity. He had, however chosen to make his cuts in the worst possible part of the business, in our sales effort and the more we lost market share the more he cut costs, and the more he cut costs the more market share we lost. The business was dying on its feet and yet he could not see that, and stubbornly refused to change tack.

The fact that neither we nor the dealers were making any money as we were filling French fields with trucks, didn't register somehow. While this policy may have saved money at the overhead level, it was catastrophic on the bottom line, with revenue falling through the floor the business was making huge losses. Then there was the further effect that with reduced in-field activity our company was becoming anonymous. He probably felt isolated and in such a position it's easy to act irrationally and perhaps to fall back on things you know you can control, as I said earlier he was a bright and clever man but he had lost his was way, unfortunately.

As a result of the locally imposed austerity programme the company had no visibility, we did not attend shows or exhibitions we did not even create any basic advertising other than free copy blagged by Alain Gignoux. If you are anonymous how does anyone know you are open for business and what, if anything you have to sell? I did not get a chance to speak to my predecessor to find out what was in his mind, and when I asked my new colleagues they responded with their normal Gallic shrugs. The most I got was "it was so, because it was so, he was the boss and that is what he wanted so that is what we did." But someone had to authorise the renting of all those fields from farmers and to organise the delivery companies to take our nice trucks form the docks to those Norman fields.

PARIS SALON

For years we had maintained a low profile on the Continent but from now on we would be we attending all the motor shows. Truck motor shows are fiercely competitive places where all the tactics of the battlefield are distilled into a frenetic two-week period and the show halls see grand strategies played out to score points over the competition. The Paris Salon was full of salesmen bragging and making Munchhausen type claims such as, "We have had 250 new customers on our stand and it is not yet lunch time" to be met with, "Oh really we have sold 10,000 trucks since Monday." All salesmen jealously guard their clients and are always on the lookout to ensure their clients are not being poached by the opposition while trying to woo new clients, a case of "It's ok for me to steal your customers but you keep your eyes off mine, or else." Salesmen are also the biggest gossipers in the world and rumours are constantly sweeping the halls, not only about who is buying from whom but on the much more important matters like which manufacturer has the best food or the best-looking girls on their stand, or who has secured the biggest celebrity to come and visit them. For two weeks the show halls are testosterone fuelled as salesmen grapple for dominance.

In terms of the scale of spending on the show stands Renault were in a league of their own and went to great lengths to ensure they dominated 'their own' show. They had all sorts of celebrities to meet and greet their customers and to impress the impressionable, but they also had some really impressive stuff like two-star Michelin Chefs cooking lunch for the guests of their directors, now that is impressive. We could not compete with this level of outlay and did not try to, so for us it was important to be innovative. Of course, for the UK Motor Show in Birmingham

Leyland spent big as well on 'our' show and we went to great lengths to dominate the event. But we never even thought about providing decent food let alone two-star Michelin grub, the best we could stretch to was stale sandwiches and dreadful tea. Even that modest level of catering cost an arm and a leg, I remember that everything had to be rented from the show organisers and for example to rent a saucer for a teacup cost about £20 for a fortnight, so the cost of the exhibition could easily surpass the million-pound mark and often did.

At the Paris Show, *Le Salon Mondial de l'Automobile*, we had a wonderfully inventive stand with a golf ball structure mimicking La Géode, a mirror-finished dome that houses an Omnimax theatre in Parc de la Villette at the Cité des Sciences et de l'Industrie in the 19th arrondissement of Paris. The dealers loved the stand and their salesmen used it to very good effect, it was understated, chic and classy, very French, once again thanks to Alain and Francois. It did wonders for our image and was well received by the press. There were many comments about the fact that we had returned to be part of the industry and it saddened me to think of the damage done to our reputation under previous regimes. The French market in particular must have wondered what we were up to, introducing a formidable brand new range of trucks underpinned by crazy spending, followed by a period of extreme austerity, which caused the company and its products to disappear from view. The French industry probably thought of us as a bunch of amateurs and it's fair to say that we had conducted ourselves with significantly less professionalism than we did in our home market. It's amazing how much harm we can cause when we think we are doing the very opposite

In a relaxed mood with a nice Frenchman talking trucks

I had made sure the world or at least France now knew we were definitely open for business and I wanted to make a flourish at the Paris Show, one of the biggest in the world. By the time of the Paris show, Sir Michael Edwardes had moved on and we had a new Chief Executive Officer, Mr Graham Day, a Canadian by birth, and a week before the show his office called me to let me know he would be at the show, I was glad we made the effort, with our stand. When he arrived we discovered he was a fluent French speaker, albeit with an accent as curious as mine (almost). He spent an hour with us and was very complimentary about our stand and my team. I introduced him to some of our most senior dealers and to some high profile customers and he charmed them, they were delighted. Then I got something of a surprise, Directeur International of Renault, Marc Villemonte de la Clergerie appeared on our stand and introduced himself to me, saying that he had heard M Day was visiting and would it be possible for me to introduce him. I was taken aback because this man was a real heavy hitter in the world of European Trucks. Naturally I introduced him to my boss and he was knocked out by Graham Day chatting to him in French, it seems that Graham and the Chairman of Renault knew each other and M Villemonte de la Clergerie told Graham his own Chairman was on the Renault stand and would like to invite Graham and I to lunch, telling us that the Chef of the day was Francois Le Notre, a celebrated cook in Paris with a big reputation.

Such civilised behaviour, this would never have happened at the UK motor show, but unfortunately we were unable to accept the invitation since Graham Day had an appointment in Paris which he could not break. When he had called me to say he would be in Paris for the show I realised this was not his only gig, but I didn't know where he was going. What intrigue, I guess he was so busy he probably just forgot to brief me! My boss hung around for a little while and then went off to his next appointment leaving me wondering what the heck was going on, there are times when even a President needs to know his place in the grand scheme of things.

Motor shows follow a similar pattern the world over, which is usually about talking yourself hoarse to anyone prepared to stop for a moment, being unrelentingly optimistic about everything and everyone all the time. Every evening after the show we had a large table reserved at a little Bistro where we could have a simple meal and catch up on the events of the day. This was also very civilised and helped to bind us altogether as a solid team sharing meals, stories and jokes. Salesmen are a great source of jokes and we had a couple of great gag tellers, the best of whom was a man called Bernard Manquin who lived near Montpellier and covered the south of France for us. Bernard had a vast fund of jokes and once he was on a roll there was no stopping him and he kept us amused each night. Francois Lacoste asked me if we did this round up at the end of the day during the UK Motor Show, and I shared a story with my team, of an incident at the UK Motor Show.

One of my colleagues in the UK was a man named John Ball who ran the English Midlands and South Wales patch for Leyland. John and I shared Stand Manager duties at the Motor Show in Birmingham and one night after the show we decided to treat our colleagues by buying them a Chinese meal in a nearby restaurant. The restaurant was in the town of Shirley and was called the Shirley Temple and it had a great reputation, according to John Ball who said he had dined there often. I suggested John should reserve a table for all fourteen and I would organise the taxis and off I went to my hotel room to change. Half an hour later I was in the first taxi and on my way to the restaurant, where they had reserved a nice round table with a lazy Susan in the middle, for Mr Ball's party of fourteen, expressing surprise that we were a wee bit early. John and the rest of the crew arrived and we ordered our meal and amid a lot of laughing, I congratulated John on booking this fine restaurant when he said "I thought you had booked it." I laughed and passed it off as one of John's jokes until about forty-five minutes later when another Mr Ball arrived with his thirteen friends for whom he had reserved a table in the Shirley Temple. Oops! No amount of explaining or showing business cards would convince the other Mr Ball that this could possibly be a mistake but it was. What an incredible coincidence, there were two Mr Balls each with a party of fourteen looking for a Chinese meal on a wet Tuesday in October in the small town of Shirley. We bought the aggrieved Mr Ball and his friends a round of drinks, apologised profusely and then left early so they could move to the table they had reserved, that was the last time I had a meal with John Ball.

One aspect that I did not find evident in the Paris Show was the 'anoraks'. At the UK shows we always had crowds of people who were not truck buyers but simply truck enthusiasts, people who knew every truck by every manufacturer going back to the dawn of time. Anoraks are always keen to discuss trucks in fine detail to display their own knowledge. These are harmless souls who collect every truck brochure and specification sheet on the stand and hoard them in vast collections. Harmless though they are they regrettably take up valuable time which is ok if the stand is quiet but they have a knack of arriving together with important people who want to buy trucks and then they can be a real nuisance. I guess truck anoraks are a UK phenomenon. As always at shows I took time out to take in the rest of the show, to see what others had on offer and what we should be looking out for in the months and years to come. Sadly, there was nothing much to get excited about, with the possible exception of a Fiat vehicle with an innovative frame and another with some fancy futuristic gadgets including a series of cameras to aid parking. I spent some time on the DAF stand speaking to my friend Pascal Mantoux, who was the boss of DAF France, there were a lot of Dutchmen keen to have a chat, it seems most of the company was in Paris for this show.

Pascal was keen to introduce me to a number of his colleagues from the Eindhoven headquarters, it is always a pleasure speaking with Dutch people they are such gifted linguists. One of the engineering managers, a guy called Harry Rheingold, asked me to guess what DAF were making during World War Two, when I told him I did not know he replied, "Nothing, we hadn't been established yet." Harry thought that was the funniest joke he had ever heard and he laughed loud and long at his witticism, and then he told me that DAF had started to build vehicles from kits of parts sold to them by Leyland Motors. I would reflect on this conversation in the not too distant future. In the meantime, I moved on to have a look at some of the other stands and leave my Dutch friends to their Dutch humour.

The Paris Show was a great triumph on so many levels, and by the end the dealers and the sales team had forged strong links with each other and with the many customers we welcomed onto our stand. By the time the show finished we were all pretty tired but exhilarated with the sheer number of customers we had welcomed. The triumph of the Salon following the successful dealer conference was a great boost to the team and just reward for hard work and creativity, and we were having a bit of fun as we succeeded in our mission to sell British trucks to the Europeans.

The Leyland Team at the end of the Salon

There was no sign of the gloomy subdued atmosphere I encountered on arrival rather there was a real buzz about the place and people were happy at their work. At the time of my arrival not many of our competitors took us seriously, we were just a little side show not likely to cause much trouble. But our mini league of nations banded together well and we were committed to the success of our project and soon the competition started to take notice of us. Sometimes taking notice evolved into being a wee bit upset when we pinched customers from the market leaders.

THE CROWN PRINCE TALKS TRUCKS

After our success at the Paris Motor Show we would exhibit at the Brussels Show in late 1986. This show was organised by Marc Lories who was Sales Director for our Benelux operation. Marc was a multi-lingual man who loved all things Belgian and was devoted to his football team Standard Liege and to cycling. He liked what we had been doing in France and felt that a similar programme would be effective in the Benelux countries. As well as picking up the French initiatives, Marc being a proud Belgian wanted his own stamp on everything we did and he convinced me that one of the best things we could do to promote our name in Belgium was to support his local cycling club who were champions of Belgium. We agreed a two-year sponsorship package and the champion cyclists proudly carried the name of Leyland on their kit and equipment in all the major cycling events around Europe.

Marc ran a small team out of Mechelen where we had a large site, most of which had been mothballed for many years, and when we exhibited at the Brussels Show there was no prouder man in all of Belgium than Marc Lories. Marc was beside himself with pleasure when Crown Prince Bernhard came on to our stand for a chat, accompanied by a large entourage of press, TV reporters and assorted paparazzi. The Prince remained on the stand for a short time and was interested in our products and our re-emergence in the Belgian Market, he had obviously been well briefed, by someone. Marc was walking on air for weeks afterwards, which surprised me a little because he could be quite cynical about a lot of things but clearly not about the Royal House of Belgium.

The Crown Prince of Belgium and a visibly delighted Marc

While in Paris I continued to be disciplined regarding my work life balance and although I worked long hours during the week, I made sure that the weekends were devoted to Isobel, Nicholas and Carrie. As a result, our family life was wonderful, the children were settled and liked their school, they were involved in sports and other pastimes and we spent weekends exploring the cities and countryside of France. We tended to dine out a lot which meant the children were well socialised and loved French food. Carrie adapted to life in France particularly well, and enjoyed the whole social razzmatazz. One rainy, blustery night we were dining in a local restaurant, Le Parasol and we dashed from the car to the ante – room where Isobel, Nicholas and I took off our coats, hung them up and went through to the restaurant. I turned to see Carrie standing in her wet coat and asked if she was ok, "Yes, Daddy", came the reply, "I am just waiting for the wee man to come and take my coat." Carrie adapted well to life in France. Our social life was wonderful and we grew ever closer as a family as a consequence of spending so much time together.

Eighteen months into the job and I was happy with the way things were going with the business and by the winter of 1986 there was a feel good factor about the place, we were doing well, sales were through the roof (comparatively) and we were actually short of stock, every time we set a target our sales team delighted in beating it. But I knew only too well that my company was something of a political football because the UK Government had that controlling interest in the British Leyland Group. The Prime Minister, Margaret Thatcher was no fan of state owned enterprises and throughout 1986 the UK newspapers were filled with speculation about the company, no doubt as a result of briefings or 'leaks' from well-placed sources. This is a normal pattern in the

UK when the Government decides it wishes to do something that might cause controversy, some flunky will brief a friendly journo and then deny everything, dismissing it as mischievous speculation. Politicians are such obvious creatures, thankfully the speculation did not impact on what we were doing in France, at least not then.

In 1986 the group decided it was in need of yet another name change. We became 'The Rover Group Plc', and it looked like we were gearing up to make ourselves more attractive to a potential buyer. The talk around the group was that we were having problems finding someone interested in a deal that included the group as a whole and there was a feeling that the negatives associated with the BL name were not helping the cause. The Truck division fancied jumping into bed with Paccar the American manufacturer which already owned Foden, the constructor based in Sandbach, Cheshire. For my own part, there was nothing I could do to influence the proceedings and as far as I was concerned all this politicking about selling the group was in another time and another place, I had become utterly absorbed in driving European Operations forward and didn't waste much time worrying about potential suitors. I was not involved in any negotiations and only those on a need to know basis were included in the briefings and that was literally a handful of people. If you can't influence the deal don't fret about it.

On 2nd December 1986, Paul Channon, President of the Board of Trade and a Cabinet Minister announced in the House of

Commons that that Rover Group was holding discussions with DAF Trucks Ltd, the Dutch Manufacturer in relation to Leyland Trucks and Freight Rover, and separately with Paccar in relation to the truck company. Didn't see that one coming, did DAF have the wherewithal to absorb a business like ours, they were a niche player without much of a profile, outside Holland. Paccar, however was a different kettle of fish and everybody in the company, myself included, was very much in favour of such an alliance.

As we left for the Christmas and New Year break, there was much to think about.

CHRISTMAS 1986

Our social life was excellent the whole time we lived in Paris and over winter that meant events with the group of expatriates whose children attended the British school of Paris. We had a very nice circle of friends and the social occasions were always high spirited and lots of fun, it seems to be the way with expats. I suspect that the type of person attracted to the expat lifestyle is the same type who likes a high octane social life. And at Christmas 1986 I was glad that we had such a busy social life to help me put thoughts of deals with other companies to the back of my mind. It was decided by the British School of Paris social committee that the 1986 Christmas do, would feature a tableau performed by the fathers of the children, who had been conspicuous by their absence from previous events. As an incentive to recalcitrant fathers it was reported that the mothers would be performing an outrageously scandalous can-can routine and that we would have to share dressing rooms.

So a group of us got together for discussions on what to do at the home of the chair of the Social Committee, Geoff Litchfield. Having been compelled to do something we tossed a few ideas about and eventually came up with the idea of doing a comedy revue, because we were a bunch of 'jokers' in more ways than one. The revue would be a combination of The European Song Contest and The Wheeltappers and Shunters Social Club and it would be called 'The Worst Joke in Europe'. The revue would be introduced and controlled by a Chairman, who would be Geordie Scotsman, Derek Hall, his lovely assistant, a London Irishman, Bill Barry and a clapometer, an Englishman Ray Applegate in a superb cardboard construction. The format was that the chairman would introduce the acts, the lovely assistant brought the contestants on stage and interviewed them. The lovely assistant was a sight to behold in a ball gown with plunging décolletage revealing an extremely hairy chest and a very large and prominent tattoo of a windjammer sailing ship. The bright red lipstick and flowing auburn tresses combined to create an effect that would not have been out of place in the bar at the end of the universe and which might have got Bill into trouble with the sailing mates with whom he spent his youth, before becoming International VP, Finance for Dow Chemical worldwide. In addition to Derek, Bill and Ray the cast for this extravaganza was:

Alastair Young, a Scotsman who would play a French waiter, complete with stripy shirt, beret and curly moustache, who uttered the immortal line, 'no you cannot have any more eggs because everybody knows that one egg is un oeuf'

Ian Crawford, an Englishman with a great line in patter, who would play a bewildered bowler hatted, business man wondering what the hell he was doing in this world.

Geoff Litchfield, an Englishman who would play the 'Hey you, Jimmy' character complete with kilt and braces, red wig and an interesting accent. Geoff asked one well coiffured lady if she had come on a motorbike, to much audience hilarity.

Davie Brown, a Scotsman who would play an Irishman with his wellies on the wrong feet, despite the L and R to distinguish them'. Davie reminisced about how he got confused on his first day on a building site when shown three shovels and told to take his pick.

Owen Quinn, a Scotsman playing a German, who told the story of a cultured English speaking German in London who asked for two martinis for him and his mate and got angry when the barman asked 'dry?' to which he replied 'nein dummkoff zwei'

The six weeks of so called rehearsal actually turned in to a one-man comedy show and we were the audience while Davie Brown had us in stitches with monologues, stories and outrageous jokes, it was a hoot. Those weekly meetings in Geoff's house were unbelievably funny, we would all be drinking Geoff's beer as we rolled around laughing as Davie moved smoothly and skilfully through his repertoire until we were sore laughing. In his capacity as chairman, Derek eventually asserted his authority and had us buckle down to getting our scripts sorted out and acquiring our outfits, in my case a German Officers Uniform, with long black boots, wee round John Lennon type gold glasses and a Groucho Marx moustache of black insulating tape, oh dear!

The night of the show was hilarious as we crowded into our dressing cupboard pushing and jostling as we tried to sort our sequence of entry. There was a lot of last minute rehearsing going on but the only person suffering from stage fright was Ray Applegate. Ray would spend the entire show inside a large cardboard box and spin an arrow to show how bad each joke was according to the audience reaction. Ray's concern was not about forgetting his lines or being overwhelmed by the audience his was more a costume concern. Ray had decided that the clapometer was a bit claustrophobic and likely to be extremely hot when the audience took their seats; he wondered if he should remove all his clothing, and wear only swimming trunks.

When Alastair suggested he might scare the stage cat not to mention the can-can dancers, Ray insisted he had a perfectly sculpted body the highlight of which was a magnificent abdominal six–pack - or so he said. Ray said it was only a question of not wishing to embarrass the rest of us in front of our wives. While this discussion was taking place, I practised goose-stepping in my knee high boots borrowed from one of the ladies, and I can tell you it is not easy goose-stepping in stiletto heels. Had German soldiers been compelled to wear boots with stiletto heels, they may have looked a wee bit less scary. There was such a lot of noise back stage as the guys ogled and teased the ladies in their frilly petticoats as they practised their high kicks. The ladies were very composed and frighteningly focussed while the guys kept yelling for the make-up girls.

Then the show started with the school choir singing a charming selection of Christmas carols, followed by the orchestra going through its paces. When the ladies came on the place went wild, it could have been Paris in the Belle Époque, with men making a spectacle of themselves raising glasses in toast to the dancers while others merely raised their glasses to get a better view. Then it was the turn of the fathers to go through their routines, the audience laughed and groaned at the appropriate times and gave us a rousing reception.

Then it was all over, and we were all rather pleased with ourselves, although Bill Barry in a plunging neckline revealing a hairy chest and a square rigger ship tattoo, haunts me to this day. The clapometer decided that the worst Joke in Europe award would go to Ian Crawford for his portrayal of a bemused

Englishman trying to come to terms with life in France. As I recall Ian did not actually tell any jokes, he merely made observations about the nature of life but his performance was remarkably insightful and deserving of an award.

DID YOU SAY DAF?

After the roar of the grease paint at the British School of Paris annual show Isobel, Nicholas, Carrie and I returned to Scotland for a few days over Christmas to visit family and recharge our batteries. We enjoyed that Christmas holiday very much and then we headed back to Paris in time for New Year. For my company the New Year started in the same manner as the old one ended with an announcement that the commercial business was being broken up, and my friends Ian McKinnon, Ric Turner and George Newburn had led a Management Buy Out of Leyland Bus.

Then on 19 February 1987 Paul Channon, President of the Board of Trade made another announcement in the House of Commons, 'Following these negotiations, Rover Group and DAF have proposed that Leyland Trucks, DAF Trucks and Freight Rover, shall combine to form a new Anglo-Dutch joint venture. As recommended by the Rover Group board, the Government have accepted these proposals, which create a company with the capability to achieve a major presence in the European commercial vehicle market.' He went on to say that the new company would be 60% owned by DAF and 40% by Rover Group and that the merger would lead to the loss of 2,260 jobs at Leyland, with the closure of one of its three remaining UK factories. This would almost certainly be the Bathgate Plant and would be a massive blow to the region and to Scotland in general. There would also be a 'slimming' programme at the Leyland site in Lancashire, at the engine plant in and the foundry.

This was dreadful news we were being condemned to death by a thousand cuts. With Bus gone and now trucks gone the company was a shadow of its former self and the rest of the business, (Car Operations and Range Rover) would remain as they were, at least for the time being. I wasn't surprised at the truck announcement just at the partner, because I knew the nature of our relationship with the government but I was very, very disappointed most of all for my team and my customers across mainland Europe. The big surprise was that it should be DAF that became the preferred 'partner' since they were very small compared to Leyland. Had it been one of the bigger names in the industry it might have been more understandable. In this merger billed as 60/40 ownership arrangement with DAF the dominant partner, this little Dutch company took control of Leyland Trucks factories across the UK, The Leyland International Business with major factories in Africa and Asia, the Freight Rover Van Business, and the massive Leyland Parts Business. Hopefully there would be the necessary substance within the company to manage such a large undertaking, because in many mergers, the 'losing side' usually suffer major casualties within their senior management ranks, and I expected this merger would be no different in that regard.

The DAF Chairman Mr Aart van der Padt had consistently made it clear that he saw no future in his company owning overseas assembly plants to build DAF trucks. What he envisaged was a series of related plants, largely owned within their own countries, building DAF designed products suited to each market, and trading components with each other. The last thing DAF wanted was any more assembly capacity of its own. So what changed? "Basically", says van der Padt, "we didn't know that in expansion we would touch on this opportunity to gain, at a stroke, Leyland's share of the British market". Van der Padt still quotes economist Peter Drucker in setting out his basic philosophy: "It's better to own a market than a mill." He goes on to say: "The UK market and Leyland's share of it, that's the interest," but points out there was one major problem in acquiring that share: DAF could not add 10,000 units to its existing assembly capacity, so to take on Leyland's home market share, it had to take on Leyland's brand new main assembly plant. The Freight Rover operation was a no brainer for a company with no presence in the van market sectors.

It is easy to see that the DAF Chairman considered that his company had won first prize in the lottery without even buying a ticket. This was an interesting analysis offered by the Chairman of DAF, but I don't think there would have been too many at Leylandians that felt as happy as he did about this 'merger'.

Reaction was swift and most of it was not good, opposition MPs were uniformly hostile to the proposals, Coventry North-East MP George Park said that it would have made more sense for the merger to have taken place in the reverse direction, given that Leyland Vehicles were the market leaders. Channon retorted that option was simply not on offer. "I am convinced that we shall see a much stronger commercial vehicle industry. The Government's own MPs representing Midland constituencies were the Government's fiercest critics during the abortive Leyland/GM talks, ironically they were now only too pleased to see the Leyland DAF merger go through, leaving other Rover Group companies in their own constituencies relatively untouched. A case of Pork Barrel politics in action. Major customers of Leyland preferred the Paccar option to provide long term stability and a global perspective. The decision to merge the company with DAF would help other British manufacturers like Foden and ERF, both of which were based in Sandbach in Cheshire. The union response was pretty muted since by this time the union movement had been neutered by Mrs Thatcher's industrial relations policies.

Even in the days before we had news on a 24/7 basis on a multitude of TV channels, the news of the 'merger' travelled quickly across Europe, it seemed as though everyone had been tuned to BBC radio, as in the war. My colleagues were worried as to what would happen to the company and naturally the first thing on most minds was "how this would affect me, will I have a job at the end of all this?" Quickly followed by "How will it affect our customers, what will become of our products, what about warranty on our trucks and what about spares and servicing who will do that?" Very soon the phones were ringing off the hook with a thousand questions and not an answer in sight, not a single bloody answer, we could only make soothing noises. Our customers, our dealers and our employees needed to be told what was going on, insofar as we could do that. With Lacoste and Gignoux I cobbled together a statement that everyone at HQ could relay to anyone who called them. It was pretty bland but it did say that all promises would be kept, and I knew that in making such a pledge, I was being optimistic to say the least. If truth is the first victim of war it is also the first victim of mergers.

The day after the announcement I was called back to the UK for urgent talks on how to make all this happen, and for a briefing on what and when we should tell those with an interest in this change in our business, the employees, the dealers and most of all, our customers. After two days in conference I was no wiser than when I arrived back in the UK but I did know that this would all happen as quickly as possible and nobody was holding out much hope for any of our mainland operations surviving the impending cull. I returned to Paris and prepared some fuller briefing documents and called our main dealers and our major customers. We tried to re-assure them by telling them that for the time being it was business as usual, our service and parts operation would still be functioning and orders which had been placed would be delivered. It came as no surprise that some customers with orders wanted to cancel and we were able to do that small service for them. More surprisingly was how many customers wanted to take receipt of trucks they had on order. That was humbling and more than we deserved.

I called round the regional offices and briefed my colleagues, called the HQ staff together and addressed them on the state of play. Lacoste and McIntosh called every dealer and briefed them from our prepared documents. In truth we did not have very much to say because there had been no real decisions made beyond the fact that DAF would absorb all Continental operations, and the Leyland name would disappear while in the UK there would be a merger of sorts, with both brands being marketed.

In the end it was as simple as that DAF took over everything and Leyland ceased to have a presence on mainland Europe. Some dealers and employees had worked for and with Leyland in its various manifestations for 30 years and now, with a single announcement from a politician obsessed with dogma it was over. The boss of DAF in France, Pascal Mantoux and I had become close friends, socialising together with our wives, and that helped the transition in France, but I had absolutely no input to what was likely to happen in any of the other European countries. Pascal and I continued to work together cordially trying to gauge what they wanted to do, and what if anything the DAF hierarchy wanted to retain from the Leyland structure. As it turned out they did not want anything to do with the Leyland Trucks infrastructure because they already had their own organisation in place, why upset that? But in the end, after much arguing, I was able to make a case for some of our dealers to be retained but DAF would only offer a second tier dealership and that was unacceptable to my dealers who defected to other marques. DAF did recruit a few of our personnel, mainly on the engineering and service side of our business and they were also keen to recruit Lacoste, McIntosh and Gignoux, none of whom were interested in moving to a competitor for whom they had little regard. I was invited to DAF's head office in Eindhoven to discuss a position within the merged the European structure but I politely declined saying I was keen to return to the UK. This was not entirely the truth, because, like my three colleagues I could not bring myself to work with a competitor.

Naturally I had to consider my own position, here I was in a foreign country with my family and my company had disappeared, and at the ripe old age of 39 I had to think about what I wanted to do with the rest of my working life. Isobel was very concerned and we talked long and hard about our options, and we decided that Isobel and the kids would return to Southport as soon as we could arrange the removal people. We had simply closed our home in England and organised general maintenance and upkeep until we returned. In my conversations at the time of the announcement I was informed that the company wanted to retain my services and I was offered the post of Sales Director for the South East Region of Leyland Cars.

This post protected my terms and conditions but I wasn't sure that I wanted to sell cars or live in the London area, but for the moment it was a lifeboat and it allowed me to concentrate on the needs of my staff, our dealers and our customers, Leyland's European based stakeholders, and to deliver the best possible outcome for them. It also allowed Isobel and I to plan our own life and our return to the UK. Having declined to talk about opportunities within the new DAF structure it quickly became evident I was persona non grata and my input was not welcome to the new owners and it was equally evident that most of my colleagues would be looking for jobs outside this new organisation. At least I could ensure that those leaving got a generous severance from British Leyland although the French State already had that in hand, with tight rules on redundancy entitlements. One quirk that I discovered was that in giving notice to a dealer, French law required a compensation package that reflected the length of time the association had been in place, regardless of the contract between the dealer and the Manufacturer. We had a universal contract in place which specified a twelve-month severance period but the law overrode this stipulation and this could have proved a costly escape clause. As it happened it did not apply since we were liquidating our business but in the ordinary way of things, had we tried to sack some dealers it could have cost a small fortune.

Not surprisingly this was one of the worst periods of my career. Having worked so hard to get this company up off its knees, seeing it prosper as never before and then to see it sold from under us, in such a brutal way to a company which was a fraction of the size and importance of our own business, was hard to take. It had been a remarkable two years, so many good things and now this. One of the biggest ironies came when I recalled that conversation with Harry Rheingold at the motor show when he told me that DAF had started out in business after World War Two by assembling trucks they purchased from Leyland in kit form. It was bitter sweet watching my colleagues leave for new jobs, we had worked well together and we had achieved much success in a short time, making the competition take note of the Brits for the first time in many years.

The fact we had achieved more in two years than we had in the previous ten was absolutely no consolation at all, every single one of us was gutted to lose something that had become pretty special in our careers. In the overall scheme of things, we were no more than a flea bite on the back of the big shaggy, careworn dog that was British Leyland. An old dog that had suffered more kicks of late than it could put up with, and in the end it simply rolled over and died without a whimper, though there were many left behind to mourn, myself included. I stayed for as long as I could but after two months everybody who was leaving had gone and there was nothing much left to do, except turn out the lights and catch a plane to England.

And with that my career with Leyland ended because the company I was now joining was the Rover Group Plc. British Leyland had lasted less than 18 years from its forced creation by the Government of Harold Wilson in 1969 and it had been my good fortune to have been with the company for almost 16 of those years. What had been a visionary decision to create a corporation to take on the might of the world, also needed courage to support the company when it wanted to close factories, rationalise product lines, drop some models and make people redundant. This policy required a Government that could resist the misguided pleading of MPs who in a frothing of self-interest feared losing their seats in Parliament if jobs were lost in their constituency. In the end neither that Government nor successive ones had the stomach for the fight and what followed was compromise, fudge and farce which consigned my corporation to a slow lingering death and left it as the butt of a thousand jokes by ill-informed commentators and two bit comedians. Do you get a hint that I was angry? well you should because I was, and I still am thirty years on.

My company with a turnover of one billion pounds per annum equally split between domestic and export, which sold one million vehicles per annum, employed 280,000 in 67 factories in the UK and 26 factories overseas was no more, it was all over in a mere eighteen years. What had started as a visionary act turned out to be simple well intentioned political misguidedness. The company struggled to compete, as plans for rationalisation and cost cutting were rejected as being politically unsellable and vote losers. With hands tied behind their backs senior managers were inevitably destined to fail and good men were fired, sacrificial lambs on the altars of political expediency and frustration. This depressing policy was more aimed at pacifying critics than supporting the establishment of an industrial giant.

My family was already back in our home in Southport Lancashire, and I took up a post with Leyland Cars which for the time being, remained as the last part of what had been the Leyland Group. I was Sales Director for the South of England, (the major region of the car business) reporting to the Sales & Marketing Director of Leyland Cars. I wasn't at all sure that I really wanted to do this job but I took it while I tried to put everything into some perspective. I threw myself into the new job with my usual energy and intensity and I think it's fair to say that I had quite an impact on that Sales organisation.

The team I had inherited were all very pleasant men, but they were not very good at making decisions, to call them indecisive would have been too kind. The infuriating thing was that the team were obviously bright and knew a lot about their dealers and their dealers' businesses but they acted as if they were in a strait jacket, like automatons always waiting to be told what to do. The other thing I found disappointing about my inherited team was the lack of energy, they all went about as if they were destined for the gallows, no joy in what they were doing. If this thing was going to work I needed to take these guys up a notch, give them some latitude in decision making and inject some joie de vivre into their working day.

I suspected that they had taken a terrible buffeting from the rip up of the corporation. All the other divisions now knew their fate, for better or worse while cars were in some sort of business limbo, waiting for God knows what. This must have been tremendously depressing for everyone left in the group to know that all the other divisions had been sorted out, but they could not even be given away. Cars division of British Leyland had been a high profile company and those who worked for the group were highly paid and highly regarded but now they had become an embarrassment to politicians, left to operate in a market place that knew they were hostages to fortune.

I arranged a series of meetings with my new team, first as a group and then on a one to one basis, to try and get to know them better, and these meetings showed me that not only were these men bright but they knew what they needed to do. The problem was that they had been conditioned to ask permission and wait for instructions, they did not want to rock the boat, I knew who to blame for that, their leaders, the dealers in no hope. The insecurity in this organisation became evident to me when I discovered at least one mole in my team during my one on one interviews, not that he admitted this but body language is a big giveaway for conspirators. This guy was feeding HQ with titbits from my meetings and to be honest I was not surprised, because I had been foisted on Cars to stir things up and some people were worried. I was careful to make sure the mole knew only what I wanted his handler at HQ to find out, but this was an organisation jumping at shadows, working against its own personnel; it needed a clear out.

During my one on one interviews, one of my dealer managers told me he was concerned about the performance of one of his dealers, so I arranged a further meeting to go through the detail with him. When we went through that review of this dealer's performance, I learned that he had been under-performing for years and was dragging down the reputation of the Company. The regional staff had poured money and effort into this guy who was a bit of a third generation dilettante, and after all the support they had nothing to show for it, he continued to be a liability. My predecessors had agreed this dealer was a waste of space but nobody had felt any need to do anything about it, because this dealer had friends in high places.

I had arrived in the company unencumbered by history or patronage, and with the clarity that fresh eyes bring I could see what was wrong and I had the fortitude of mind and spirit to want to do something about it. After issuing an improvement notice accompanied by a warning about future performance I fired this dealer, the first time in many years that anybody had taken such drastic action and it sent shockwaves through the company and the dealer network. How novel was I among my new car colleagues? Even more novel was the fact that I told the man myself and did not leave the odious task to one of my subordinates. Now that was really novel!

Without any emotional baggage, I had no problem doing the right thing, and it served notice to the rest of the dealers about meeting their commitments. If you don't value your franchise, why should your dealers? The message that had gone out from Sales before seemed to be "Please try harder, but if you can't that'll be ok, as long as you are nice to us." At least that's how it came across to me, dealers pleased themselves and meantime Sales shovelled large amounts of dough their way by means of sales support while market share plummeted. Nuts to that!

The first group wide sales meeting I attended was held in Longbridge, attended by my fellow regional directors, our boss the director of sales and marketing and some of his head office colleagues. The chair of the meeting asked everyone to introduce themselves with a short bio and I discovered I was the only attendee not to have been raised in the rarefied atmosphere of the car sales organisation and the only attendee who had worked in departments other than sales. While there was a lot of firepower and intellectual horsepower in that room it was all emanating from an extremely narrow experience base and it was more than a little incestuous. The agenda was set to produce a formulated outcome and reminded me of my earlier experience as the newbie at the Truck Sales & Marketing monthly management meetings, where I was also the outsider. When it was my turn to make a

presentation I started by telling them why I had sacked the dealer and how I intended proceeding with the others. When I said my piece I was reminded of Ian Roberson's great quote when referring to the reaction of MPs in the House of Commons to the theft of the stone of destiny from Westminster Abbey. I could "feel a shiver run round the room looking for a spine to run up".
© *Ian Robertson Hamilton QC*

Back in the office I had a message to call one of the dealers which I duly did to be told he had some concerns he would like to discuss with me privately, could he come and see me, please? I asked if it might be better for me to call on him to which he readily agreed, so we made an appointment for the following day, before which I pulled his file to make sure I was as much up to speed on outstanding matters as it was possible to be. The following day he told me that he had evidence that one of my managers was defrauding the company and he was afraid he might have compromised himself, by being party to some skulduggery. He showed me what he had which basically showed that the manager in question was awarding dealer support subject to the dealer using a named company to carry out marketing activities. Providing support conditionally is normal but usually it is conditional upon improved performance not on using a particular company for marketing. This was not correct but not criminal, however the company this guy was using was his own company which he ran through his wife and his brother, and that was definitely verboten.

Not surprisingly the guilty manager was the smartest of all the guys I had inherited and he was running a slick operation, unfortunately not for his employer but for himself using his employer's money and that was fraud, so I fired him. We had to go through the whole dismissal rigmarole insisted upon by HR despite the guy admitting his crime, there was no question of prosecuting him, we wouldn't want anyone to know we were so sloppy that such a thing could happen. Ironically after this man left our employ, one of the dealers told me that his marketing company was the best they had ever used, very professional and on the ball. But the control and authorisation protocols for Dealer support were so weak there might have been another dozen scams going on that I did not know about it. While spying on new Directors was ok, it was maybe too much work to ensure company funds were spent properly and managers were kept on the straight and narrow. Those at HQ who were keen to keep tabs on me did not seem to be able to summon the wherewithal to sack incompetent dealers or fraudulent managers. Maybe they were too worried about keeping a clean external profile, and as I said earlier the carve up of the Corporation must have had a profound effect on the whole team.

Once again the company was using me to put its house in order, and I was back in my accustomed role of the fixer, a person prepared to face up to hard decisions and to do what was necessary. For most of my career in the Leyland Group I had been working as a Company doctor in all but name, and I was happy to do so. My career had been stimulating and I loved the challenges I was presented with and above all I loved the great buzz from making things better. But now, I was not happy at Leyland Cars, I did not like the products, I had little time for my immediate colleagues and I definitely did not like the culture or the work ethic. This was a radically different industry from Trucks and I was clearly not a "Cars man" by temperament or breeding. But I continued in the role, commuting down to London on Sunday evening, spending long days trying to knock my team into shape and returning home Friday nights.

THE SCOTTISH MAFIA

One Saturday morning, three months into my role with Leyland Cars, I was getting ready to take the kids down to the beach when I got a call from my old pal Ian McKinnon who was now Chairman of the Leyland Bus Company Limited. Ian had been Managing Director of Medium Light Vehicle Division and it was he who helped me as I metamorphosed into an Engineering Manager from being a Financial Controller. He had kick started my meteoric rise through the organisation and was another mentor to whom I owed a great deal. We had kept in touch, through all our respective moves and when I went to Paris in 1985, Ian had taken over as Managing Director of Leyland Bus Worldwide Operations. The Transport Act of 1985 had deregulated bus services and the Thatcher Government continued its massive deregulation programme for transport services. The Bus industry was in a state of flux and progressively over the next few years the pace of change quickened as bus passengers coped with the privatisation of the National Bus Corporation and all its offshoots, the Scottish Bus Group and the bus operations owned and managed by Councils large and small all around the UK. It was quite a time to be in the UK Bus Industry and there were some interesting players emerging at that time. The momentous year of 1987 when I was winding down Truck Operations on mainland Europe, following the so called merger with DAF, Ian McKinnon and some colleagues had bought the bus operations from BL and the Government in a classic MBO. The other members of the buy-out team were Ric Turner, George Newburn, Jim McKnight and John Kinnear, and so the Scottish Mafia was born. Only Ric was not a Scotsman by birth although he was definitely a Scotsman by adoption. When Ian called he asked me how I was enjoying my role at Leyland Cars to which I replied frankly that I was not enjoying it in the least and I intended to move on. "How about meeting up for a cup of coffee?" asked my old pal. "Sure," I said "when would you like to meet up, I can only make weekends because I am away Monday to Friday. "How about now?" Was Ian's reply.

So we agreed to meet in a restaurant in Preston, which was halfway between his home in Lytham and my home in Southport. I explained to Isobel and the kids that this could be very important and asked Isobel if she would take Nicholas and Carrie kite flying on Southport sands to allow me to meet up with Ian. Isobel agreed and so off I went to see what was on Ian's mind. When I arrived at the restaurant to my surprise Ian was accompanied by Ric and George, it was to be an MLVD re-union and the cup of coffee merged into lunch and an afternoon of talking. Over lunch my pals described the process of the MBO and outlined what they had achieved since they the completion of the buyout. In the space of a few months they had repaid the venture capitalists and taken back their equity, they had implemented a significant cost cutting exercise and, freed from corporate and political restrictions, made the company much more effective, re-focussed the product line and re-organised the factories to increase capacities. Ric took me through the financials and the company was strong, very strong.

All in all, it was pretty impressive, but they had a problem and that was Sales, and the Sales & Marketing Director had now left the team for pastures new. They told me they had been struggling with Sales for a couple of years and had recently parted company with the man whom they had inherited on taking over the company in 1985, before the MBO. At the end of this long spiel, Ian said "Owen the company needs you and anyway, you started off in buses up at Workington, this job is your destiny. When can you start?"

I said "If that's a job offer, I accept.

Submitting my resignation came as a shock to Leyland Cars, it was not well received and I understand why, at that stage the rump of the Leyland Group had been shaken by the massive changes and was struggling to establish credibility with the buying public both at home and in the export market and this was not a good time for senior people to be quitting. I felt bad because Leyland had given me so much and I had been so happy in my career with MY company. Although I felt like a bit of a traitor, I also knew that I had given the company everything and I had achieved a lot for the company as well as for myself. I was really unhappy in the car side of the business and I needed to move on. On a happier note, there were people at Leyland Cars who sighed with relief when they heard I was leaving; they could now retreat back into their cosy shell as they awaited the lingering death that was inevitable to my mind. My contract notice period was three months, part of which I spent back in Paris finalising the details of the DAF acquisition, not that there was much regard given to my input. My spell in Paris went quickly because I was very busy and then I was back in the UK and getting ready to take up my new post with the brand new private company, Leyland Bus Limited.

And now I would be Director of Sales and Marketing for Leyland Bus, and take an equity position in the company. I would have the opportunity to work with a bunch of like-minded individuals in Ian, Ric and George. We had all been very close in my time at Bathgate and I knew them to be consummate professionals who knew how to take decisions and make them stick. I knew the other directors quite well and they too, were all professional operators. This would be some boardroom, with a great combination of intellectual horsepower and street smarts. It was also a delicious irony, I had joined the BL Corporation at Leyland Bus Company and now I would be leaving BL to once more join Leyland Bus, this time as part-owner of the Company. Isn't life strange?

This was going to be quite an adventure.

"You know what you could be, tell me my friend why you worry all the time what you should be"

© Mike Heron

About the Author

Passionate Scotsman and European, enthusiastic granddad and professor of fun, fun, fun to three wee boys. Whimsical gardener, retired revolutionary, avid reader, fan of Napoleon and Paul of Tarsus, lifelong pilgrim, part-time Hospitalero, expert floor scrubber and maker of beds, devotee of the idiosyncrasies that make people interesting.

Owen Quinn July 2018

<caminopilgrim15@gmail.com>

Made in the USA
Columbia, SC
05 August 2018